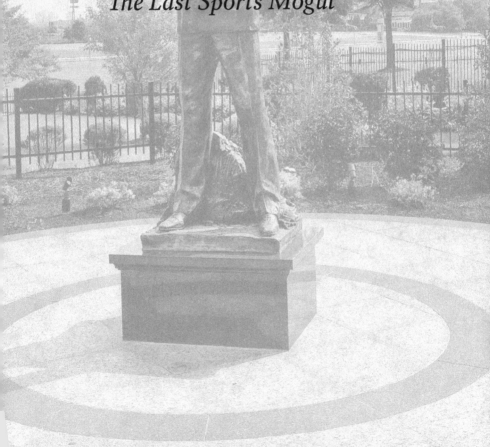

ED SNIDER

The Last Sports Mogul

ED SNIDER

The Last Sports Mogul

Alan Bass

TRIUMPH
BOOKS

No part of this publication may be reproduced, stored in a retrieval system, or transmitted, in any form by any means, electronic, mechanical, photocopying, or otherwise, without the prior written permission of the publisher, Triumph Books LLC, 814 North Franklin Street, Chicago, Illinois, 60610.

Library of Congress Cataloging-in-Publication Data available upon request.

This book is available in quantity at special discounts for your group or organization. For further information, contact:

Triumph Books LLC
814 North Franklin Street
Chicago, IL 60610
(312) 337-0747
www.triumphbooks.com

Printed in the United States of America
ISBN: 978-1-62937-984-5
Design and editorial production by Alex Lubertozzi

Photos in first insert courtesy of: Martha Snider (p. i, ii); the Philadelphia Eagles (p. iii–top); and Comcast-Spectacor (p. iii–bottom, iv, v, vi, vii, viii). Photos in second insert courtesy of: Martha Snider (p. ii, iii, iv–top); Jay Snider (p. iii–top); Comcast-Spectacor (p. i, iv–bottom, v, vii); Drew Katz (p. vi–top); the University of Maryland (p. vi–bottom); and Zack Hill (p. vii–top, viii).

Contents

Preface

IF THERE WAS one thing that could be said about Ed Snider, it was that his life inspired a vast array of opinions about himself at all ends of the spectrum. And there is not a soul who knew him who didn't shape one of these decisive, passionate opinions. There are those who loved him, who would spend their lives praising his work and when asked about him, still declare proudly, "Anything for Mr. Snider." There are also those who spoke out loudly against some of the decisions he made in his career or his personal life. But whether he was viewed with contempt or admiration, there was no denying the magnitude of his influence on the sports world and the city of Philadelphia. Those he worked with held an enormous amount of respect for him. To these devoted members of his staff, he was always "Mr. Snider"—a man to be looked up to, esteemed, and made proud. But despite all of these opinions of a man many placed on a pedestal, deep down, he just wanted to be known as "Ed."

The beauty of Ed's life is the dichotomy between his simplicity and complexity. He was simple in the way he was open and uninhibited by a social mask. He wore his heart on his sleeve. As one former employee said to the *Philadelphia Inquirer*, "There was never any doubt whether the Flyers won or lost. All you had to do was look at Mr. Snider." As a young Philadelphia Eagles executive in the 1960s, he was known to lead by example, rather than by demand. "The only contribution an owner makes is making sure there is good management," he once said to the *Philadelphia Daily News*. When Ed was at work, he wanted solely to complete the task at hand, with no interruptions or disruptions. When he was with his family, he wanted nothing to do with work. Ed was always one to simply live in the present and love whatever he was doing at that instant.

But Ed had a deeper complexity that supplemented his otherwise straightforward nature. Those who knew him fell into one of two categories: those who thought he was passionate and loyal, and those who thought he was ruthless and would run over his own mother to get ahead. Even those closest to him acknowledged that he could be quite difficult at times—the two sides of Ed Snider. There are many people who excoriated him regularly and spoke of him quite terribly, while scores of people revered him. Those who knew him intimately understood that his life was not black and white—there was a lot of gray to Ed.

While you could find many who would vouch for either side of the argument, what is irrefutable is his business acumen. NHL commissioner Gary Bettman may have shaken his head and laughed at the constant late-night calls he received from Ed every time he felt a referee had it in for his Flyers. But ask Bettman who the most influential, helpful, and passionate people in the NHL were during his lengthy tenure, and Ed would rank near the top. Even those who hated Ed with all their might acknowledged what a brilliant man he was—nay, had to be—to have the level of success he achieved.

Ed's professional life was a balancing act between two competing, and usually extreme, arguments. Was he solely responsible for the start of the Flyers organization, or was he riding on Jerry Wolman's coattails and claiming the credit? Was he a responsible NHL owner who allowed those he hired to do their jobs, or did he meddle in every hockey decision the club ever made? Was he the most brilliant sports owner Philadelphia has ever seen, or was he the sole reason the Flyers failed to win another Stanley Cup after 1975? The questions are endless, as are the positions one can take from one extreme to the other.

In the early 1960s, before the Flyers even existed, Ed showed how progressive and forward-thinking he was when it came to his businesses. Those who worked with him recognized it immediately, while journalists who covered him at the Eagles and eventually the Flyers were floored by his visions for future greatness. He was referred to by '60s sportswriters as "a man of this generation," "a man with great foresight," and "a man who envisions some good in everything he undertakes." They described his philosophy as "do your best, and ask no more." Ed, they said, "enjoys living and the challenges life presents."

As the years progressed, the contrast between the two perceptions of him were even more apparent as his influence increased and those near and far began to form their own opinions. There was nothing in life Ed wanted more than to win at whatever he was competing in—football, hockey, business—often times to a fault. Ed was called a man of contradictions, ruthless, cold-hearted, a sore loser, a sore winner. "He's complex," said Bill Putnam, the Flyers' first president, to the *Philadelphia Inquirer*. "He doesn't fit any of the molds. There are times when he's extremely generous, happy, easy to get along with. And then, sometimes, he's just a bitch on wheels." One former coworker called him "a smart S.O.B...a very astute guy," but then acknowledged to the *Philadelphia Inquirer*, "I don't care for him as a human being. I've told my children that's one guy I don't want them to emulate."

Ed's character is one of the strongest anyone who knew him had ever seen. Despite one former associate admitting, "Nobody gets to the top without some carnage," Ed was nothing if not honest and straightforward. He told you exactly what he thought and never felt bad about doing so. All he expected from everyone around him was hard work and the highest level of commitment. Give him anything less, and he would show you the door; show him the loyalty he desired and the same passion he had for his companies, and he would do anything and everything for you. His loyalty and generosity towards those he loved were legendary. He had a wonderful sense of humor, even if it only came out at certain times. Whether he was playing pinball at Frank Clements Tavern in downtown Philadelphia, singing and dancing to Billy Joel on the ride home, or sailing through the Caribbean, his take on life was whimsical.

The words "enthusiastic" and "passionate" may not even do justice to Ed's personality. A man of superlatives, who viewed everything as "the greatest," whether it was a steak he was just served in a restaurant or a new building he walked into for the first time, he saw life as one grand opportunity after another. His view of the world was often overly simplistic, labeling people as "good" or "bad" and seeing situations as black and white, leaving very little room for discussion.

He was also perhaps the last ever self-made sports mogul. Many before him built their wealth solely off the value of a professional sports team, but it is difficult to point to one who did so after Ed. Nowadays, with the lowest-end NHL squad valued at hundreds of millions of dollars, it is impossible to enter the sports ownership world unless you are already independently wealthy. Ed was worth little when he started the Flyers with a small group of partners. With a few loans from local financial institutions, his simple goal was to grow hockey in Philadelphia, a sport that had had an up and down relationship with the city since the late 1890s. A few years into his Flyers career, he was still millions of dollars in debt. Over the subsequent decades, he built an arena management company, a ticketing technology firm, a concessions company, a sports marketing company, a sports-talk radio network, and a 24-hour television network, not to mention an NHL team that ranks as one of the most successful of the last 50 years, both financially and in on-ice success. At the point Comcast purchased the majority of the organization from him in 1996, its value had ballooned to nearly $100 million—a far cry from the $2 million that he paid for the right to an NHL franchise in 1966. More importantly, his organization became a family for those involved—just talk to any player who ever wore the orange and black or any employee who spent a few years in the organization. Nearly every one sees themselves as a Flyer for life.

In addition, his contributions to the National Hockey League are immense—even years after his death, the league's business model is still fresh with his fingerprints. When he joined the hockey world, the sport was well behind its competitors, all of whom already had national television contracts. The NHL, however, had always been a regional sport, and its owners were often laughed out of the room when they met with the major networks. Ed recognized these regional strengths and foresaw the benefits of having strong regional TV deals for each team, bolstered by a solid national contract, which would help spread the game. Forty years later, with Ed still serving in the league, the NHL signed its first billion-dollar national TV deal. At the same time, each team continued to make a fair share of money through their own individual, regional network deals.

Ed utilized his experience with the NFL-AFL merger to warn his NHL brethren of the dangers of fighting with the World Hockey Association, and suggested they merge after the rival league's first season. He was mocked and ridiculed, but seven years later, after salaries skyrocketed and NHL owners were bleeding profits, the league finally heeded his warning. Ed also understood the benefit of having multiple businesses intertwined to help boost the finances of his hockey club. Now, more often than not, NHL franchises are owned either by multifaceted companies or individuals who have branched out their businesses in the same way Ed had already done in the 1970s.

This book profiles the life of Ed Snider in a way no other work has done previously. It starts even before his birth, in an attempt to search for the roots of his financial acumen, entrepreneurial spirit, and raw ambition. It walks through his childhood in greater Washington, D.C., as he fought anti-Semitism and watched his family build a thriving grocery store business from the ground up. It follows Ed as he graduated college and searched for what he wanted to do in life, from CPA to record company executive. It traces the start of his relationship with Jerry Wolman; his early, mostly unexplored work running the Philadelphia Eagles; and delves into the messy, devastating breakup with his business partner and close friend. It follows him as he twice prevented the relocation of his NHL franchise that had yet to play a game, then proceeded to turn a fledgling Philadelphia hockey organization into the Flyers, Comcast-Spectacor, and eventually a billion-dollar business. And, of course, it delves into his philanthropy and his family, exploring the relationship he shared with his children and grandchildren, who were the bedrock of his being. Ed's life was fascinating, to put it mildly, even if the pros and cons of his decisions and management style can be debated in a Philadelphia bar into the wee hours of the morning.

The companies that exist because of him employ thousands of people across the country and include the Philadelphia Flyers, Comcast-Spectacor, and all of its subsidiaries. The nonprofits that exist due to his contributions include the Ed Snider Youth Hockey Foundation, the Snider Foundation, the Ed Snider Center for Enterprise and Markets at the University of Maryland, the Sol C. Snider Entrepreneurial Research Center at the University of Pennsylvania, the National Museum for American Jewish History, the National Foundation for Celiac Awareness, the Institute for Cancer and Blood Diseases at Hahnemann University Hospital, the Ayn Rand Institute, and many more. He was named by *SportsBusiness Journal* to its "Top 50 Most Influential People in Sports Business" list and, in 1999, the *Philadelphia Daily News* named him Philadelphia's "Greatest Mover and Shaker of the Millennium."

The high-powered friends he developed while living in California saw him in a casual way Philadelphia had not, but they discovered his stature when they would visit the city for a Flyers game. These Hollywood superstars and billionaire businessmen were often stunned when, as one friend described, "The seas would part," as Ed walked down the street or a hallway. It was not just that he owned the hockey team—Ed had taken the nation's former capital by storm as a young entrepreneur and became its pride and joy through his ambition, work ethic, and toughness—three qualities Philadelphians respect more than anything. In short, one could plausibly argue that Ed Snider was the most influential Philadelphian the city has ever seen.

Some may disagree with decisions he made as the owner of the Flyers. Some may speak negatively about his management tactics. But no one can dispute the influence his work has had in his community, both on a micro and macro scale. During the 1976 Stanley Cup Finals, a fan hung a sign over the second deck of the Spectrum: WIN OR LOSE, YOU'VE GIVEN PHILLY A LOT TO BE PROUD OF. YOU'LL ALWAYS BE #1 TO US. What Ed gave to Philadelphia was a leader who cared so deeply about his city and so deeply about his team, that sports fans throughout the region had little choice but to jump on the bandwagon and go along for the ride.

Ed's personality can be summed up very simply. Ed was:

- Ambitious and entrepreneurial, possessing an intelligence that those who worked with him had never seen before and have never seen since.
- Incredibly conservative when it came to politics, yet surprisingly progressive when it came to his business and social issues. An Ayn Rand acolyte, he consistently provided a full-throated defense of capitalism and the benefits it brought to society.
- Generous and giving, spending hundreds of millions of dollars over the course of his life (as well as posthumously) to support causes in which he believed, as well as supporting members of his extended family, solely because he felt it was his duty to share his success with those he loved.

- Extremely difficult to work with, possessing an anger and demand for perfection that scared many employees away over the years. At the end of the day, his vote was the only one that mattered.
- A person of surprisingly low emotional intelligence when it came to personal relationships. More often than not, when problems arose, with friends, family, or romantic partners, his only instinct was to simply move on.
- Most importantly, head over heels in love with his family—he would do anything and everything for his children and grandchildren and was pained when anything came between them, even if it was of his own volition.

Like most of us, Ed had wonderful parts to his personality, yet also had a dark side that was often troubling. Far from presenting him as an angel or a devil, the best way to go about telling the story of his life is to show all sides of him, letting the reader develop their own conclusions and decide for themselves how to perceive him.

However you choose to view the life of Ed Snider, it is clear that even if the Flyers ceased operations tomorrow and Comcast-Spectacor shut their doors forever, his legacy would live on through his incredible philanthropy. That altruistic behavior often caused those close to him to do the same, whether it was through his family's charitable foundation, the Ed Snider Youth Hockey Foundation he built, his support of various Jewish nonprofit causes, or the work his children now do in the nonprofit community. One hundred years from now, regardless of the Flyers' success or even existence, Philadelphia's culture and well-being will have been partially shaped based on the work Ed did throughout his life. That is his legacy. That is the story I want to share with you.

• • •

GROWING UP in the Philadelphia region and a hockey fan since I was six years old, Ed always loomed high above everything else in Philadelphia. Others may not have been able to name the mayor of their city, or even their own local politicians, but everyone knew Ed Snider. He was larger than life, even if you knew nothing about sports. His philanthropy, his love of all things Philadelphia, and his overall contributions to the city are immeasurable. Long before I was a writer or a businessman, I followed him with great interest. When he gave an interview, I read or listened. When he was in his owner's box on a night I was in the crowd, I watched him from afar as his fist pumped with each goal, or as he threw up his hands with each perceived officiating mistake. As the Flyers rose and fell through each season, so did Ed.

As my business and writing careers progressed, my view of him began to evolve. I saw him less as the owner of a local sports team and more as a visionary—a builder of a sports business empire who was years ahead of his time. As Comcast-Spectacor grew and the Flyers consistently ranked as one of the top organizations in sports, my interest piqued and I strived to learn more about his life.

Although I didn't know him personally, I was fortunate to have met Ed a few times in my life. The first time was as an intern in the Flyers' community relations department in 2009. We were prepping the Spectrum for a final, black-tie gala that he was holding for family, friends, and members of the Flyers organization before it would be demolished the following year. A group of us were escorted to an office on the executive level of the Wells Fargo Center to pick up some supplies and head across the parking lot, when he exited his office to see what we were doing. As soon as his door opened, everyone in the vicinity whipped their heads around as if a rare, exotic animal had just walked in front of us. We were all starstruck and, quite frankly, nervous as could be to see him. He asked who we were, and after introducing ourselves, he stuck his hand out with a smile and said, "Hi, I'm Ed Snider."

Stories had passed through the organization of how tough he was, how demanding he was, how every little thing had to be just right. Some he worked with were terrified of him. But not us, not in that moment. He was so warm and welcoming. It was just four words, but his body language and his tone said, "Welcome to my organization, I'm so happy that you're a part of it." His genuine smile and excitement to see new faces conveyed a deep love and respect for his life's work— traits that trickled down throughout the entire company. Despite his sadness at the closing of the Spectrum, the building into which he poured so much blood and sweat, his enthusiasm at being able to share it one last time with those he loved was infectious. As we wheeled flat-beds of boxes across the Philadelphia Sports Complex, we were giddy, even more enthralled with our tiny contribution to the greater good.

Later that season, I had the opportunity to have an extended con-versation with him for my first book, *The Great Expansion: The Ulti-mate Risk That Changed the NHL Forever*. Over the course of an hour, he regaled me with stories from the early days of the Flyers with chuckles, thrilled at the opportunity to relive the struggles he over-came and the roadblocks he inevitably bashed through. His contribu-tion to that work only increased my desire to learn more about his life. I would also be remiss if I did not bring up the time my wife and I ran into him in line at the Wells Fargo Center's Chickie and Petes—even Ed, with his luxurious director's lounge dinners, could not turn down a bucket of crab fries. A man of the people, for sure.

In 2013, I spent the day with then Comcast-Spectacor COO Peter Luukko, profiling him for a story that would appear in *The Hockey News*. Coincidentally that day, the organization won a big contract to manage an arena—a project they had been bidding on for the pre-vious few months. Everyone was ebullient and already in the plan-ning stages for what came next. While eating dinner with Luukko, I watched as he politely interrupted Ed's meal to let him know the good news. Ed smiled but didn't say much—he didn't need to. After nearly

50 years of building, he had the pieces in place within his organization to ensure that his vision continued without the need to be directly involved in each decision. It was at that moment I told myself that one day I would write Ed Snider's biography.

This book represents years of compiled work from across the hockey world. In my own published works, Ed was always prevalent. In my first book, *The Great Expansion*, Ed was featured not only as the founder of the Flyers, but as a progressive-minded owner who wanted to change an NHL still refusing to step into the present and move toward the future. My second book, *Professional Hockey in Philadelphia: A History*, chartered the many professional hockey teams that played in the city from the 1890s through the present day. His partnership and feud with Jerry Wolman were a big part of the Flyers chapter. The research for that chapter further cemented my desire to write this book.

But many others need to be involved in order to properly craft an accurate narrative of a man who has been all over Philadelphia for half a century. The research for this book includes scores of interviews with those close to him throughout his life, from family and friends to business associates, opponents in the hockey world, reporters who covered his teams, former employees, and more. Nearly 50 hours of interviews and 450 pages of interview transcripts were utilized to build the story you now hold in your hands.

Ed's family provided endless resources to make this book a reality. They shared stories, documents, photographs, videos, archival information, and even financial records to support and reject many theories or stories that existed in the public realm. Nonetheless, although this book was sanctioned by the family, they had no say in the structure or final product, no right of approval. The book remains independently written to give an accurate, unbiased view of their patriarch.

The media archive for Ed's life reaches into the millions, in terms of word count. From 1963 through his death, he is mentioned in upwards of 100,000 news articles across the world. Hours of existing interview archives, pages of transcripts, and never-before-seen works, both written and vocal, were utilized in this project.

Many of the quotations used in this book came from interviews I conducted myself, but a good share also came from media sources from the last 60 years. All quotes obtained elsewhere are noted in the text. Some quotes from years ago were adjusted for proper grammar or spelling, but in no cases were the contents of the quotes changed. Quotes and information coming from some interviews I conducted are not cited, in order to keep the anonymity of those sources—many still work for Comcast-Spectacor or an associated company and others simply did not want their name connected with an anecdote. Nonetheless, any claim of fact has been confirmed with at least a second source, and often times documentation. When a fact could not be definitively established, it was either omitted or included with explanation.

When I first sat down to outline how I envisioned this project taking shape, I had to make a promise that the book would not become a history of the Flyers. Rather, I wanted to make sure that it centered solely on Ed and his life—whether it included vast amounts of chapters on the Flyers or not. As time progressed, however, it was evident that my issue would not be in holding back on the Flyers content, but in finding specific examples in which Ed was directly involved with the team's day-to-day operations. You will notice in these pages a surprisingly low amount of Flyers material. That is not to say that Ed was not involved. But in speaking with hundreds of people, both casually and on the record, it is very clear that, while Snider's fingerprints are all over, there is no evidence of a single instance in which he demanded a specific hockey decision be made.

To best understand Ed Snider and the traits that ended up propelling him to the fame he eventually enjoyed, it is crucial to go back as far as the family's genealogy allows. Not only does the history help illustrate the time period in which Ed came of age, but it also helps to color the development of the man who would one day claim Philadelphia as his own. Therefore, the story starts well before Ed was born and follows the Snider family as it makes its way to Washington, D.C., and eventually Philadelphia.

This book will be viewed from varying perspectives: it is a book about the business of sports and how one man turned his passion into a career. It is a book about hockey and how the Flyers built arguably the most successful expansion franchise since the days of the Original Six. It is a book about philanthropy and utilizing one's own success for the greater good. It is a book about family and the difficulties of balancing a career with the desire to always be with the ones you love. Choose any lens with which to interpret the following pages and there will be something useful to color your own life. We can all learn a lot from Ed Snider, whether it is how we want to act or how we want to avoid acting in a given situation. In either case, he will always and forever have something to teach us.

Growing Up in Washington, D.C.

IT WAS DECEMBER 28, 1909, when Yankel and Tsipe Schneider arrived at Ellis Island on the SS *Uranium*, sailing from Rotterdam, The Netherlands, in search of a new life. With over 1 million Jews chased out of Russia since 1880 through pogroms—organized massacres that occurred in the early 20th century—the Schneiders felt it was crucial to pack up all they could carry and leave their small village of Rafalovka.

Rafalovka was a tight-knit, familial community, a typical shtetl—a small Jewish village that existed in Eastern Europe at the time. Founded in the 17th century, it sat about 225 miles west of Kiev (at the time, part of the Russian Empire, but now part of the Volhynia region of Ukraine). By the 1800s there were just 70 Jews living in the town, but by 1897, the town population had grown to 2,038, over half of whom were Jewish. The Schneiders are believed to have been blacksmiths by trade, a contrast with many of the other residents, who were mostly artisans and shopkeepers.

Zivel Schneider was one of 13 children (only eight appear to have survived to adulthood). Zivel married Esther Breznok, and the couple themselves had eight children, one of whom was Yankel. He and his wife Tsipe had five children at the time, Sol (born in 1906), Louis, Sophie, Harry, and Samuel. As the 20th century began, the family was naturally quite concerned about their well-being in the Russian

Empire. Jewish settlements were regularly torched, villagers were regularly murdered, women were often raped. It was a terrifying time for anyone of Jewish descent, and when the pogroms came just a bit too close for comfort, the Schneiders made their way across Europe and found passage to the United States.

When they arrived in their new country, their Yiddish-German names were changed at immigration, as was often the case at that time. Yankel became Jacob, while Tsipe became Jennie. The family name was Americanized to Snider. Thus, Jacob and Jennie Snider and their children disembarked from their ship and headed toward St. Louis, Missouri, where they would make their new home. Shortly after settling, they moved across the state to Kansas City, where they tried to make a go of their new life, though they certainly had their fair share of struggles.

The family was poor, and putting food on the table each night was a challenge. Jacob worked as a street merchant, while Jennie raised the children. Young Sol helped his father peddle fruits and vegetables from his street cart, while the other siblings pitched in as they could in between their schoolwork. Sol also sold newspapers on the street to help the family save money. When Sol was in his late teens in the 1920s, he met Lilian Bonas.

Her parents, Sam and Toby Bierszunski, were born in Poland. But, like many areas of Europe, Warsaw was also a dangerous place for Jews of that era. The country was ruled by a rotating cast of Germans, Poles, or Russians, depending on who had won the most recent war. Sam's family was able to buy their way out of military service when they desired to leave the country. When they immigrated to the United States in 1904, Sam's uncle told him that no one would be able to spell their last name. Their surname was therefore also Anglicized, to Bonas. Similar to the Sniders, they moved to St. Louis in 1906.

It is assumed, like countless others, that both families had ended up in St. Louis because of the 1904 World's Fair. The region's population grew by nearly 30 percent in the first decade of the 20th century. Sam worked for the St. Louis Street Car Company for $1.25 per day. Struggling for money, food was scarce and the family warmed themselves beside a coal stove that sat in the middle of the dining room. Lilian was born in St. Louis in 1907 and never strayed far from her home town until there was reason. In 1913, Sam and Toby, with Lil and her five siblings (one of the Bonases' children had died in childhood in Poland) relocated to Kansas City.

Lil was a troublemaker as a child. She was expelled from her school for consistently not paying attention to the teacher and was subsequently enrolled elsewhere. When she and her sister, Tammie, graduated, her parents had to split up and attend two schools' graduations. Her parents sent her to camp as well, but when Lil decided she was not enjoying it, she hid in the back of a bakery delivery truck leaving the camp and made her way back to Kansas City.

It was there that Lil is believed to have met Sol. Sol and Lil had a brief courtship that was nearly interrupted when Sol's older sister, Sophie, followed her husband across the country to Washington, D.C. When Sol decided to join her in traveling to the East Coast, Lil made a life-changing choice to come along as well. The two first filed for marriage in Jackson County, Missouri, and married on April 13, 1926. They then trekked toward the nation's capital—Sol was 19 years old and Lil just 18—and headed toward a new life together. They settled at 4810 Georgia Avenue in northwest D.C.

Much of the rest of the Snider family followed, and Sol and his brother, Sam, continued their father's entrepreneurial ideas by opening a small corner grocery store named Snider Quality Market. At the time, Washington, D.C., was still a town of the American South. Anti-Semitism was prevalent, and Jews were not allowed to work in government jobs. Jewish families often made themselves useful to their anti-Semitic neighbors by finding work in essential businesses that the public needed in order to survive. Groceries were the perfect outlet for that entrepreneurial spirit. The market stocked everything from fruits and vegetables to cigars and liquor and, as time progressed, the business was successful and provided enough cash outflow for both families to comfortably pay their bills. It also helped that Lil worked for Mutual Life Insurance in Baltimore for a few years to supplement the family income.

In March 1928, Lil gave birth to the couple's first child, a daughter named Phyllis. Despite their modest success in business, Sol and Lil were far from living on easy street and disaster was always around the corner. In 1929, Sol was robbed at gunpoint one night as he was walking home from locking up the store. When he got to Eighth and Taylor, he was forced to give up the entirety of the day's $800 receipts, leaving him penniless for a day's work, showing just how fragile the family's young success was. In fact, in late 1932, Sol, Lil, and Phyllis went to live with Lil's sister, Cecil, for a few months because they were struggling financially. Sol saved furiously until January 5, 1933, when he stood in the middle of the living room, held up a bank book, and proclaimed that he had accumulated $2,500, to which his family cheered wildly. The next day, on January 6, Lil gave birth to Edward Malcolm, the first and what would be the only son in the next generation of Sniders. The family soon moved into a new home at 412 Oglethorpe Street in the same neighborhood.

As young Eddie, as he was known, slowly grew up, the family business expanded. Years later, Sol would gather a group of local grocers to form an alliance called IGA (the root of the acronym is unknown, though it probably was something akin to "Independent Grocers Association") and a new conglomerate called "Food Town," in which the individual stores purchased their goods together in order to obtain discounted rates from their suppliers. This allowed them to compete with the larger grocery store chains.

At this point, the extended Snider family was full of businessmen and entrepreneurs—one was a restaurant owner, another owned a nightclub. It was always in their blood. It would be apt to describe Eddie's upbringing as solidly middle class. They were moderately successful in their business endeavors, but not wealthy. They never again struggled to put food on the table, but they surely had to count every penny to ensure it stayed that way.

One of the ways they were able to be economical was through the use of the grocery store. When fruit and vegetables were near-rotted, Sol would remove them from the store displays and bring them home for Lil to use. A master in the kitchen, she would regularly cut out any rotten parts of the produce and include them in family dinners. Nothing went to waste if she could help it. The family would regularly dine on delicious fruit salad crafted by hand from the matriarch, her prowess in the kitchen turning a business loss into a thrifty treat.

Sol worked long hours in the grocery store and never once complained about it. He knew what was necessary to keep his family happy and was thrilled to do so. He was loving and easygoing and outwardly affectionate toward his children. He was a large man with a hearty belly laugh, one that would resonate throughout the house or the store. He also carried with him many superstitions, which manifested themselves in various habits, including an insistence on keeping a pair of solid metal dice on his desk with the "four" and "three" face up. No one dared move them from "Lucky Seven" to any other digits, lest Sol find himself with any bad luck. Many of his superstitions were passed down to his children and even some of his grandchildren over the course of many years.

Lil was a character who was loved by everyone in the neighborhood. Her tough exterior act often covered for the fact that she doted endlessly on Eddie and loved him to pieces. Her rough upbringing and travels across the country to reach the American Dream taught her that family was the most important thing in her life. In good times and bad, her parents and now her husband were always there for her, and she was determined to be there for her children as well. Not that her upbringing didn't also create the bossy personality that she became known for—she was extremely intense, a trait that she would pass onto her son and then some.

However, Lil's quirkiness was also a sight to be seen. Known later in life as "the Great Condenser" among some of her children and grandchildren, she would regularly organize, to a fault. When Eddie went off to college, she cleaned out his room, including the hundreds of baseball cards that he meticulously collected throughout his childhood. If she saw a half-eaten bag of chips in front of an unopened bag, she would open the new bag and dump the remainder of the initial bag on top to save space. Similarly, she would take two different jars of jam—even if they were different flavors—and combine them into one jar. Not only did she do this in her own house but also her children's houses once they got older.

Eddie's childhood was a simple one that did not leave him wanting for anything. Despite his stories later in life that they grew up quite poor, there is no evidence to support that claim. But he certainly had struggles, as most children did. The Jewish son of an immigrant, he was bullied as a young schoolboy and often teased for his cultural heritage. At least one time, but possibly more, Eddie was confronted on his walk home from school, where some older kids threw his glasses on the pavement, pushed him to the ground, and chanted, "Jew boy, Jew boy, don't you cry, you'll be a rabbi by and by." Young Eddie would wait for them to finish, pick up his broken glasses and walk quickly back home. Although it did not happen often, the episode scarred him for many years, leaving him fearful to be alone.

He countered those fears by joining up with groups of friends who could protect each other, and garnered a reputation for being a bit of a tough guy himself. Although he didn't partake in any cruel, bullying activities toward others like the ones he experienced, he developed a swagger that only grew as he progressed toward adolescence and into adulthood. His confidence bordered on arrogance, but he could make up for that with his charm. Nonetheless, one of the lessons these difficult childhood memories taught him was that no matter what you do, you should never allow yourself to get beaten up without putting up a fight. Eddie's Uncle Sam used to tell him that, when he was younger, he would intentionally walk through anti-Semitic neighborhoods with a big Star of David on his shoulder, goading any residents into challenging him. Eddie would laugh and applaud at the story of his heroic bravado. So long as you can protect yourself, he believed, you'll always have a chance at whatever you want to do.

One of the people who helped him develop that sense of toughness was his sister, Phyllis. With a six-year age difference between them, she was a prototypical big sister to young Eddie. She often rolled her eyes at what she perceived was overly loving treatment he got from some of the adults in the family. She called him a wimp and a baby (terms that she continued to use through the entirety of his life) and joked that he was a tough guy who constantly got beaten up. When he was young, she once let his baby carriage roll down the street because she was annoyed at him, before realizing she was going to have to chase after it herself. But she would also take him around, showing him the ropes and acting as a protector of sorts, albeit with tough love.

Parts of this tough reputation may have also been established accidentally. In later years, he often told a story about a large, older boy at his school named George Kafalas. One time, Eddie was interested in a girl that, unbeknownst to him, was seeing George. When it was discovered, Eddie received a stern message to meet outside the school at the end of the day to fight. Thin and lanky, Eddie was not a fighter. He talked the talk, but knew better than to get into a physical brawl, which he would probably lose. Later that afternoon, when George began to remove his coat in preparation, Eddie grabbed the larger boy's arm, twisted it behind his back, and broke his arm. (It is helpful to note that, the stories he told in later years were often exaggerated, but were generally not outright lies. So, in this scenario, perhaps the arm was not in fact broken but injured enough to incapacitate the bully.) George ran away, while Eddie was hailed for his bravery— despite his tactics being less than gentlemanly.

Events, as well as people, were important influences on young Eddie. During most of his formative years, news of the ongoing World War II colored his perceptions, and he would read and hear stories of his fellow Jews in Europe being persecuted and murdered by the Nazis. Although he was quite young and could not necessarily do much about it at the time, it was something that bothered him endlessly. As someone who had experienced some anti-Semitism, he shuddered at the thought of European children similar to him being pulled from their homes and placed in concentration camps simply because of their religion. Although he did not show it in his youth, it was a scar that stuck with him for the rest of his life.

His personality was also shaped by the fact that Eddie was treated like a prince by the rest of the local family. When Lil's sisters followed the family to the East Coast, four of them settled in the same apartment building. With no sons among them, Eddie became the superstar and could do no wrong. The only male of his generation, he was doted on and spoiled to whatever extent they could. When he asked for money, they gave it to him. When he needed an excuse, they provided it for him. Even his sometimes naïve father would hand him cash just moments after Lil chided him for requesting money from his parents. The sisters would often show up unannounced, much to the chagrin of Lil. Nonetheless, family always came first and she would welcome them with open arms.

Lil loved her son so much that she often saw right past any potential faults, which taught young Eddie that he could get away with nearly anything he desired. As a young teenager, he would often leave the house for school in the morning and play hooky, instead choosing to spend the day with his friends. When the school called Lil to inform her that Eddie hadn't shown up, she would refuse to agree with their assessment. "Yes, he did," she would say. "I saw him leave, he did go to school."

"No, Mrs. Snider," they would reply, "he's not in school today."

"Oh, yes, he is," she would repeat. "He left for school this morning promptly."

In the same time period, many Jewish children were enrolled in Hebrew School in preparation for their bar mitzvah, the Jewish coming-of-age ceremony for 13-year-old boys, and Eddie was no exception. But, when months passed and Lil had yet to receive the date for his special day, she went to the temple and asked what the problem was. The rabbi was dumbfounded, having never met Eddie, who never attended. In the end, Lil had to make a deal and pay a nominal fee to secure a date for her son's bar mitzvah. To help him study, Eddie was given a recording by the rabbi of the reading for that day—he simply memorized the Hebrew and performed admirably, with almost no lessons.

The family was somewhat observant (Lil kept a kosher home for some time), but most importantly, they were always very proud of their religion and partook in the cultural parts of it with great enthusiasm. Lil would regularly cook holiday meals for the family, where everyone would get together and celebrate. The family would rarely go to synagogue, perhaps only on the high holidays of Rosh Hashanah and Yom Kippur. But they utilized their cultural heritage as a means for family closeness, a typical style for many Jewish families.

As Eddie progressed through his teenage years, Sol began experiencing some health problems related to diabetes. Although Lil often worried about him and took great care in preparing appropriate foods for his condition, Sol was a lover of all edible goods and generally consumed whatever he wanted. With Sol's condition occasionally making him unable to work as much as he needed, Eddie would regularly help out in the grocery store. He would do everything, including sweeping the floors, rearranging the displays, and arranging the meat at the butcher's counter. In his later years, he would often reminisce about scrubbing the vegetable drawers each night and taking great pride in ensuring they were pristine. In fact, it is quite plausible that his future perfectionist tendencies were born out of his grocery store work. When he mopped the floors after closing each night, he wanted to make sure there wasn't a single spot anyone could find. From a young age, Eddie worked hard to ensure everything was done just right, a precursor to his business style years later. No task was too menial for him, from unloading trucks to cutting meat, to stacking cans and boxes.

He quickly learned how to properly arrange items to make them sell better and how to market products accordingly. Eddie even had an opportunity to develop his already budding charm while working in the store while it was open. He would pile fresh corn in an attractive way and wait for the rush of middle-aged women to enter the store for their regular shopping trips. He would lean on the display with a charismatic smile on his face. "See this fresh corn?" he would say. "We just got it in, it's tender as a mother's love." The corn would be sold out in minutes. Eddie also would spend hours making margarine in the back and packaging it for sale. It would come in large blocks of white, and his job would be to add yellow food coloring, mix it up, shape it, and present it to the customers. For the rest of his life, he refused to eat margarine, always demanding butter be available for his meals.

His father was very laid back as a manager, even toward his own son. He gave Eddie free rein to learn at his own pace and make his own mistakes. He didn't restrict his son from any area of the store, allowing Eddie to develop a great love for all things food-related. A trait that stuck around until the day he died, Eddie would forever be a master at picking out fresh produce, choosing the best cuts of meat, and knowing when a canned good was no longer healthy to eat. Through the decades that followed, he was consistently picky about the food he ate. He knew what quality ingredients looked, smelled, and tasted like, and he refused to eat anything subpar. All of this traced back to his many years at Snider Quality Market.

One of the key qualities that Sol had, often unbeknownst to his own wife, was his generosity and willingness to help anybody in need. He would give money to those who asked for help, and often times even those who did not. Years later, when Sol passed away, hundreds of people showed up to his funeral, with scores of them telling Lil their own individual stories of how Sol financially helped them through a difficult time. In her typical, sarcastic tone, she would reply, "Well, *that's* where our money went!" Eddie surely stowed that trait in the back of his mind, planting the seed for his future generosity to others.

But Eddie's childhood was strikingly average, similar to most young Jewish boys at that time. Starting at age 12, he was sent to Camp Cody each summer, a two-month, all-boys, overnight camp in New Hampshire. With about 80 percent Jewish attendees, mostly from Baltimore, Washington, D.C., and Pittsburgh, Eddie attended for four summers and made a name for himself as one of the most competitive and athletically capable campers. For perhaps the first time in his life, people would publicly see how much he simply hated to lose.

The campers partook in various athletic competitions, from water polo to soccer, from baseball to field hockey. He excelled at baseball, staking his role as the catcher—a logical choice for the young leader, since the position often dictates the pace of play and guides the pitcher through the game. Eddie quickly became known as the camp's top water polo player, a natural talent in the pool. At the end of camp each year, the counselors would divide the campers into two teams, gray and green, to compete for top billing. Eddie was the first pick for the team each year, earning him the endearing nickname "First Choice Eddie." In his fourth year, he was named an assistant counselor because of how much he was liked by both the campers and the camp's owners. He showed great leadership and responsibility, and his go-get-'em attitude was always one that put a smile on the faces of those around him. He told his bunkmates of a girlfriend back home named Fippi, whom he would write letters to multiple times per week each summer. Girls were always a topic that interested him, perhaps nearly as much as winning whatever activity in which he was partaking.

Eddie was admittedly not a great student, even as he entered high school, though not for lack of intelligence. He cared much more about his buddies and the ladies than he did his schoolwork. But he was perhaps one of the smartest kids in his age group, a reason why his grades didn't suffer. He was always able to finagle his way to acceptable marks from his teachers. More understandably, Eddie was not the most well-behaved student. He was not quite a class clown, but he found school less important than other parts of his life. And he was not shy about letting his often immature mind take over in the midst of class.

For one assignment, Eddie was instructed to read an Edward Lear poem to his class, entitled, "The Owl and the Pussy-Cat." At one point in the poem, Eddie recited the phrase, "O lovely Pussy! O Pussy, my love, What a beautiful Pussy you are." Naturally, he exploded in laughter, causing the class to do the same. He was sent to the principal's office, where he showed no remorse for his actions. He would continue telling this story for the rest of his life, laughing just as loudly at the poetic phrase in his seventies as he did when he was a teenager.

When Eddie began attending Calvin Coolidge High in D.C., his personality began to take a more concrete shape. As would be the case for most of the rest of his life, he found an inner circle of guys to hang out with. In high school, his posse was called "The Playboys," for reasons one would most expect. They had jackets made up, would have a pack of Lucky Strike cigarettes on their arms, hang around, leaning on cars, smoking (a habit that he would keep for decades), chasing girls, and satisfying their overactive libidos—typical '50s, fast and loose types of guys. Everyone in the group received a nickname. Eddie's was "Tadpole," a moniker he received during his camp days and one he would loosely use sporadically throughout his life, whether to name a boat or as his email address in later years. No one is certain exactly where and how the nickname originated, though there are multiple possibilities. While it could have been attributed to the way he walked, his body type, and even lewder suggestions, most plausibly it was created at Camp Cody because of the large goggles he wore while swimming. Regardless of the origin, it is a nickname he kept for many years, to be used only by his closest of friends.

When Eddie was 16 he received a red Pontiac convertible, which he proudly drove all around town. He was one of the few students with a brand-new car, and he made sure everybody knew it. He also developed a taste for expensive, extravagant clothes at this time. If Eddie wanted something, he could simply ask his Aunt Cecil or Aunt Tammie, and they would gladly provide whatever he needed. His dandy clothes became a trademark that continued throughout his life, especially as he became more successful. His suave looks, along with his reputation, would often get him noticed by those in his peer group. Most importantly, for Eddie, it would garner him the opportunity to meet and flirt with scores of girls, something that would become extremely important to him in his mid-teens.

Even before his high school years, Eddie always had a deep interest in girls. So it was not a shock when that interest expanded during his high school years. Always playing the field, it was unusual for him to want to settle down with someone. Yet, coming from a family dominated by strong-willed and strong-minded women, it is unsurprising that Eddie developed a preference for partners who mirrored those qualities. Even if it was not his initial goal, he would be stricken by the women he met who were independent, confident, adventurous, and mature for their age. As he progressed through high school and began looking for someone permanent, those are the traits to which he was naturally drawn. With that in mind, it wasn't long before he met the first woman who would truly capture his attention.

2

College, Christmas Trees, CPA, and a Record Company

ONE OF THE MEMBERS of Eddie's group, Jerry Lilienfield, became his best friend. The two went everywhere together, hung out with the same crowd, and were attracted to similar women. When Eddie was 18 and a senior at Coolidge, he and his buddies would regularly hang out at a nearby deli. One day, he walked in to see Jerry having lunch with his girlfriend. Eddie, as was typical, leaned up against the table and struck up a conversation with the young, attractive woman, who identified herself as Dobbie Gordon. Always a bit flirtatious and suave with the ladies, Eddie continued chatting until Jerry, trying to protect his own relationship, mentioned that Dobbie had an identical twin sister.

"Really?" Eddie said, getting excited at the prospect. "How old are you?"

"Fifteen," Dobbie replied.

"Oh," he said, a bit dejected. "Tell your sister to call me when she's sixteen."

On that note, Eddie left, most likely forgetting about the interaction. But less than a year later, when Dobbie, Jerry, and Dobbie's sister, Myrna, were driving around the area, Jerry pointed out Eddie's Pontiac in a nearby parking lot. Myrna called out for them to stop the car. She got out, wrote a note, and placed it on Eddie's windshield, giggling as she ran back to her friends. When Eddie came out a few hours later, he saw the piece of paper on his car that simply said, "I'm 16 now." Smirking, he knew exactly what it meant and got into the car to track down his suitor.

Myrna and Eddie hit it off right away. Eddie was a textbook bad boy, while Myrna was petite, attractive, and exorbitantly social. She and Dobbie were inseparable and would constantly be looking for ways to get into trouble together. Myrna was also quite adventurous, never seeming to be satisfied until she tried something even more daring. (Later in life, she would sail across the world, including multiple transatlantic trips.) One time, she ran into a friend while gassing up the family car, and the two got on a plane to Florida without telling anybody. She would always return, but not before getting into some crazy situations.

Eddie's reputation as a ladies' man was well-known throughout school, and Myrna's parents were initially a bit hesitant about their daughter's new love interest. But Myrna knew what she wanted. She was quite independent and had a strength to her that Eddie appreciated and even craved at that time, perhaps reminding him of a piece of his own mother's personality. Eddie enrolled at the University of Maryland, the local school, which was typical for the family. Any time a future grandchild or nephew chose to go to a non-area college, Lil would not understand. "There are a lot of good schools in Washington," she would say. "Why do you have to leave? Your family's here." Eddie fulfilled his mother's wishes and stayed close by. During that time, he and Myrna continued to date, dreaming of bigger things together and pining for their future. And so Eddie bought a diamond ring and presented it to Myrna, just 17 and still in high school. Without blinking an eye, she accepted. When he desired something, he went after it full force until he achieved his goal, even as a teenager.

Both families were ecstatic, and the Sniders threw a large engagement party for the soon-to-be-married couple at their home. The

Gordons had warmed somewhat to Snider and accepted him as their future son-in-law. But while that side of the family was lukewarm on Eddie, the Snider side of the family had fallen for Myrna, just as Eddie had months earlier. The antics among the family members were always entertaining, including when Myrna and Dobbie planned to play a prank on the loving and jocular Sol. People started ribbing him that he couldn't tell his almost daughter-in-law apart from her twin sister. "Are you kidding?" he boomed, "I would know my Myrna anywhere!" So, at the engagement party, the two went into a room and swapped clothes without Sol knowing. When they returned, Dobbie went up to Sol and asked, "Am I yours or not?" Sol cracked a big smile and said, "Are you kidding? Come here, baby! I'd know you anywhere!" When Dobbie revealed the joke, Sol turned red in the face and the entire room erupted in laughter. It was always in good fun, and the families continued to remain close as Eddie and Myrna inched toward their wedding day.

The duo was married the following year at the B'nai Israel synagogue on 16th Street on July 11, 1954. With Dobbie serving as the maid of honor, Phyllis's husband as the best man, and Eddie's guys surrounding him in support of the next chapter of his life, Eddie and Myrna tied the knot. The two were bound to be unstoppable, what with Myrna's wild side and Eddie's determination and refusal to lose at anything. They found an apartment on New Hampshire Avenue in Silver Spring, Maryland, and embarked on their new life together.

Getting married and going off to college did not stop Eddie from being "victim" to his often-overbearing Jewish mother. As the newlyweds slept in their new home, Lil would call her son, waking him up, and tell him it was time to go to school. Myrna and Eddie would roar with laughter, rolling their eyes at how ridiculous it was for his mother to still be that involved when her son was in his twenties. But they smiled, knowing it was done with love—her strong personality simply did not allow for her to act any other way.

Eddie graduated from the University of Maryland in 1955 with a degree in accounting. Over the course of his four years, he excelled in all of his business courses, while earning average marks in his other courses, for a GPA of just over 3.1. His course load was heavily skewed toward his business degree, with a number of advanced accounting courses in which he received A's.*

With a brilliant mind for numbers, he aced the CPA exam and quickly got a job with a firm that assigned him to be the accountant for a local gas station. According to the story Eddie told for the rest of his life, on his first day, he opened up the owner's ledger and saw that the guy was making $25,000 a year running this gas station, while Eddie was making just $5,000. At the end of his first day, he returned to his boss and asked him when he would make that much money. His boss thought about it and replied, "If you work really hard, maybe five years." Eddie handed him the ledger and quit. "I think I'm gonna own a gas station," he said, tongue-in-cheek. The story reeks of classic Snider bravado, and in reality it's more likely he sat down at a dusty, cramped desk covered in grease and oil, already irksome to someone who prided himself on cleanliness and appearance. He had no interest in working in this dirty atmosphere and most likely decided right then and there to find a new career. If he could find a way to work for himself, he wouldn't need to worry about anyone else's workspace.

Still close friends with Jerry Lilienfield, the two decided to team up on various business ventures to try and make some money. The first attempt was Christmas trees—a venture that he later admitted was quite odd for a young Jewish boy. But business was business, and if Eddie saw an opportunity to make money, he wasn't going to argue about the business model. They also sold Easter Lilies on a street

---

* Interestingly, an elective course Eddie took in his junior year was called "The Governments of Russia and the Far East," a curious choice considering his life-long hatred for communism and the Soviet way of life. He aced the course.

corner in the spring. He would come home and dump the change on the floor of the apartment so that he and Myrna could sit down and count their savings. The endeavors were moderately successful, but they wound up scrapping the plans when Jerry came across a new opportunity in which they both saw great potential.

Jerry discovered a warehouse with a half million phonograph records just sitting in boxes, collecting dust—recent records, overstock that simply had not sold as well as anticipated. He shared the information with his best friend, and the two of them together gathered enough money to purchase the lot and open their first company, Edge Limited (EDdie + GErald = EDGE). Eddie approached his Uncle Harry, who owned a cabaret-type of nightclub called Casino Royal in D.C., to ask for some help that he knew his family would always provide. He walked through the front of the house, then backstage, where he had to walk through the girls' dressing area to get to his uncle's office in the back. Harry gave his nephew $5,000 to help jumpstart the new business, and Eddie and Jerry moved the records to Myrna's parents' basement, where the duo created the startup's home base.

The first batch of records sold quite quickly—Eddie placed racks in his father's and others' grocery stores throughout the region, where shoppers grabbed the impulse buys like candy in the checkout aisle. Although Eddie had plenty of money to repay Harry's loan, he continued to pay it at the previously agreed rate of $50 at a time, allowing him to return to the nightclub and walk through the girls' dressing area time after time—quite on brand for the high-testosterone entrepreneur. Nonetheless, Edge Limited started to see some modest success. Eddie quickly made deals with various record companies to supply him with the inventory he needed to keep his customers' store racks filled. Eventually, the two piled records into the trunk of Jerry's car and drove up and down the East Coast, searching for new business. They went as far north as Atlantic City, placing new record racks in retail shops along the Eastern Seaboard.

The duo even enlisted Myrna and her sister, Dobbie, to help them with sales. With the two being young, attractive, and extremely extroverted, they were superstars at charming the mostly male shop-owners and selling the inventory with which Eddie and Jerry had filled the Gordons' basement. Eventually, they even started placing some records in regional big-box stores, which helped them move even more volume than they initially anticipated. The opportunity was now available for the business to develop beyond their wildest dreams.

Desiring to expand, Eddie helped found the National Association of Record Merchandisers, now known as the Music Business Association, even serving as its first president in 1958. Although Edge was moderately successful and there was potentially a method for them to take the company national, there were a few problems. First, the company did not have nearly enough capital to expand to the size needed to match the demand. There simply was not enough cash flow in the business model to support a national expansion. Second, the business was getting too big for Eddie and Jerry to handle on their own, and every time they hired people to whom they could delegate, problems seemed to arise, forcing the duo to step in and perform the duties themselves. Third, and perhaps most importantly, Eddie simply hated it. He loved owning and running his own business, and knew that's what he eventually wanted to do, but he couldn't stand the constant packing of the car, store-to-store selling, and the days and weeks on the road. The money was great, but he was not enjoying the work— leading to another lifelong lesson he always attempted to impart on others. Money could never be the reason for an entrepreneurial endeavor. It had to be something you were deeply passionate about, something you could do every day with continued joy. The record business did not fill that need for Eddie. Instead, he came home each day exhausted, dejected, and resentful toward his work.

After long discussions, the two decided to call it quits and close up shop. It is not known if they simply closed or sold off the business, but it is certain that, if they did sell it, it would not have been for very much money. The company had no assets other than its inventory and there would have been little to no value for any potential buyer. Nonetheless, the two were happy with their modest success and were thrilled to go into the next chapter of their careers.

For Eddie, that meant a job offer from Capitol Records in their famous cylindrical building out in California. He was intrigued by the notion and brought it home to discuss with Myrna, but she was not a fan, to say the least. She loved being close to her family and was inseparable from her twin sister. To move across the country at a time when regular long-distance contact was near impossible (and certainly not affordable) was not something she was willing to do. Always putting his faith in his loving partner and trusting her every step of his early adult life, he agreed and turned down the offer.

In the late '50s, Myrna gave birth to the couple's first child, Craig. Over the next few years, they would welcome Jay, Lindy, and Tina to the family as well. At this point, it became even more evident that Eddie was dependent on Myrna for nearly every part of his personal life. Despite his business brilliance and his ambition, he was nearly incapable of taking care of himself without the help of his wife. She would cook his meals and bring him drinks, and when she was out for the day or on vacation with her family, he would inevitably cause some mess that she was later forced to clean up. While she was gone one day with her sister, Eddie called her, explaining that he was trying to make coffee but there was a terrible smell. After trying to troubleshoot over the phone, Myrna realized that her husband had taken the rubber-bottom coffee pot and put it directly on the stove, melting the pot and causing dangerous fumes to rise throughout the house. Another time, home alone for the night, he set newspapers throughout the hallway and around his bed before going to sleep, that way he would hear if someone came into the house and was walking toward his bedroom— he would wake up with just enough time to do something about it.

He would also begin developing some of the food habits that would be a trademark in his later years. One of these was his incredible love of and reliance on Heinz ketchup. He put it on almost everything and if it was not available, he would go nuts. Multiple times he would ransack a relative or friend's cabinets when they advised him they did not have Heinz for the meal they were about to enjoy. This ransacking often included him throwing items across the kitchen, desperately trying to find a hidden bottle that had long been forgotten.

Eddie may have been useless when it came to homemaking, but with his business now closed, he was facing a new issue: what to do with his life. He was ambitious and laser-focused on anything he put his mind to, but he needed an opportunity, one he hoped would come knocking soon. That opportunity came through his brother-in-law, Earl Foreman. Phyllis had begun dating Foreman when Eddie was a teenager. Foreman had recently returned from his service in the military, for which he had earned a Bronze Star. With the age difference between Foreman and Eddie, along with the difference in life experiences, Foreman became a makeshift older brother to the young Snider. Eddie would share his baseball card collection, but the two bonded over Eddie's requests for advice on this cute new girl he met (Myrna). Foreman obliged and was always there to help his brother-in-law in whatever he needed. The two were very close, acting more like brothers than most biological siblings. Foreman was a large part of Eddie's teenage years, and their friendship blossomed into a relationship that would eventually result in the start of his career in professional sports. He became one of Eddie's closest friends and confidants.

An attorney by trade, Foreman became acquainted with a young, up-and-coming Jewish businessman named Jerry Wolman, a builder in the Washington, D.C., region who was nearly six years Eddie's senior. Wolman had a weekly card game with some of his friends. When one of those friends invited Foreman to join them one night, he introduced himself as an attorney, which piqued Wolman's interest. Needing someone to help him close a few small deals he was pursuing, the two began a business relationship that continued growing exponentially.

When Wolman's father suffered a stroke years earlier and became debilitated, Jerry dropped out of high school to run the family business, the Shenandoah Produce Company. Similar to Eddie, Jerry learned by doing all of the menial tasks in the company, even selling over-stocked produce door-to-door as a 10-year-old to help his father's fledgling business. From a young age, the similarities between the two men, in terms of upbringing and personality, were striking.

A few years later, in their twenties, Wolman and his wife, Anne, decided to leave Shenandoah, Pennsylvania, in search of a better life. With almost no money to their name, they got in the car and agreed to pick up a hitchhiker. Wherever he was going, that's where they would settle. The winning city was Washington, D.C. The two found an apartment that cost them under $10 per week. He found work as a paint store salesman, where he slowly met various builders and developers, ultimately becoming enamored with the profession. Eventually, he decided to take a leap of faith and entered the real estate development world himself. In addition to his inherent talent, his passion for his work was unrivaled. "There's nothing like it," Wolman said in a *Philadelphia Inquirer* feature written in the 1960s. "You start with vacant land; you put in the foundations, watch the steel go up. And one night you pass by and see lights in the windows and you know you've created something."

By the 1960s, Wolman was worth over $35 million. His company had built over 4 million square feet of office space, shopping centers, and motels, in addition to 25,000 housing units. He worked with his brother and regularly put in up to 18 hours of work each day. Those who worked with him said he had a photographic memory and a keen business acumen.

Each time Foreman closed a deal for Wolman, in addition to the attorney's fee, Wolman would often give him a cut of the asset, which resulted in Foreman generating for himself and his family an immense amount of income at a young age. Wolman and Foreman became like brothers, introducing each other to their group of friends and family. One of those family members was Sol Snider, who Foreman had grown close with ever since he began dating Phyllis. Sol was always a fan of a businessman with an entrepreneurial spirit, and Wolman fit that description marvelously. The three would often go to lunch and socialize, discussing crazy business ideas and regularly keeping in touch. Despite a 20-year age difference between Sol and Wolman, the two got along amicably.

A few years later, Wolman discovered that his boyhood team, the Philadelphia Eagles, was for sale. In 1963, with Foreman's logistical and financial help, he entered an auction and gave the highest bid at $5,505,000—then the highest price ever paid for a professional sports franchise. The bid was accepted, and at 36 he became the youngest owner in the National Football League. Perhaps the best description of Wolman comes in the form of an answer he gave to a reporter when asked why he overpaid for the Eagles franchise: "Because I fucking wanted it," he said. With Foreman owning 48 percent of the new venture, the two began putting together a plan for how to run the organization.

In the midst of his bidding for the team, Wolman returned to Washington, D.C., and after chatting with Foreman, discovered that, with Wolman overseeing his construction company and Foreman keeping his home base in Washington, they would need someone to oversee the day-to-day operations of the Eagles organization. Eddie had recently stopped his involvement with his record company and was looking for a new career. It is possible that Sol Snider mentioned to Wolman that his son had a brilliant business mind and a work ethic that rivaled anyone. It is also not out of the realm of possibility that Foreman himself pitched his brother-in-law to his business partner.

Regardless of exactly how it happened, Wolman, slightly aware of Eddie's previous record business, was intrigued by his raw ambition. Wolman saw a bit of himself in the budding entrepreneur and often placed his trust in like-minded people who saw the world in a similar way. Eddie was dazzled by Wolman's attitude and his penchant for going after a dream with no second thought. The two quickly became close friends, earning Eddie a valuable spot in Wolman's group of close advisors. After chatting with him, the builder invited Eddie to join the Eagles front office and run the organization. Despite the offer forcing him to move away from his family, Eddie was enthused by the proposal. He and Myrna agreed that, despite not wanting to be far away from their respective families, it was close enough that they could regularly arrange visits in either city. With bright eyes and dreams for the future, the young couple packed up their bags and moved to this new city, Philadelphia, eager to start the next chapter of their lives.

3

Joining and Running the Eagles

ON DECEMBER 6, 1963, Philadelphia technically met Ed Snider for the first time. In the announcement of the team's purchase, Wolman revealed the ownership split between him and Foreman. When asked by the *Courier Post* why he would own the majority, he responded with a smile, saying, "Because I'm smarter," eliciting laughs from all of the surrounding reporters. Snider was introduced as "a 31-year-old public relations director with the group." In reality, Wolman wanted him running the team and had also given him a future option to purchase 7 percent of Foreman's shares for $70,385.

Within weeks, Snider's position was upgraded to team treasurer, and the duo gathered their newly acquired Eagles employees in the team offices. With everyone in a conference room, Wolman stood before them and introduced himself and his business partners. "I'll be around," he told everyone, "so I'll have the opportunity to meet with each of you one on one." But with Wolman jetting off to Chicago quite often to oversee a new, major construction project, he needed someone to be in charge while he was working from afar. That is when he presented Snider to his new employees as the man who would run the Eagles during his regular absences.

Snider garnered a similar respect as Wolman, but in a very different way. While Wolman was always smiling, friendly, and lackadaisical in a charming way, Snider was focused, driven, and stern about his work.

He went around meeting one on one with each of his new employees to ensure they understood his expectations. Information was his best friend. He requested daily reports from each department and was furious if a day passed without one being placed on his desk. Running a professional sports organization was his big chance to make a splash and he was not going to blow it by expecting anything less than perfection. Some would occasionally get annoyed with Snider's tough, demanding attitude, but there was complete respect for him and his work ethic. As one former employee said, "He got everybody in line."

As he walked the office, Snider, who demanded to be called "Ed" or "Eddie" (though most continued to call him Mr. Snider), would tell employees, "You better anticipate my questions." Consequently, when they would gather in his office to go over the day's reports, Snider would inevitably come up with the one question they had not expected. Employees quickly learned about Snider's extraordinary level of intelligence, quick thinking, and business acumen. He had a gift for seeing a situation and cutting right to the chase, leading his employees in the right direction and then letting them find the correct answer on their own.

While Snider was busy attending to the day-to-day operations, Wolman was making a name for himself in Philadelphia as well. The Eagles owner was known by all those around him to be the most generous person they had ever met. He would regularly give $100 tips to valets, waiters, and others who worked for him. When he visited his children at camp in the summers, he would give $100 bills to their counselors as thanks. If an employee needed a few dollars for cab fare, Wolman would whip out a $20 bill and tell them to keep the extra. There were stories that often popped up of Wolman's indulgent kindness, including a situation where he anonymously covered the expenses for someone's medical bills. Whether or not the specific stories are true, it helps to illustrate the level of generosity that Snider observed from his boss, even if it was occasionally over the top. As

Snider became more successful in business in later years, his generosity also became legendary, though it was never quite as in-your-face as Wolman's. Nonetheless, it was through this relationship that Snider learned how important it was to treat those close to you as well as possible. Snider's generosity in his Eagles days was apparent, if not more practical—though any level of kindness would seem insignificant relative to Wolman at the time.

Wolman would give just about anything to those close to him. In fact, he even claimed later in life that he infused Snider's record company with cash during a period of struggle. While Snider forever denied it (and the evidence suggests that the two did not even meet until after Snider closed down his record company), there is no doubt that, if Snider had ever asked, Wolman would have done so without question. Early in Snider's Eagles tenure, he and Myrna were finally able to purchase their first home—Wolman claimed that he gave them $83,000, but financial documents from Snider's personal archive show that it was a loan, which was eventually paid back in full. What is inarguable, though, is that Wolman provided Snider with the opportunity to see serious financial success for the first time in his life. The two had grown incredibly close, vacationing together with their spouses and regularly socializing outside of work. Emotional and overly grateful for his friendship, Snider penned this note to his boss just after he and Myrna settled on their home:

> For the first time in my life, I have the desire to write a letter, the nature of which I have never had occasion to write before. Jerry, I got the biggest thrill of my life today—the combination of sitting in the little company and writing a check in excess of $83,000.00 for our new home while everyone's eyes popped out and then going over to the home and realizing that this magnificent place would be where Myrna, the kids, and I would be living. All of this added to the exciting,

challenging, and wonderful opportunity that you have given
to me with the Eagles. I only hope that my close association
with you will give me the insight to acquire the many wonderful characteristics that you so naturally come by—generosity,
consideration, humor, instinct, vast intelligence, unequaled
common sense, humility, understanding—I could go on forever. Even more important is the fact that my overwhelming
ambition is to see that you get much more than your money's worth. Jerry, the finest thing that could happen to any
man is to have you as a close friend—and the fact that this is
the case with me overwhelms me dearly. Having answered
so many letters thanking you for this or that in the past year,
I feel strange in writing one myself—but the simple spoken
word could never adequately express my feelings—I just
choke up. There is nothing that is within my ability to do
that I would not do for you, should you ask. Eddie.

The letter highlights just how beautiful a relationship the two
enjoyed in the 1960s. There was a mutual love between the two, the
sort of emotional attachment that two men have for each other when
so much of their lives are intertwined and their values aligned. Wolman and Snider also spent much time together outside the office.
They would regularly double date with their wives and spend many
nights hanging out at Gatsby's, a restaurant in Narberth, Pennsylvania, where many of the bigshots in Philadelphia would relax. The two
liked the same foods, enjoyed similar vacation spots, and even had
similar tastes in women. The Eagles owner was charming and social,
able to disarm a room with a smile. He was generous, always willing
to go above and beyond to help someone, even if he did not know
them. Their personalities jibed well, and one can see the later stages
of Snider's business personality take root from his days looking up to
Wolman.

Those close to Wolman also called him the most charismatic person they had ever seen. He thrived off making his employees feel special. He would take the time to get to know them, genuinely showing care for each of them and their families. He also was exorbitantly passionate about his work, whether it was construction or his football team. After purchasing the team, he had a big green limousine with a silver eagle on the front of the hood so that he could show off the love he held for his organization. Just about everyone who met him fell in love with him, just like Snider did as a young man. The two together made a dynamic duo.

Right from the get go, Wolman and Snider both made themselves quite visible to the public. Snider was regularly on the Eagles sideline, often wearing pointed Italian shoes, peg pants, a skinny tie, and hair greased back just so. He walked with the same swagger he had as a teenager and with the confidence of a man who had been running professional teams for years. Just days after the sale to Wolman was announced, the two flew to St. Louis to watch the Eagles play the Cardinals and made themselves available to the press after the team's loss. They were visible from the start, showcasing the passion and care they had for the football club, whether it was on game day or in the front office.

In Snider's capacity, he oversaw the entire organization, both the business and football operations, though any major decision was of course subject to Wolman's approval. Shortly after they took over the team, which had just experienced a horrendous 2–10–2 record, they fired head coach Nick Skorich and began the search for a new one. Wolman was interested in the Bears' George Allen, a young defensive coordinator at the time, but Bears owner George Halas convinced the naïve Wolman that Allen wasn't head coach material (because he didn't want to lose the future Hall of Famer). Instead, Wolman hired Joe Kuharich, a former coach of the Notre Dame football team, Washington Redskins, and Chicago Bears, and currently working in the league office. Kuharich never had a winning season in six campaigns between stints in Washington and Chicago, but he and Wolman clicked instantly in their first meeting. Kuharich was given a five-year contract and complete control of football operations.

As the 1964 football season progressed, the team seemed to be in a better position than the previous year. With Kuharich believing the team needed a boost of young talent, he sent star quarterback Sonny Jurgensen, who spent part of the 1963 season injured, to Washington along with halfback Jimmy Carr in exchange for 24-year-old quarterback Norm Snead and defensive back Claude Crabb. He also moved fan favorite and five-time Pro Bowl wide receiver Tommy McDonald to the Dallas Cowboys for three starters. McDonald was so jolted by the move that he briefly considered retiring after the news broke. Nonetheless, Wolman had made his point—he wanted Kuharich to make the team his own and gave him carte blanche to remake the roster as he saw fit.

As the 1964 season was coming to a close, the new coach had already tripled the previous year's win total to six and Wolman was sold. He approached Snider and informed his partner that he wanted to give Kuharich a long-term contract. Snider was not convinced. He and Kuharich had butt heads through most of the first season, and Snider felt he was difficult to work with. Wolman pleaded his case, but Snider held firm. At the end, Wolman insisted that it was his team and if he wanted to reward his coach, that was what he was going to do.

A few days before the final game of the season, Wolman announced that he had signed Kuharich to a record 15-year contract worth $60,000 per year, a significant raise from the $40,000 he made in his first season. The contract was longer than such coaching stars as Tom Landry, who only received a 10-year contract from the Cowboys, and Paul Brown, who also received a 10-year deal from the Cleveland Browns. Even the legendary Vince Lombardi, who was two championships into a seven-year span that saw the Green Bay Packers win the league's title five times, only had a five-year contract.

Philadelphia was stunned at the news, but Wolman displayed his usual confidence. Not only was he giving out this unprecedented contract to a coach who just had a losing season, but he was promoting Snider to vice president and treasurer of the team. "He has full authority to make any and all decisions relative to Eagles' operations," Wolman said to the Associated Press. Although it was not publicly announced at the same time, along with his new title, Snider received a similar 15-year contract to run the organization. The assumption is that Wolman rewarded Snider for going along with the Kuharich signing, despite his disagreement. That was the kind of loyalty Wolman expected and loyalty that Snider eventually learned to appreciate as well.

The duo continued to turn heads around Philadelphia. At the 19th annual Sportswriters and Broadcasters Dinner in January 1965, Wolman was one of the guest speakers, flanked by Snider, Kuharich, and other team executives. The media ate them all up, touting Wolman's personality and Snider's youthful exuberance. Their beloved football team, they believed, was finally in good hands. They were only five years removed from winning the NFL championship, but the team had fallen hard. The fans needed heroes, and Wolman and Snider seemed to be the pair to fill the void.

Philadelphia had always been (and still is) a blue-collar city. Fans of each of Philly's teams just want to see players and owners care as much about the team's success as they do. If the fans can live and die with each win and each perceived slight from an opposing fan, why shouldn't those who work for and run the team do the same? There was no better example of this than in the 1965 preseason. During a 37–0 beatdown by the Redskins, tempers were already boiling from the embarrassment. With Snider and Wolman in the stands, along with Wolman's wife and kids, Washington fans started yelling anti-Semitic slights at the executives.

"A Jew should not own a football team!" one yelled. "The game's too rough for their little white hands!"

"Jews shouldn't own the Philadelphia Eagles!" another screamed.

Wolman, unwilling to take the abuse, punched three fans in the face. A skirmish ensued, with Snider jumping in to protect his owner. At Snider's insistence, it took multiple officers, who were initially standing around watching, to break up the fight. Wolman was fuming as Snider walked him out of the building and back to the safety of the team. But the Philadelphia fans responded to the raw passion that the two continued to show in running the team. Just before the start of the season, the Eagles announced a team-record 48,254 season tickets sold. The stadium was now nearly full for every game, with 60,000 fans regularly piling in to watch their beloved Eagles.

Even at this early stage, it is very easy to see the roots of Snider's eventual business success. Not only was he passionate about the free market and doing what he could to give his team and league an advantage, but he was also extremely progressive when it came to managing a professional sports team. Ahead of the 1966 NFL Draft (which took place in November 1965), the Eagles spent an unheard-of $200,000 on their scouting efforts, including outfitting their draft day hotel suite with eight phones to use for nearly 48 straight hours, in an attempt to get a leg up on their competition. The more information they had at their fingertips, he figured, the more likely they were to have a better draft than their counterparts. Snider was heavily involved in the team's draft, not from a football standpoint, but from a strategic perspective. He loved learning about the various techniques for evaluating talent, collecting differing opinions from scouts and helping shape them into a decision. It was something he continued to utilize for decades.

Just a couple months later, the NFL signed a massive television contract with CBS, a deal that would bring in $18.8 million for each of the next two seasons and one that shocked the traditionalists because it dropped the local blackout rule. For years, the NFL restricted televised games based on when the local team was playing. If the Eagles were playing at 1:00 PM on a Sunday, no other NFL game could be presented on the region's airwaves at the same time. Even when the local stadium was sold out, the NFL still refused to broadcast other games, much to the dismay of their fans.

But the new deal was pushed by those like Snider, who saw the future of the business before their eyes. Split among 15 teams, the contract amounted to over $2 million for each team over the course of the following seasons. The old guard in the football world complained about television potentially keeping fans away from games, which would sacrifice valuable gate revenue. But Snider knew that theory was baseless, as it had already essentially been disproven.

"We don't believe the change will hurt our attendance at all," Snider said to the *Philadelphia Inquirer*. "If we thought it would take away as many as 100 regular fans, we would have opposed it, regardless of the money involved. We like to believe that if the fans have a choice between seeing the Eagles play or watching another game on TV, they'll be at our game. If they can't come to our game, we'd rather have them watch another NFL game on TV than an [American Football League] game."

His concern for the AFL came from a place close to home. Unbeknownst to many, Snider was working behind the scenes with the higher-ups in Philadelphia to secure a new stadium for the Eagles. Since 1958, Franklin Field had housed the Eagles on 33rd and South Street, just west of the Schuylkill River. A luxurious-looking stadium when it was completed in the 1920s, it surely had its own charm. But 40 years later, it was antiquated and not fit for a professional football team. At that time, The Pennsylvania Railroad and Madison Square Garden wanted to partner to build a new arena on the railroad tracks at 30th Street in Philadelphia. With Franklin Field sitting just a few blocks away, Snider opposed that plan, of course, but was interested in making inroads on a similar project. He called Paul D'Ortona, president of the Philadelphia City Council, to discuss his wild idea.

The *Philadelphia Daily News* once described the politician as "a no-nonsense, money-for-the-neighborhood kind of " guy. An Italian immigrant, he cared deeply for Philadelphia and in coming up with ways to improve the city. Upon hearing the idea, D'Ortona immediately invited Snider for a ride. They drove down to a swampy area of South Philadelphia at the corner of Broad Street and Pattison Avenue. The only structure there at the time was JFK Stadium, the rickety old venue that housed the Eagles for a few years in the 1930s. D'Ortona had a dream to put a brand-new sports stadium in that area to draw people to South Philly.

"I just loved the area," Snider reminisced years later to the *Philadelphia Daily News*. "I loved the confluence with I-95 and 76. The subway stop was put here at the same time. Coming up from Delaware, coming in from New Jersey, coming down from the Northeast on 95, coming in from Philadelphia and the rest on 76—I didn't want people having to fight through congestion in the center of town."

A few days later, after creating a business strategy that would work for both the city and the team, Snider called D'Ortona and told him he wanted to build a new football-baseball stadium on the north side of Pattison Avenue. Working with Phillies owner Robert Carpenter Jr., the two teams hatched a plan to partner together to erect a place they could both call home. In 1964, the voters approved a $25 million bond issue to finance a potential new stadium, giving Snider the green light to begin the formal process. As part of the agreement, the city agreed to give the Eagles exclusive football use of the proposed new stadium, attempting to prevent a potential AFL team from being introduced to the region.

But problems quickly arose with regards to the AFL battle. Founded in 1959, the league was becoming a serious thorn in the NFL's side. Players were being lured away to the rival league with big bonuses, inflated salaries, and promises of future success. The Eagles, meanwhile, tried their best to hold on to as many players as they could. More importantly, though, to keep their market value and their monopoly on football fans in the region, Snider negotiated that exclusive stadium deal to protect his and Wolman's team. But Philadelphia Mayor James Tate fought the deal the Eagles signed with D'Ortona, claiming that the city did not have the right to negotiate an exclusive deal with the Eagles. In reality, he was reportedly conducting secret negotiations to lure an AFL franchise to the city to help line the city's treasury. Tate claimed the city could support two teams, but Snider was not going to let it happen while he was in charge.

The situation led to a very public battle between Tate and Wolman, as the two traded barbs through the media. It came to a head in May 1965, when Wolman filed suit against the city to force them into signing the previously agreed upon exclusive contract. D'Ortona remained on Wolman's side, but Tate held the power and continued to create headaches for the team. After a blue-ribbon committee was established by the judge to force Wolman and Tate to come to an agreement, Wolman offered to cut the length of the exclusive deal from 30 to 15 years and also promised to underwrite any deficits the building incurred through operations. Tate held firm on his end, but by the end of June, the AFL had had enough with the politics and announced they were not considering Philadelphia for an expansion team. Days later, the Eagles came to a deal with the city, granting them exclusivity in the new stadium for 10 years, with the lease auto-renewing for two additional 10-year terms—though in those subsequent 20 years, the city had the right to permit an AFL team to use the stadium. The team had fought off Tate's bullying tactics for at least a decade.

As it was, though, the federal government was beginning to create additional headaches for those like Snider who were trying to get ahead of the game. At the end of 1959, the Washington Redskins signed a new, 29-year lease with the District of Columbia Armory

Board, which granted them the exclusive use of D.C. Stadium for professional football. After the AFL was created and a group of Washington businessmen were looking to apply for a franchise, they submitted a complaint to the U.S. Justice Department, claiming the restrictive covenant violated the Sherman Anti-Trust Act.

In October 1965, Frank J. Barry, the Interior Department's solicitor general, reported his findings in front of Congress. Because the government owned the land on which the stadium was located, and because of the District of Columbia Stadium Act of 1957, the federal government had the right to oversee any deal regarding the use of the stadium. He found that:

> The landlord has agreed to make the facility available, for professional football purposes, exclusively to the Redskins. The effect of the covenant is to foreclose all competitors to exhibiting professional games in the Washington Market. Exclusive agreements foreclosing much less than all the available facilities have been held to violate the anti-trust law.... The Redskins are, by virtue of being the only professional football team in the District of Columbia metropolitan market, a monopolist.... The act of excluding all competitors from the market conclusively demonstrates that it is using its position to maintain its monopoly position, and is therefore prohibited by section 2 of the Sherman Act. (Congressional Record 27834)

Snider was horrified at the ruling, claiming to the Associated Press that it "would invalidate stadium contracts of almost all NFL clubs." The deal was essentially the same that Snider had negotiated with the city of Philadelphia. Not only did he feel the government was overreaching to control the fate of private businesses—something he despised—but he was concerned for the well-being of his own organization. Snider was at one of the heads of the table when it came to battling with the rival American Football League and he was not planning to back down.

The Eagles vice president was one of the key members of the NFL committee that began negotiating with the AFL to end the rivalry and merge the two leagues together in 1966. Although NFL Commissioner Pete Rozelle was the only one to make public statements regarding the negotiations, Snider was one of many NFL team executives to provide counsel to Rozelle as he attempted to navigate perhaps the toughest test the league ever faced. When, in June 1966, the two leagues agreed on a deal to end their petty war, Snider had developed a hatred for league rivalries, instead seeing that it was more beneficial to all parties to come together to fight for the same goal—expanding the sport throughout the country. This experience gained by settling disputes between rival sports leagues would come in handy years later when he went through a similar ordeal in the NHL.

But at the time, the Philadelphia market never seemed to dictate the desire for a second football team anyway. The fans loved their Eagles and would support them no matter the circumstance. Snider was never bothered by the legal troubles related to his exclusive lease, allowing him to move forward on plans for the new stadium. As the project progressed, it was clear that the stadium was going to cost much more than initially planned. When the number reached an estimated $41 million, Snider was forced to return to the city, where there was heavy opposition from the politicians. Snider, not one for dealing with government regulation or any sort of red tape, was furious at the delay. He called Philadelphia a "red-hot sports town," and berated the city for using politics to deprive the fans of something they deserved. He noted that over 12,000 fans regularly paid to see the 76ers play at the rundown Convention Hall. Over 75,000 fans showed up to watch the Navy–Notre Dame football game at the antiquated JFK Stadium. And the Eagles consistently sold-out Franklin Field, a stadium that was showing more age each week. Imagine what each team could accomplish with a proper, modern facility?

During his days with the Eagles, Snider regularly involved Myrna with his job, a strategy he would utilize for the remainder of the marriage, regardless of the business in which he was involved. Snider leaned on his wife for social functions and business ideas that he felt he was unable to execute on his own. In fact, some have claimed that Myrna ended up writing the original iteration of the Eagles fight song, which would only be used for a short time before being temporarily retired. (Of course, the cheer would return years later in a shorter, more recognizable fashion and is now used throughout each Eagles game.) That claim is nearly impossible to verify, but it is plausible based on her involvement elsewhere in the organization. She was instrumental in creating the cheerleading squad that is now so prevalent at football games. Games needed to be livelier and more engaging, in her opinion, especially in between the whistles. There was too much down time, and she felt it needed to be filled by any means necessary—specifically in getting women more involved in the sport. A fight song would have fit in just perfectly with the atmosphere she was trying to create.*

With Wolman and Snider running the show, the Eagles' top two made for a dynamic duo that was taking the sports world by storm. Both of them were well-respected throughout the NFL, despite being much younger and more progressive than most other executives in

---

* The creation of the original Eagles fight song is often credited to two Philadelphia ad men in the 1950s. The original version was much longer and only slightly similar to the current iteration of "Fly, Eagles, Fly." The first time a fight song began playing regularly at Eagles games was in the mid-1960s, which tracks with the theory that Myrna was somehow involved.

the league. Their colleagues loved the youthful energy each possessed and especially loved Snider's focus and passion for his team. During an NFL convention in Hawaii, Snider once blindside-tackled Pittsburgh Steelers' coach Bill Austin as a prank. His enthusiasm was infectious, and those around him always seemed to want to work harder to match his ambition. The two had a vision for the evolution of the business of professional football, and other owners were going to have to keep up or be left behind.

Snider's time running the Eagles coincided with inarguable financial success for the organization. According to documents Wolman filed with the SEC in 1968, the team's revenue increased 32 percent in the few years since he purchased it. The organization was extremely profitable, generating millions of dollars for Wolman's coffers, much of which was attributable to the league's new television contract—a fact that was not lost on Snider as he progressed in his career. In a 1967 letter, Snider outlined his duties with the Eagles. They included speaking at local events, speaking to the media on behalf of the Eagles, approving all operating budgets, negotiating player contracts, supervising the team's scouting system, approving the team's preseason schedule, approving ticket prices, and "having the final decision in any and all matters pertaining to the operation of the club."

And despite the team's lack of on-field success—the Eagles had just one winning season by 1968 and failed to make the playoffs in each of the Wolman-Snider years—Snider was a visionary and one who impressed even the staunchest of potential critics: the Philadelphia media. In a 1966 profile by the *Republican and Herald*, Snider was described as an "energetic and vital young man who knows how to utilize every" second of his valuable time. "At age 33, a man of this generation," it continued. "A man with great foresight. A man who envisions some good in everything he undertakes, and then strives to make it the best. Ed Snider has that wonderful quality of leadership."

By example, rather than demand, he has been able to gain the respect and loyalty of people in his charge and the business and civic leaders of the community. He conducts himself and the operation of the Eagles on the higher level." It was clear that Snider had a firm handle on running a professional sports organization and learned the steps required to make it successful, which he was about to use as other business opportunities arose.

4

Saving the Hockey Team

IT WAS MARCH 1965 when the National Hockey League announced it would be doubling the size of the league by adding six new teams. However, this garnered almost no media attention in Philadelphia and therefore did not register with Snider, who was busy strategizing the Eagles' future. This potential new business venture only revealed itself in conversation with Bill Putnam, an old banking buddy from Morgan Guaranty Trust Company in New York, who Wolman and Foreman utilized to secure the loan to purchase the Eagles years earlier.

Putnam and Snider kept in touch throughout the years, and when Putnam informed him he was leaving to go to Los Angeles to work for Jack Kent Cooke, who was working on his own bid for one of the two west coast teams that the NHL planned to award, Snider was confused. He asked if an NHL franchise was available for purchase. Not just one, Putnam replied, there were six available—two in the west, two in the central, and two in the east.

Almost immediately upon hearing this news, Snider was hit with two prominent memories. In the early 1960s, during his days running Edge Limited, he was in New York City having a cocktail with Juggy Gayles, a sales manager for Carlton Records and a business friend of Snider's. Instead of dinner, Gayles opted for a hockey game, which his counterpart knew nothing about. Having never seen a hockey game in his life, Snider was curious at best, if not somewhat uninterested, to see the Montreal Canadiens play the New York Rangers in Madison Square Garden. When the puck dropped, he was stricken and fell in love with the game—specifically the play of Rangers goalie Gump Worsley, a Hall of Fame talent in the prime of his career. The bulky goalie, standing at 5'7" and 180 pounds, did not look like a typical athlete, which stunned Snider, whose familiarity with athletics was more from football than any other sport. He loved that Worsley looked like a typical fan off the street, rather than a chiseled athlete, along with the fact that he played without a mask, giving the crowd full view of their superstar. Although Snider didn't attend another hockey game for quite some time, that memory remained in the back of his mind.

A few years after that first game, while visiting Boston as a member of the Eagles, Snider went to Boston Garden with a friend to see his hometown 76ers play the Celtics in an NBA matchup. While exiting the arena, he turned his head to see hundreds of fans lined up at the box office. He asked his friend what they were waiting for, to which he learned that the NHL's Bruins put 1,000 tickets on sale each game-day morning. What shocked Snider even more was that the Bruins, at the time, were in last place. Unbeknownst to the Eagles executive, hockey was the hottest ticket in Boston. Even legendary Celtics' coach Red Auerbach used to publicly complain. "The Bruins open the door, and the Boston Garden fills up every night they play," he told the *Miami Herald* in 1966. "We keep winning titles and have to hustle and scratch to draw a sellout crowd." Indeed, between 1957 and 1966, the Celtics made the NBA Finals every year and won nine championships. The Bruins failed to even make the playoffs between 1960 and 1967, finishing last place in the league six times during that span.

With the Eagles financially healthy and a new football-baseball stadium a potential reality (what would eventually become Veterans Stadium), these memories had Snider turning his attention to the other section of the swampy stretch of land, the spot across Pattison Avenue, next to the decrepit, nearly abandoned JFK Stadium. Snider was intrigued when Putnam told him of the league's expansion plans. Like the rest of the sports world, he knew major league hockey was often closed off to outsiders.

The NHL had been a six-team league since 1942. The squads are historically referred to as the Original Six, even though the league's history goes back to as early as 1917. With six healthy franchises to their name, the league was content to continue operating in such a small region. As late as February 1965, NHL President Clarence Campbell made public statements bashing the idea of expansion. The league was selling to about 95 percent capacity at that point. The teams were profitable, albeit on a small-business basis, but owners were happy. Despite being regularly excoriated by the media for the perception that they refused to let outsiders into their little club, those on the executive board were insistent that expansion was not an option.

Fortunately, New York Rangers president Bill Jennings wasn't quite as hard-nosed as the rest of the executive board. Jennings was a graduate of Princeton and Yale Law School, eventually becoming the counsel for the Madison Square Garden Corporation, which owned and managed the Rangers. He was known as the league's most progressive member, helping to establish the NHL's New York office in the mid-'60s and constantly pushing for an evolution of the sport's business model. At least seven times between 1962 and 1964 he tried to convince his fellow owners of the merits of expansion. Each time, he was shot down. But once there was no longer room for financial growth at the gate, the owners realized they needed additional revenue streams. They confidently approached television networks for a national deal, but were stunned to find out that no one was interested in broadcasting a league that only had four teams in the United States, all of whom were closer to Canada than the rest of the country. Essentially, the league realized that in order to get their TV contract, they needed two teams in California (Los Angeles and the Bay Area), two more teams in the middle of the country, and two additional teams on the East Coast.

Coincidentally, around the same time period, 76ers owner Ike Richman had engaged Snider in a few brief conversations about Wolman's interest in building an arena so the basketball team could move from Convention Hall to a more profitable building. With a back-of-the-mind appreciation for hockey, an understanding of hockey's success in similar-sized cities, along with Richman's predicament, it all clicked in Snider's mind. A hockey franchise and basketball franchise could share the same arena, along with a healthy schedule of concerts and events, thereby making the building a profitable enterprise for Wolman and give each franchise the opportunity to succeed financially as well. Snider had a tendency to be influenced by those with whom he was involved. In this case, it was a construction expert in Wolman (along with those who were aiding his efforts in constructing Veterans Stadium). This certainly put him in the mindset to dive headfirst into this potential new project.

With his idea in mind, he asked Putnam, who had already been in touch with the league, if he thought the NHL would be receptive to a bid from Philadelphia. Putnam wasn't certain, but gave Snider the phone number for Jennings, who headed the league's expansion committee. Snider immediately contacted Jennings, who at first acknowledged that Philadelphia was one of the largest markets in North America, larger than multiple existing franchises. Yet he was perturbed by the lack of success for minor professional hockey teams that Philadelphia had iced in the previous few decades and was more concerned about the city's brief, but disastrous history with the NHL. The Philadelphia Quakers were born in 1930 when the Pittsburgh Pirates hockey team relocated as they attempted to fix their arena issues. Owned by famed fighter Benny Leonard, the Quakers had arguably the worst season in NHL history, going 4–36–4 and finishing in last place. The team lost a great deal of money and averaged just 2,500 fans per game. The franchise was forced to fold after the 1930–31 season.

Other professional teams graced Philadelphia ice in the decades that followed, but most did not have great success, mostly due to the shoddy state of the Philadelphia Arena on 46th and Market, the only indoor ice rink in the city suitable for professional hockey at the time. Snider was somewhat aware of those issues, but he was convinced that the market was there for the taking, if the team was operated properly and placed in the right facility.

When told by Jennings that the only requirements were a $10,000 application fee, a $2 million expansion fee, and a building that could house at least 12,500 fans, Snider asked him to keep their potential bid a secret so that they would have no competing bids from the city. Other cities, such as Los Angeles, had numerous potential owners vying for a franchise. Snider wanted a guarantee that, if Philadelphia was to be awarded a team, it would be his. He hung up the phone and ran into Wolman's office to explain what he thought was a gold mine of an idea. Wolman had the construction contacts and Snider had the ear of the higher-ups at City Hall. The Eagles owner was ecstatic at the prospect of creating a new building and sports franchise and wholeheartedly agreed with his vice president's plan. Wolman put Snider in charge of the project, but kept his own name as the headliner. He assumed, and accurately so, that since he was the more well-known among the two, it would increase the project's prospects for success. (It was not unusual for Snider and Wolman to partner on other business ventures during this time. In the '60s, they even opened an establishment called The Classroom, a nightclub where they would often hang out at night instead of going home to their wives.)

Snider's first call was to the city. Paul D'Ortona had first introduced Snider to that swampy plot of land in South Philadelphia a few years earlier when they were discussing the new Eagles/Phillies stadium, which was slated to begin construction in the coming months.

This time, Snider asked about the possibility of erecting an additional building for a hockey team on the adjacent plot of land. D'Ortona was thrilled at the idea and took Snider right into the mayor's office to meet with Mayor Tate. They called into the office the city solicitor and the city's finance director, and on the spot they all agreed to expedite the paperwork needed to build a new arena in the lot next to JFK Stadium. Knowing he still faced an uphill battle with the NHL, Snider asked Tate to send a letter to Jennings and Campbell to ensure them that the league would have Philadelphia's cooperation and support for the new building and a new franchise. They did it right then and there.

As the bid ramped up, Snider, who was still running the Eagles' day-to-day operations, found himself struggling to find enough time to work on the hockey project. In one of his regular conversations with Putnam, the banker acknowledged that the opportunity with Jack Kent Cooke in California was not working out the way he had hoped. Snider immediately invited him to come back to Philadelphia to run the city's bid for an NHL franchise—which Putnam accepted hastily. Putnam was named the president of the club and bought in with 25 percent ownership. Snider and Wolman each owned 22 percent, along with Snider's brother-in-law Jerry Schiff, another 22 percent stakeholder. The other 9 percent was held among various minor investors. Snider would work with the city to ensure the project progressed, while Wolman handled the construction and financing of the building. The plan was for Putnam to completely run the franchise, while Snider and Wolman oversaw it from afar.

Putnam, with the help of Eagles director of special events and publications Hal Freeman, worked tirelessly on their pitch to the NHL, which they would make in Montreal in front of the league's Board of Governors. The group sent a brochure to the NHL advertising Philadelphia as a potential hockey town, according to Jay Greenberg in *Full Spectrum.* "On the cover was a picture of a hockey player in a red and gray uniform, with a yellow Liberty Bell in a circle on the front of the jersey," Greenberg wrote. "Entitled 'The NHL in Philadelphia,' it blamed the city's past hockey failures on the poor facilities. The brochure emphasized the area's 5.5 million population and the base of established spectator support for the other major league teams." All the while, Snider was traveling to and from New York, meeting with representatives from the NHL over dinner and drinks to ensure their bid was on track.

On February 8, 1966, Putnam and Wolman traveled north to formally meet with the league executives, while Snider remained in Philadelphia, optimistic that when the group was awarded their franchise, he could immediately announce the news at a press conference at City Hall. But the meeting did not initially go as planned. Black Hawks chairman Jim Norris was insistent that Philadelphia couldn't support an NHL franchise, calling it "a lousy sports town." Others in the room were also less than enthusiastic about the city's spotty hockey history. Nonetheless, there was a glimmer of hope, as the other owners were impressed with the potential new arena and how supportive the city was of the construction process.

But neither Putnam nor Wolman were optimistic. Publicly, they were going up against Cleveland, Louisville, Buffalo, Pittsburgh, and others. In the board room, though, Philadelphia was battling solely with Baltimore for the final eastern franchise, and the Maryland city had a strong history of minor-league hockey over the previous few decades. The Associated Press reported that Wolman had attended this meeting, along with other big shots from around the sports world, including the Pittsburgh Steelers' Art Rooney, Los Angeles Rams owner Dan Reeves, Buffalo Bills owner Ralph Wilson, and others.

When Putnam left the meeting, he was so certain of the team's failure that he told his wife he would soon be out of a job. But when the phone rang, Jennings was on the other line. "You're in," he said. Despite their hesitance about the city's hockey history, it turned out that the league's decision was simply a numbers game. Baltimore's

Civic Center would only hold 12,700 seats for hockey because there was a permanent stage on one end of the arena. Philadelphia's building, created specifically for this NHL bid, would hold more than 15,000. The league, whose main source of revenue at this point was ticket sales, only had one choice. Philadelphia was named the final recipient of an NHL franchise on February 9, 1966, with Baltimore listed as the first alternate.

At a press conference the next day, Snider, Wolman, and Putnam cheerfully discussed the details of their bid, announcing for the first time their planned arena in South Philadelphia (which would eventually become known as the Spectrum). The city was stunned, with almost no inkling of their plan to bring hockey to the city. The media also got a chance to meet with Snider and Putnam, who Wolman confirmed would be in charge of the hockey team. "We'll get going right away now that we have a franchise," Wolman said. "We have guaranteed that the arena will have a minimum of 15,000 seats. Actually, we may have as many as 16,500."

"I think our guarantee of a new building helped sway the Board of Governors in our favor," Putnam told the *Philadelphia Inquirer*. "We had to convince the league that Philadelphia would support major league hockey."

Snider went into specifics, explaining that the arena would be placed in the originally planned parking lot for the proposed football-baseball stadium at the intersection of Broad, Pattison, and 11th Street. Within an hour of the announcement, calls were already flowing into the Eagles front office from fans looking to buy season tickets for the hockey team.

The next week, the *Philadelphia Daily News* posted the following: "Notice is hereby given that Articles of Incorporation have been filed with the Department of State of the Commonwealth of Pennsylvania at Harrisburg, PA," it said. "The name of the corporation is Philadelphia Hockey Club, Inc." Almost immediately, Hal Freeman was transferred to the new arena's management and Lou Scheinfeld of the *Philadelphia Daily News* was named vice president of the hockey club.

Snider was then put in charge of securing the financing for the new team. Wolman promised him the first of the $2 million that the group needed to pay for entry into the league. Snider quickly secured the other million in a loan from Fidelity Bank. But in the meantime, Wolman had received an offer from two investors, whose names have been lost to history (but whom Putnam once identified in his notes as "McConnell" and "Wetenhall," according to *Full Spectrum*), to purchase 100 percent of the hockey team. Wolman called a meeting between himself, Snider, Putnam, and Schiff to discuss their options. The assumption was that the investors wanted to relocate the franchise, but when Snider asked Wolman to where, his partner refused to say. The offer would have netted the group a collective $1 million profit on a team that had yet to play a game. Schiff agreed with Wolman that it would be prudent to sell the franchise. Putnam, however, disagreed, not wanting to throw away months of hard work. Snider didn't believe they could even legally sell a franchise that was only conditionally awarded by the NHL. To his understanding, all they owned was the promise of a franchise—which essentially had no value. Wolman, not having a unanimous vote, dropped it.

Simultaneously, Snider was confronted with a serious issue from Foreman. The contractor in charge of constructing the Spectrum, McCloskey, was not being paid. Stunned at the news, the duo delved deep into the new building's accounts and saw that there was almost no money, despite the fact that they had drawn from their loan in order to make payments. Upon further research, they realized that Wolman had been taking money out of the Spectrum's accounts and rerouting it to a major construction project in Chicago.

The John Hancock Center was going to be the jewel in Wolman's crown. The building design called for 100 stories made up of 46,000 tons of steel, 1,245 panes of glass, and 552 crown lights that could be seen all throughout Chicago. When completed, it would tower over the city at 1,506 feet, taller even than the Empire State Building. But in mid-1967, Wolman received a call that would change his life forever. After just 20 stories of construction, the partially built structure was already settling as if it were at full height. An in-depth investigation found the culprit to be the concrete caissons, which hadn't been poured correctly. The construction would need to be torn down and the footings re-poured. For a project this size, Wolman didn't have the capital to finance additional construction without revenue coming in, as usually happens during construction. Within months, he lost somewhere between $6 million and $20 million, all but wiping out his fortune. In an attempt to save himself, he utilized Spectrum funds (and those from other areas of his empire) without informing any of his business partners.

Infuriated that his partner would dare jeopardize their new business endeavor, Snider approached Wolman and informed him he was no longer interested in working with him on the hockey team. With very little money to his name, Snider offered Wolman a swap: in exchange for Wolman's 22 percent of the team, Snider would give him his 40 percent share of the Spectrum, along with some other business assets, leaving Wolman as the sole owner of the new building. Wolman took the deal, and Snider subsequently bought out Schiff's share of the hockey franchise, along with the shares of other minor investors.* As part of the deal, which Foreman helped negotiate, Snider remortgaged his home, borrowed $75,000 from two banks, and left himself in perhaps the most financially risky position of his young life. With 60 percent of the shares, Snider now held the majority ownership of the new team, while Putnam retained 25 percent. The duo was still looking

---

* This trading of interests is supported by documentation from both Snider's and Wolman's financial archives, including documents filed publicly by Wolman with the SEC in 1968.

for someone to purchase the last 15 percent of stock in order to help finance the fledgling franchise. Publicly, though, they attempted to downplay any potential financial issues.

"Jerry Wolman is rearranging his holdings with all of his partners," Snider announced to the press at the time, trying to combat any whispers. "And this is just one facet of the arrangement. He intends to stabilize his finances and stop the rumors which are floating around the city. This transaction does not mean Wolman has lost faith in the ownership group or Philadelphia as a hockey city. Jerry just thought it in his best interest to sell his 22 percent, which was really meaningless. His main concern is football."

With the due date for the NHL expansion fee coming up in less than two weeks, Wolman suddenly informed them that he no longer had the money to lend to them. Panicking, Snider and Putnam ran endlessly around Philadelphia trying to gather any dollar they could, in an attempt to save their franchise. Putnam sold three years of the team's broadcast rights to Kaiser Broadcasting, who owned channel 48, for an upfront payment of $350,000. Snider borrowed $150,000 from friends and family. For the last $500,000, Snider called Bill Fishman, president of ARA Services (the company that would eventually become Aramark), which had already given a $2 million advance to the Spectrum in exchange for the food service rights at the new arena. Fishman was amenable, but needed to find a bank that would take his ARA stock as collateral.

Throughout these tumultuous months, Snider and Myrna were stressed beyond belief—but they never let it show. Their children do not even recall there being issues at home. The couple tried endlessly to ensure that work stayed at work, even if it seemed their entire life could come crashing down within days if they could not find a solution. Snider had never in his life been in such dire straits when it came to a business decision.

The money was due on Monday, June 5, 1967. On Saturday, the duo was still short $500,000. Fishman had mentioned that he was waiting for a reply from Provident Bank. Putnam wasn't interested in waiting. He called Roger Hillas, one of the bank's executives, at home while he was outside mowing his lawn. Hillas picked up the phone and ultimately agreed to provide the loan. The check was cut on Monday morning—the group finally had their $2 million expansion fee.

Snider remained in Philadelphia and sent Putnam, Scheinfeld, and PR man Joe Kadlec to Montreal to pay for the franchise and meet with the press. As soon as the banks opened, Snider walked in, ready to wire $2 million north of the border. As he got up to the counter, the lights in the bank went out. With a single turn of his head toward the outside, he realized that the power was out all over. A blackout had hit a 15,000-square mile stretch from New Jersey to Maryland and as far west as Harrisburg, Pennsylvania. With no phone lines working, Snider couldn't even contact Putnam to let him know what was going on. His partner sat in the Montreal hotel room, breathing heavily, begging for some sort of contact from Philadelphia.

Somehow, word got to Montreal about the blackout, and the NHL owners, along with Campbell, waited impatiently for the last of the new expansion franchises to present their check. At that point, enough rumors had spread about the Philadelphia group's financial struggles, which made the existing six teams quite skeptical about their ability to come up with the money. The potential owners for the Baltimore bid were standing in the lobby, smirking, holding their own $2 million check, with the full expectation that, by day's end, they would own the final NHL expansion franchise.

Near midday, though, the power was restored and Snider wired the money through New York and up to the Royal Bank of Canada. Putnam and Scheinfeld ran across the street from their hotel to grab the cashier's check, which was made out to "National Hockey League."

Halfway across the street on their return to the hotel to hand the check over to the league, Putnam stopped and realized there was a mistake. Each expansion team's check was supposed to be written directly to one of the existing six teams—the newspapers reported that the Philadelphia franchise wrote its check to the Toronto Maple Leafs, but all of the principals involved recall it being the New York Rangers. They returned to their hotel room and called Snider. "Oh my God, I'm going to have a heart attack," he said, shaking his head. He had the bank cancel the check, reissue it, and sent his representatives into the hotel conference room to finally pay for the franchise.

They barged into the room, handed the check to Campbell, who looked at it, handed it to Jennings to examine, then put it down on the table. "That will be all," he said, with a stern look on his face.

"Do we have the franchise?" Scheinfeld asked.

"If the check clears," Campbell replied. Scheinfeld asked for a receipt, but Campbell simply repeated, "That will be all."

As they returned to their hotel room, Scheinfeld called Snider. "How did it go?" Snider asked.

"I think okay," Scheinfeld said.

"What do you mean, you think? Did we get the franchise?"

"I think. He didn't say yes, he didn't say no. He said, 'If the check clears.'"

Snider took a deep breath. "Did they give you any certificate or anything?"

"They gave us nothing."

"Oh, God," Snider said. "I shouldn't have sent you up there." One can envision a young Snider, head in his hands, laughing nervously at how ridiculous the whole charade was. He had put his entire life on the line, yet he couldn't even get a receipt from the NHL showing what he had purchased.

Nonetheless, the media scrum that ensued in the hotel lobby minutes later confirmed that Philadelphia, indeed, had been granted their franchise. Questions arose from all angles about the ownership group, the strategy for building the team from the ground up, along with who would be involved on the hockey side of the organization. Most of that, including the team name, had yet to be decided, but this much was certain: Snider was now the majority owner of a major league hockey team in Philadelphia. The city's NHL franchise still had a long way to go before taking the ice for the first time, but Snider could at least breathe one short sigh of relief before the next storm commenced.

Breakup with Wolman

AFTER SWAPPING SHARES with Wolman, Snider again found himself in a financial pickle. Bill Fishman of ARA Services chose not to exchange his loan for shares of the team and demanded to be repaid. There was still 15 percent of the team that had not yet been sold, and Snider needed that money in order to pay back the $500,000 that he owed to Fishman. On a whim, he called Joe Scott, whom he knew through his work with the Eagles.

Scott was a local businessman, a beer distributor who had grown his young company, Scott & Grauer, into one of the largest beer distributors in the world. A well-respected and well-known man in the Philadelphia business community, Scott had met Snider during an advertising campaign with the Eagles in the mid-1960s. The two kept in touch, Scott impressed with Snider's tenacity and Snider impressed with Scott's business sense. Snider was in need of capital, and the banks were not giving him the help he needed. He also was in need of a strong business partner who could help him grow the team into a marketing success. A few times before the team took the ice in 1967, Snider had offered Scott the chance to buy into the hockey club, but each time he had politely declined. But less than a year after selling his company and retiring, Scott was starting to drive his wife, Pat, crazy. So, according to *Full Spectrum,* when she answered the phone and listened to Snider's desperate pitch, she handed Scott the phone and said,

"Ed Snider has a proposal for you. You are going to say 'yes.'" Scott, intrigued by the idea, mentioned to Snider that he did not want to be in a large group of investors and countered Snider's offer with stipulations of his own—he wanted it to just be himself, Snider, and Putnam. He insisted on having a job with the team as well. Snider agreed, and the ownership group for the Philadelphia hockey team was set. With Scott, Snider felt he had a better chance of securing additional, desperately needed financing for the franchise that Snider and Putnam may not otherwise have been able to get.

The group went to six banks and were rejected by each one. Disheartened, the three men approached their seventh and final option, Girard Bank, with a less-than-optimistic mindset. But, to their surprise, they were met by Girard president Steve Gardner, who revealed that he had grown up in Boston and had great exposure to the Bruins as a child. The bank's vice president, Bill Baer, was involved with the Harvard hockey team while in school. The two made a pitch to their board and secured a $1.5 million loan to help finance the operations of the new hockey team.

In the meantime, construction on the new building progressed quickly and efficiently. The Spectrum, in fact, was built based on a deal with the city that gave the group the best possible chance to make the endeavor profitable. The city kept ownership of the land, while the building became what is known as a leasehold improvement. In exchange for not using public funds to finance the construction of the arena, the city agreed not to charge real estate taxes. In essence, the team was improving city property by putting a new arena on the spot, which would be used for the public benefit.

This team, which was starting to see itself come together from a competitive perspective, still needed a name. It was decided that a contest would be held for residents of the region to name the new Philadelphia Hockey Club. Thousands of suggestions rolled in, including Quakers and Ramblers, allusions to the city's first NHL team and their most recent professional hockey team. But Snider and Putnam wanted a new identity, something that evoked a modern flair. The duo continued throwing ideas around, including Liberty Bells, Lancers, Raiders, Knights, Keystones, and more. Nothing stuck, until one night when Snider, Putnam and his wife, and Phyllis and Earl Foreman were coming home from seeing a show in New York City. While sitting at a Howard Johnson's restaurant at a rest stop on the New Jersey Turnpike, Phyllis was musing about the speed of the sport and players gliding across the ice. Impulsively, she threw out the name "Flyers." Besides the alliteration that rolled off the tongue, the group loved the motion and excitement that the new name conjured. Just like that, the hockey team had both a name and an almost completed building in which to play.

With Snider working to get the building ready for the Flyers inaugural season, he placed Myrna and her sister, Dobbie, in charge of designing some of the interior of the Spectrum, as well as the uniforms for the arena workers. Snider vetoed Myrna's idea for pink coveralls for the janitors, but the two ladies hired New York designer Levino Verna to design the usherettes' outfits. They agreed on a dark orange top with an orange- and pink-striped miniskirt, along with hot pink tights. The ice crew wore silver jumpsuits, while the male arena workers wore blue. Eventually, the uniform was changed to shades of pink, orange, green, and blue. The bottom line was that Myrna and Dobbie wanted the color scheme inside the Spectrum to be as dazzling and wide-ranging as the events hosted in the Spectrum—and Snider wanted his wife and sister-in-law to help as much as possible.

But even as the calendar raced toward the Flyers' home opener, the building wasn't completed. The construction was done, but the interior was not ready as quickly as they had hoped. With Wolman's financial troubles becoming more serious, the group was no longer able to count on his capital. Snider put on hold various amenities that were originally scheduled to be in place for opening night. They eschewed wall paint at a savings of $30,000. The $800,000 television studio was delayed. The electronic turnstile system, costing $23,000, wasn't installed. Even the boards for the ice rink were delayed—the Flyers had to cancel their two home exhibition games because of it. Only when Snider bribed a union guy were the boards delivered and installed just in time for the first game. At the end of each day, Snider would meet with his executives, sometimes into the early hours of the morning, trying to figure out what still needed to be done. But even though the building was still missing a few details, it was essentially complete in time for the Flyers home opener. With just 16 months between ground-breaking and completion, the Spectrum had been built without a single penny of taxpayer money.

The first public event in Spectrum history was held on September 30, 1967—the Quaker City Jazz Festival, a full-weekend celebration of some of the greatest jazz musicians of the era. Through the weekend, thousands of people piled into the building to listen to stunning performances by stars such as Stan Getz, Dionne Warwick, Dizzy Gillespie, Herbie Mann, Jimmy Smith, and more. Saturday's event was attended by just under 10,000, but Sunday's concert was sold out. The *Inquirer* praised the sightlines of the new building and complimented the comfort level of the plush red seats. The festival featured a revolving stage, allowing everyone in the arena to get a quality view of the main event.

For the first five months of its life, the Spectrum had already filled its calendar with a variety of events in a way few arenas in the country did at the time. In addition to the full home seasons of the Flyers and 76ers, the building scheduled the Moscow State Circus, the Ringling Brothers Circus, the Ice Capades, the U.S. Figure Skating Championships, Holiday on Ice shows, a fight between Joe Frazier and Tony Doyle, and various concerts. From the get-go, business was good.

In the midst of all of this, Wolman's struggles continued to escalate. The relationship between him and Snider continued to unravel as the summer progressed, though no one is certain exactly why. It is important to mention at this point that there are many legitimate theories, each backed by some evidence. There is a plethora of possibilities, many of them personal and none of them ever told. Yet those close to each man have pondered aloud as to what may have occurred in the months preceding the Flyers' first game. There are some who believe Wolman and Myrna got too close for Snider's comfort, which heightened the temperature before their eventual breakup. Snider told many close to him during his life that he believed Wolman and Myrna were having an affair, though there is no evidence to back up that claim. Even if it were untrue, simply the thought of it would have enraged Snider and certainly led to a massive power struggle, and even a sudden end to their relationship.

The two had already shared a fairly frosty relationship once Snider caught Wolman taking money out of the Spectrum's account, but the battles did not get personal until late in the summer of 1967. For his entire life, it was typical for Snider to never take a business issue personally. If there was animosity toward someone, it meant that they did something to harm him. That an affront was made toward Snider is not out of the question from either side. Myrna was understandably unhappy with Snider's behavior when it came to their marriage. He and Wolman would spend many of their evenings at the nightclub they owned and would arrive home much later from work than other coworkers who left much earlier.

There is also a possibility that Snider finally realized that Wolman had spent many years overinflating his wealth and realized that his business partner and boss was actually sitting atop a house of cards. Wolman was incredibly overleveraged, and by the time his financial empire began crumbling, Snider perhaps saw, for the first time, that his mentor and close friend was not what he claimed to be. There is a story told that, in September 1967, Wolman and Snider held a meeting at the Eagles' offices where Snider, in a fit of rage over a major business disagreement having to do with Wolman's financial troubles, leapt across a conference table and attempted to grab Wolman by the neck. Unfortunately, with no one from that meeting still alive, it is impossible to determine the truthfulness behind that claim. And without any of the principals around, and with Snider forever refusing to discuss the memory, it is nearly impossible to say with any certainty what transpired over those few weeks in 1967 when the power structure of the Philadelphia sports scene shifted.

At that time, Wolman quickly needed an infusion of cash, or the empire he spent years building would crumble. He approached his partners with a loan proposal he had received that he claimed would solve their problems. According to those who were in the room, Wolman spoke of an eight-figure loan lined up from a group of Kuwaiti oil tycoons. In order to obtain the loan, Wolman would need to package all of his assets as collateral—the Eagles, the Spectrum, Connie Mack Stadium, his construction company, Yellow Cab, everything. More importantly, the loan required the Flyers to be involved as well, despite Wolman's lack of ownership in the team at this point. Snider, Scott, and Putnam sat and listened as Wolman pleaded for their shares in the hockey team. Since Snider owned the majority of the team, the decision was ultimately up to him.

Snider's initial thoughts were ones of confusion. He couldn't see why the Flyers would be a necessary addition to the deal. The team had exponentially more debt than assets at that point—they hadn't even played a game yet. It was rumored that perhaps the goal was to flip the Flyers to the previously denied Baltimore group for a quick profit. But even if Snider was willing to give up the team, he certainly wasn't able to pay back all of the loans he had personally guaranteed. At that point he owed millions to various banks, friends, and family, plus an additional mortgage on his home. Even if he wanted to sell the team, he couldn't. But more importantly, he believed in the Flyers. A lengthy discussion ensued between Snider and his partners, in which they badly wanted to do something to help their friend, but concluded that, because they were unwilling to part with the franchise, nothing could be done. It has been reported that Snider initially agreed to help Wolman but later changed his mind. It's also been suggested that Myrna was the one who knocked some sense into him and convinced her husband to keep his shares of the hockey team. Regardless of the method, the end result was the same.

After informing Wolman that he was unwilling to give him the Flyers, Wolman was infuriated. He believed that, after all he had done for those around him, including Snider, he was owed the help that he was once promised by his former business partner. Wolman may have recalled Snider's letter to him years earlier, but much had changed since then. Instead, Wolman felt as if Snider was driving the last nail into the coffin that would ultimately send him into bankruptcy.

Separately from Wolman's woes, Eagles coach Joe Kuharich was also becoming blatantly more hostile toward Snider in the Eagles office. Snider, still running the football club, would spend his mornings at the Eagles offices and the afternoons and nights overseeing his partners who were running the Flyers and the Spectrum. Kuharich began berating Snider in team meetings, speaking ill of him in front of other employees, and being otherwise abrasive. The two had a fairly chilled relationship in the first place, but now Kuharich felt that he was the only one show-ing up each day and doing the required work. He felt that since Snider wanted to spend so much of his time with the hockey team, he no longer had a right to try and run the football team as well.

While Snider was being berated by the Eagles coach, however, the fans had made up their own mind as to who was at fault for the current state of the team. During the Eagles on-field struggles, fans would regularly chant, "Joe Must Go," demanding a change at the head coach position. That the fans were unhappy with the leadership of the team enraged Snider, who felt the fault lay with him as the team's vice president. Just a few weeks earlier, Snider had been featured in the *Philadelphia Inquirer* in his capacity as the head of the Eagles organi-zation. He was still the public face of the football club. But that didn't matter if his owner no longer had confidence in him. When Kuharich shared with Wolman his feelings toward Snider, the Eagles owner, already furious at his former business partner, finally had an excuse to pull the trigger. Snider knew something was coming.

The Eagles threw a party for their employees the night of October 18, 1967. Snider was present, in body if not in spirit. Those in attendance noted that he was a bit introspective, unusual for someone who always attacked each day with fire and passion. He leaned over to one of his employees and said, "You're going to hear some things." His colleague replied, "I've already heard some things." Snider looked at him and said, "You're going to hear some more," and left the party. Word traveled quickly through the office, and most everyone had an inkling of what was about to happen.

The next morning, October 19, the day of the Flyers' home opener, Wolman fired Snider from his position at the Eagles. Wolman, in an autobiography published before his death, claimed that he drove to Snider's house and fired him while he was shaving and preparing for the Flyers game. Snider, before his death, claimed that he asked Wolman for a buyout of his contract that morning and then was blindsided that evening when the media reported that he had been fired. Lou Scheinfeld vividly recalls Snider arriving at the Spectrum before the home opener already upset about the situation, which suggests Snider's account was not accurate, although it is certainly possible that Snider was upset over a blow-up between the two, and not necessarily at being fired. Those who worked for the Eagles at the time recall it happening in the office, in front of many ears. Regardless of where it occurred, Snider was infuriated. Despite his newly found passion for the Flyers, the Eagles were his career and he fully expected to keep both positions as time progressed. He loved his job and was crushed at losing it. He wasn't even certain that Wolman had the legal right to fire him—he had a long-term contract, which included an option to purchase 7 percent of the team. Just a few weeks earlier Snider was center stage representing the Eagles at the groundbreaking for what would eventually be known as Veterans Stadium. Now he was sitting alone in his Flyers office, desperately looking for a safety net.

Snider called Foreman, who owned 48 percent of the Eagles to Wolman's 52, and asked for legal advice. Foreman, unaware of Wolman's decision, was stunned. As business partners, he expected to be informed of any major decision—and firing the head of the organization would surely fall into that category. Yet he was uncomfortably stuck in the middle. Wolman was his longtime business partner, but Snider was his brother-in-law. He didn't want to take sides, but he also knew that Snider's contract needed to be honored. He called Sol Snider, a regular confidant to whom he could bring personal struggles for discussion. Sol's response was, "Blood is thicker than water."

Rather than fight with Wolman initially, Foreman and Snider went directly to the NFL in New York City to meet with commissioner Pete Rozelle. Despite having a sympathetic ear, Rozelle said that there was nothing he could do, that Wolman had the right to choose who did and did not work for the team. Snider and Foreman walked outside onto the sidewalk, where Snider declared, angrily, yet confidently, "I think I'd like a hot roast beef sandwich with mashed potatoes to celebrate being fired." Sitting in a luncheonette with Foreman and *Inquirer* reporter Joe McGinnis, Snider talked about how painful it was for his seven-year-old daughter to read the newspaper that morning and cry.

Even during one of the lowest moments of his life, Snider still dressed and acted in a way that commanded respect from those around him. During the lunch, McGinnis described Snider as someone who "always reminded you of either a head waiter or a hairdresser. Always smiling and ready to bow. He dressed well but always a little too much. Pointed-toe shoes, tight pants, French cuffs every day. Often, after being with him for five minutes, you felt you should slip a dollar into his hand. Then you noticed the jewels in his pinky ring and the feeling went away."

Picking at his roast beef sandwich, Snider spoke with a variety of emotions—sadness, confusion, anger, and perhaps worst of all, vulnerability. "You can only have one man running an organization," he said to the *Philadelphia Inquirer*. "And when you have two strong personalities in the same place, this kind of thing is bound to happen."

With no help from the league, Foreman's training as a legal expert took over and he immediately called for a meeting of the Eagles board of directors to fight Wolman's move. But, at the end of the day, Wolman was the majority owner of the team and had the right to do what he wanted. Foreman grudgingly relented and focused on negotiating a separation package for Snider to compensate him for the remaining years of his contract with the Eagles. Snider was in just the third year of a 15-year deal and wanted to be compensated for both the remaining 12 years and his 7 percent option. After intense discussions among the group, Wolman agreed to pay Snider $923 per week for one year, along with two additional $120,000 payments. The Eagles owner then called for a press conference the next morning, October 20.

With Wolman, Kuharich, Snider, and Foreman in attendance, the mood was dour, to say the least. "I'm enjoying this," Kuharich said from his position.

"Maybe next time it will be your party, Joe," Snider retorted.

"It happens every day," the GM/coach replied.

Kuharich was basking in the glory of seeing his foe pushed out of a team that was now clearly his. But he also was angered by the media interest in a person he deemed to be irrelevant. "I've never seen anything so ludicrous," he snapped. "You're here for nothing. If I got fired, there'd be two people here." He continued, "Why is everyone so surprised? The guy Snider spends 60 percent of his time with the hockey team.... What's he doing for the Eagles? You only get a couple of hours work out of him a day. He comes in at 12:00 o'clock. What's the big deal? What's the surprise?"

"He's unbelievable," Snider said, giving Kuharich his now famous glare. "I've never bad-mouthed him. I won't start now. He's just following the party line." Meanwhile, Wolman sat on the other end of the dais, dejected, dressed in a black, pinstriped suit. When reporters wanted to know who would run the team on a day-to-day basis, Wolman simply stared at the ground and remained quiet.

According to the *Philadelphia Inquirer*, as Snider left the office after the press conference—his office cleared out and his name already removed from the door—the employees who had grown to love him were in mourning. A cleaning lady approached him, saying, "Sorry to see you're leaving, Mr. Snider."

"I don't tread where I'm not wanted," he said with a smile, stepping into his limousine.

Within weeks, Wolman began talking with various media outlets, claiming he had funded the Flyers' expansion fee and that he provided the ownership group with the capital to run the team. Snider held his tongue, preferring to focus on his management of the hockey franchise. But when Wolman persisted and reporters continued filling up Snider's call sheet looking for comment, Snider opened his desk drawer, gathered all of the relevant documents, and called Fred Byrod from the *Inquirer*. He presented all of his loan documents, promissory notes, and other documentation showing the money he borrowed from friends. Byrod perused the documents, confirmed their authenticity, and published the full, then unknown story of how Snider saved the young franchise. He confirmed that in exchange for Wolman's share of the debt-ridden hockey club, Snider traded his 40 percent share of the Spectrum, his 14 percent of Connie Mack Stadium, and his 10 percent share of an Allentown apartment project in which he and Wolman were involved. "Would you say that was running out on Jerry?" he asked.*

But Wolman forever refused to agree with his counterpart's story. "[Snider] is capable of being ruthless—I know from experience," Wolman said in a 1973 interview with the *Philadelphia Daily News*.

---

* All of the financial transactions are supported by the S-1 Jerry Wolman filed with the SEC, along with financial documents from Snider's personal archives.

"Eddie is bright and determined. I don't think he'd let anything stand in the way of financial success."

Years later, in an interview with the *Philadelphia Inquirer*, Snider reminisced about the saga through the lens of his objectivist philosophy. "Jerry didn't put me in a position to do anything I've ever done in my life," he said. "I put myself in that position. What you have to understand about life, what you have to believe in is a mutuality in any kind of relationship. I thought what we accomplished, we accomplished together. He doesn't owe me anything. I don't owe him anything."

Despite his lifelong perturbation with Wolman and his associates, Snider never denied that his former business partner was instrumental in creating the foundation for success that Snider eventually enjoyed. Without Wolman's name on the project, the Spectrum would never have been built, and without the Spectrum, Philadelphia would never have been granted an expansion franchise. Multiple times in his life, he admitted that, in 1966, if he had knocked on doors for help or went to the city by himself looking for support, he may have been laughed out of the room, despite his role in helping get the new football-baseball stadium off the ground. It was only with Wolman's public backing that Snider was able to get the hockey project going in the first place.

Many have argued on both sides of the story for the half-century since. Wolman claimed Snider turned his back on his business partner. Wolman associates claim it was more of a walkaway—the end result being the same, but the intention being less malicious. Snider claimed he was simply trying to save a hockey team that he believed would be successful in Philadelphia. With the benefit of hindsight, one can see which entrepreneur came out ahead in the long run. But at the time, no one could have accurately predicted how everything would ultimately play out.

"I loved Jerry Wolman," said Lou Scheinfeld years later. "And Ed knew it. But look, I was a reporter, I'm trained to be objective, to get both sides of the story. Ed was tough. Either you were 1,000 percent

with him or you were the enemy. And I didn't feel that way." Scheinfeld insisted to Snider that he could continue working for him while
still maintaining a friendly, professional relationship with Wolman.
There are very few people who remained close with Wolman while
also remaining in Snider's orbit—his sister, Phyllis, was one of them.
But those close to him were saddened by the breakup. "It was too
bad," Scheinfeld continued. "They went from Damon and Pythias to
Cain and Abel. It went from love to hate. But watching them together
in the good days, man, they were some team. They were just so good
together. But you know, a lot of marriages break up."

One of the ironies of their split was the similarities in personalities and how Snider's continued to develop as he became more successful in his career. We can now see how much Snider eventually
became like Wolman, in terms of how he trusted and loved those close
to him. While much of it was due to Snider's own upbringing and
the nature of his family, there is no doubt that Wolman's incredible
generosity, charitableness, and loyalty to those around him rubbed off
on the budding sports entrepreneur. Snider would ultimately spend
his later years with a tight-knit group of managers who were often as
loyal to him as he was to them. Of course, there were many ways in
which Snider and Wolman differed, but the parallels that can be drawn
between them at various stages of their lives are striking.

The true, underlying reason of the breakup may never be known.
What is certain is, at the time, Snider was doing his best to save a
hockey franchise that had millions of dollars of debt to its name before
the team even stepped onto the Spectrum ice. Even the most astute of
businessmen would not have been able to guarantee or even foresee
the level of success the Flyers would eventually enjoy. All Snider had
was a fiery passion and perhaps a stronger desire than anyone else in
the sports world to make the situation work to his benefit. And the best
way to do that would be to make the hockey team and the Spectrum
succeed.

6

Jumpstarting the Flyers

WITH ONLY A FLEDGLING hockey club to his name, Snider had a monstrous task in front of him. Even from the start, most were still unaware of his existence, let alone that he had been in charge of the hockey team from day one. An Associated Press story on October 27 falsely referred to Snider as "a lawyer" replacing Wolman as "majority owner of the Flyers," even though Clarence Campbell and various news sources confirmed that Snider's former Eagles boss was never the majority owner. Nonetheless, it shined a light on the task he faced: to lead this new club to a level of on-ice and financial success.

One of the first hockey-related business moves the organization made was to hire Bud Poile as general manager and Keith Allen as their coach. Having worked on the West Coast with Jack Kent Cooke for some time, Putnam knew Poile from his work with the San Francisco Seals of the Western Hockey League, while he was familiar with Allen from his work with the Seattle Totems (also of the WHL). The two came highly recommended from the hockey community and provided their expertise in the sport to Putnam to help build a solid foundation for the organization's on-ice success.

At the suggestion of Poile, Allen, and Putnam, Snider then purchased the Quebec Aces, a minor league hockey team, and utilized them to develop young Flyers players. With the Spectrum not yet ready, the team brought their players to Quebec for a six-week training camp so everyone could get acquainted. It was there in Quebec that Snider met with the players, further developing his understanding of hockey, a sport with which he was still mostly unfamiliar. Although his expertise was not in the sport itself, he surely had something to teach the young players from a public relations standpoint. The players were stunned that this 34-year-old man was the owner of the team. But they quickly recognized he held himself in a way that commanded the utmost respect of anyone in his vicinity. Although he was friendly and warm to the players, his eyes had an intense fire, immediately intimidating many of them, whether or not this was his intention. He taught some of the players how to present themselves and how to speak with the media, always looking someone in the eye and never showing weakness in their actions. Leadership came from the top, and he always led by example, right from day one.

After training camp ended, everyone returned to Philadelphia to begin what would be the incredibly difficult job of kickstarting a new franchise in a notoriously tough sports city. Even during the first few days, getting the team going was a challenge, to say the least. To create hype for the new franchise, the organization arranged a parade through the city, ending at City Hall. All of the players were loaded into cars and driven through an otherwise empty city. Heads turned, as confused onlookers wondered who these people were. Many jeered, while others gave the middle finger. One person yelled that they would be in Baltimore by the end of the season. By the time the team got to their destination, the mayor was nowhere to be found. Even he did not want to be associated with the disastrous event.

The Flyers dropped their first two games, but the team brass remained optimistic as they returned to Philadelphia with a 1–2 record for the home opener. Yet, when only 7,812 fans showed up for the Spectrum's first hockey game, Snider became worried. His concern was magnified when, for the second home game a few nights later, less than 6,000 attended. The team needed to sell an average of about 12,000 seats per game to break even, and while they knew it would take some time, they didn't expect to be at half that level at the start. They looked internally to figure out what could be improved in the public relations department. With no prior experience, they asked Chicago owner Bill Wirtz who was in charge of sending out the Black Hawks' press releases. "We don't send out releases," Wirtz laughed in response. "We sell out every game, why should we send out releases?" Such was the NHL in the 1960s—the Philadelphia ownership group was on their own to figure it out.

As the calendar rolled toward November, Joe Scott came up with an idea. Adults were set in their ways, he thought. It was hard to convince them to try something new. But what if the Flyers could attract young people to their games? Scott was a huge hockey fan and was convinced that getting fans in the building for just one game would convince them to return again and again. Scott offered free tickets to schools in bulk—the building had nearly 10,000 empty seats for each game, what did it matter how many he gave away? Although it was a struggle at first, eventually a few schools accepted the offer and brought a number of students to the game as a treat. Scott would continue to reach out to any school in the area who won any sort of championship and offer free Flyers tickets as a reward. If Scott could get the younger generation interested, they would inevitably drag their parents to a game, thereby multiplying the spread of this wonderful sport. Plus, the parents would need to purchase their own ticket to attend with their kids. Even school bands would occasionally attend in the upper deck and entertain those around them during the game. Scott would make personal visits to every company he had ever done business with, charming them and trying to convince even a few to come down to South Philadelphia to give this new team a try. Slowly, but surely, word got around, and more and more people would make their way to Broad and Pattison.

As attendance increased slightly, the Flyers were about to give the team's marketing efforts an enormous boost. On November 4 they traveled to Montreal for a matchup against perhaps the strongest team in the league: the Canadiens. Playing in the Montreal Forum, the most famous hockey arena in the world, the ruthless Montreal fans were taunting the new expansion club even before the game started. They began yelling things like, "They belong in the Eastern Hockey League!" But from the drop of the puck, the lowly expansion team controlled the game. Powered by Leon Rochefort's hat trick, the first in team history, the Flyers defeated the eventual Stanley Cup champions 4–1, eliciting the first of what would be many bursts of emotion from their passionate owner. With a big grin on his face, he offered his first-ever public words on his team's on-ice play. "It's like a baseball player playing his first game in Yankee Stadium," he said to the *Courier Post*. "They rose to the occasion and played their hearts out. They kept the pressure on the surprised Canadiens, who never recovered." With a dominant win that caught national attention in the hockey world, the Flyers began seeing an increase in advanced ticket sales against Original Six squads. "The future looks bright," said Putnam. "Hockey is a great, action-packed game. It can't help but catch fire here, too."

Snider, as early as the first season, was showing his players the passion and care that would become a trademark of his management style. After each game he attended, win or lose, he would go into the locker room with a big smile and shake every player's hand, thanking them for their effort that night. Occasionally, after a big win, the handshake would be replaced with a bear hug as he spoke lovingly of his team. After a loss, the smile would still be there, but the players could sense the pain he felt.

Through November, the Flyers defeated four of the Original Six teams: Montreal, Boston, New York, and Detroit. In fact, after they beat the Red Wings, fans began chanting "We're Number One!" at their hockey club, which had just leapfrogged Los Angeles to sit in first place in the newly created West Division (which housed all six expansion clubs). On top of that, attendance began improving. The team hit nearly 10,000 fans for the first time at the end of October, and by the middle of November, they had already set a team record with a gate of 11,267 against the Rangers, then broke that record the following week with 12,086 fans in attendance to see the Flyers play Detroit. With the team seeing success on the ice, attendance continued to increase.

As the calendar turned to 1968, the team surpassed 250,000 in season attendance, with crowds regularly reaching close to 15,000. Snider subconsciously harkened back to that night in Boston when he and Celtics coach Red Auerbach traded playful jabs about sports. At the time, Auerbach bet Snider a dollar that hockey would never make it in Philadelphia. This early in the team's life, he could already foresee collecting his winnings. His bet with Auerbach was one thing, but he had spent months dealing with members of the pessimistic Philadelphia media as well. "You can see who turned out to be right," Snider jabbed at the press—though in the same sentence he acknowledged that even he was surprised at how quickly the project showed success. "I honestly thought it would take two or three years to build this," Snider said to the *Philadelphia Inquirer*, ecstatic at how quickly Philadelphia seemed to be taking to his team. With attendance steadily increasing and the team winning, the national media began paying attention to Philadelphia hockey.

In fact, even the local papers started giving the Flyers their fair space. Snider was jubilant when the Flyers received equal billing in the *Philadelphia Inquirer*, the *Philadelphia Daily News*, and the *Evening Bulletin* as the Eagles, who had perpetually received the most attention. He did not hide the animosity he still held toward his previous employer, either. After the Flyers defeated Los Angeles 7–2, equaling the offensive output the Eagles had managed against their rival Giants in a humiliating 44–7 loss, Snider was quick to point out the fact to broadcaster Stu Nahan, so he could let his audience know. The bad blood was perpetuated by the media, who had already seen glimpses of Snider's legendary competitiveness. When, during a December 17 Eagles game, a plane flew overhead with a trailing sign calling for Joe Kuharich's dismissal, the joke running through Philadelphia was that Snider must have gotten his pilot's license. On top of that, Wolman had buckled to his financial troubles and began preparing his assets for bankruptcy. With the Eagles on the way down and the Flyers on the way up, Snider was beginning to garner media attention as the hot new sports owner in town.

Even at this early stage of his ownership of the team, one could see glimpses of the aspects of his personality that would eventually see him build the organization into an empire: astute business acumen; a concern for the health of the sport as a whole rather than just his franchise; and most importantly, commitment to and passion for every player who put on the orange and black of the Flyers.

After the Flyers defeated Toronto in a hard-fought battle on the road, Snider and Myrna were waiting at the Philadelphia airport at 1:30 in the morning to greet the team on the tarmac. The players were pleasantly stunned. It was extremely rare for any NHL owner to show that sort of care for the players, who were often treated by franchises at that time as easily replaceable, low-level employees. On top of that, Snider spoke publicly about his vision for hockey's future. "This sport has tremendous growth potential, and I would like to see it remain a healthy sport," he told the *Philadelphia Inquirer.* "Each team, by virtue of its attendance and a moderate amount of television and radio receipts, can make a reasonable profit."

Media attention increased exponentially when Wolman officially declared bankruptcy, causing many to flock to his former business partner for comment. "I feel very sorry for Jerry Wolman and what he and his family are going through," Snider said to the *Philadelphia*

Inquirer. "No one wants to see a man go bankrupt. But that is all I will say on the subject of Jerry Wolman. I've been silent until now. I'll remain silent. I did my job with the Eagles. We have a good organization. As good an organization as there was in football. I'm not responsible for what has happened since I left." Snider, always the brilliant marketer, would take every Wolman question and pivot the answer toward the Flyers. "We have a fine organization here," he continued. "But I still didn't think we would do as well as we have. We have a good chance—if we keep going like we have since the first of the year—to end up in the black. I honestly thought it would take two, maybe three years to build up the proper following. I always knew hockey would go here, but I thought it would take longer because of all the expansion teams. Philadelphia was the only one which didn't have a built-in following from a high minor-league team. I think a big thing that helped us was that a lot of fans lost interest in the Eagles at about the same time we were starting back in the fall. These fans seemed to turn to us as an outlet."

But with everything going smoothly, disaster struck in February 1968. During an Ice Capades show, a fierce wind ripped a 150-foot by 50-foot section of the Spectrum roof off, hitting a few people in the parking lot (but only causing minor injuries) and allowing light to shine through to the event floor. Upcoming events were canceled while they attempted to repair the damage. Just two days later, the building was declared fixed and reopened for a 76ers game. On March 1, however, three more sections blew off the roof in another wind storm, causing Mayor Tate to shut down the building until further notice. While in reality, it could have been fixed within a few days, the issue became a massive political football in the city, further delaying the fixes required for the new building.

Upon further investigation, the city acknowledged that the Spectrum's roof was an "economy" roof, specially requested by McCloskey during the construction and approved by the Board of Building

Standards. It was March 1967 when they granted the architect a variance for a roof that was vulnerable to "uplift," but they were assured it would be accounted for in the design. On top of that, the city never even received the final plans for the Spectrum until the roof issue occurred, when it should have been submitted well before the building opened. The Spectrum had enormous numbers of violations throughout and had apparently never been issued a Certificate of Occupancy before its first event.

With Snider not having been involved in the building's construction, he was both shocked and embarrassed. Not only was the building now associated with him because of his Flyers, but the hockey team would have to play the remainder of their season on the road. Financially, this had the potential to be disastrous, considering the organization was not yet profitable this early in its life. Publicly, he acknowledged that the team had insurance for such an event and would be fine, but privately he was panicking. The building would be fixed with little financial loss due to that insurance, but the organization had more than 11,000 tickets sold for each of the remaining Flyers home games, not to mention the other events scheduled over the following month. The lost revenue would be a killer for a team desperately trying to balance its books.

Almost immediately, Snider received a call from Bill Baer, the vice president at Girard Bank that had given him a large loan months earlier, according to *Full Spectrum*. The bank was impressed by the team's early financial prowess and already had a large amount exposed and committed to their continued success. It would be irresponsible to let the team flounder because of an issue they had nothing to do with. The smarter thing, from the bank's perspective, was to ensure their investment was protected. Baer asked Snider how they would handle the situation, and Snider replied with a shrug. Baer asked how much they needed, and Snider replied that it was about $1 million. "It will be in your account tomorrow morning," Baer said.

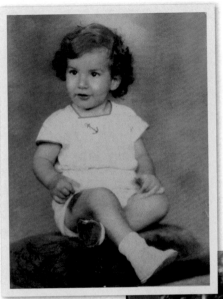

Edward Malcolm Snider, known as "Eddie," was born on January 6, 1933.

As a child, Eddie experienced bullying and anti-Semitism. This led him to develop various "posses" throughout his life to ensure he was never alone, along with a tough-guy mentality that meant you never let anyone intimidate you.

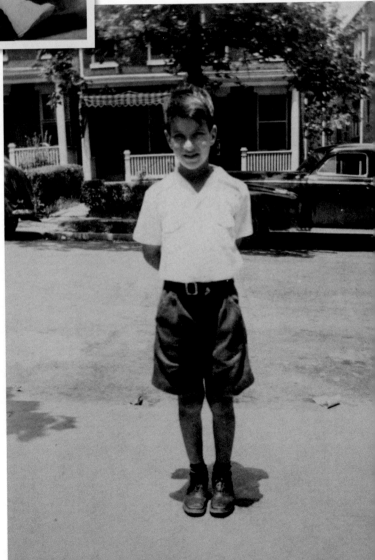

Eddie was exposed to entrepreneurship at a young age, as he watched his father start Snider Quality Market and grow it into a successful small business. The store (above) carried produce, meat, canned goods, tobacco products, alcohol, and more. Eddie regularly helped out in all areas of the store.

When Lilian found out that Eddie had not been attending his Bar Mitzvah sessions with the rabbi, she had to pay the synagogue extra to secure a date for the ceremony. At left is the Snider family at Eddie's big day (from left to right): Phyllis, Sol, Tsipe, Lilian, and Ed Snider.

From the moment he was hired to run the Philadelphia Eagles, Snider commanded respect from almost everyone who worked for him—save for head coach Joe Kuharich, pictured at right between Snider and brother-in-law Earl Foreman.

When Snider saw an opportunity to add an NHL franchise to Philadelphia's sports offerings, he approached Jerry Wolman to see if he was interested in building a new arena. Wolman enthusiastically agreed, culminating in the construction of the Spectrum. At the groundbreaking (below), Wolman was front and center, while Snider was second from the right.

One of the first hires the Flyers made was Keith Allen as their head coach. He would eventually serve as their general manager and build two Stanley Cup–winning teams. He and Snider, pictured at left, would remain as close as family until Allen's death in 2014.

The Flyers built their team through the 1967 expansion draft, where they selected players who would still be around when they won their Stanley Cups in the 1970s. Snider (below) sits at the front right, with Bernie Parent standing behind him. Keith Allen is standing in the center, with Joe Watson to his right. Joe Scott and Bill Putnam are seated first and second from the left.

Snider had a deep love for anyone who wore the orange and black of the Flyers and treated them like family. Here, he shares a moment with defenseman Jimmy Watson, who played for the organization for ten years.

Perhaps no player had a closer relationship with Snider than Bob Clarke. After Clarke rejected a generous offer to join the WHA's Philadelphia Blazers in favor of remaining with the Flyers, Snider told him he would never forget it.

Snider was the best person to be around when the Flyers were winning, but you wanted to stay out of his way when they were losing.

Snider had a soft spot for any employee who worked for him from the start, perhaps none more than broadcaster Gene Hart, seen here laughing with Snider after a game.

Snider was incredibly intense when watching his Flyers. Usually seated next to Myrna (pictured to his left), he experienced a wild ride of emotions during each game.

Unlike modern owners, who are often off to the side during a championship celebration, Snider was front and center all night during the 1974 Cup win.

Snider forever said that winning the Stanley Cup in 1974 was the top moment in his career.

Just like that, Snider's problems were again healed at the last second by a benevolent banker.

But despite the bank being his savior, Snider was miffed at the way the city was treating his personal problem like a game. He was a stickler for government overreach. If there was a problem, they should come to him and he would fix it. Instead, politicians threw nasty comments against each other in the newspapers, seeing who could one-up the other in hopes of scoring political points. Meanwhile, Snider just wanted his team to have a home in which to do their job. "The situation has me so upset that I can't eat," he told the *Philadelphia Inquirer*. "This is supposed to be the major leagues, you know? This supposedly is a major league city."

After making his pointed comment at the city's higher-ups, Snider stayed out of the public spotlight over the following weeks while the city fought with itself about the Spectrum. Nonetheless, the Flyers played their remaining home games on the road, most of them in Quebec City at the Aces' arena. By the end of March, Philadelphia had their act together and the Spectrum was finally fixed. Though, just a couple days later, the roof leaked over Section 8 and gave a few fans a bath. Putnam's reply to the *Philadelphia Daily News*? "I don't give a shit. People sit out in the snow to watch the Eagles."

With most of the roof issues seemingly behind them, the Flyers traveled to Quebec City for the already scheduled penultimate game of the year, the first of back-to-back games with their cross-state rival Penguins. Despite the Flyers losing to Pittsburgh in Quebec, putting their record at just .500 with one game left, all eyes were on the Kings, who were playing the Oakland Seals in their final game of the season. Los Angeles needed a win to remain in contention for the division title—anything less would hand the championship to the Flyers. Having landed in Pittsburgh just after midnight for the second game, the entire Philadelphia team gathered in their downtown hotel as their owner tried to find out the score of the West Coast game. With a phone to his ear, a newsman shouted toward Snider, "It's all over. You're the champs." Not wanting to believe it, Snider called Pittsburgh's United Press International office to confirm the news. When they informed him that, yes, the Kings tied the Seals 2–2, Snider tossed the phone and commenced a raucous celebration with his team.

Snider and Putnam shared a handshake and a hug, while players emptied into the hallway, whooping and hollering. The owner invited everyone into his suite as he opened one of many bottles of champagne. "Here's to the greatest team in the world!" he yelled, pouring the bubbly into a nearby glass. "The Stanley Cup is next!" The team cheered and began an all-night celebration that extended into a Pittsburgh bar down the street. With Snider joining them in jubilance, the players stayed out until 5:00 in the morning, knowing that the result of their final game did not matter—they would finish in first place regardless. Though the team ended up losing in the first round to the tougher, more vicious St. Louis Blues, the inaugural season, despite its many ups and downs, was a resounding success.

If nothing else that first season, Snider had established how he wanted his organization run: like a family. He treated the players like they were his own children—and his own children were as present as he was in the building. His four kids were at almost every game, while Myrna was by his side night after night. In fact, she was often even more loved than him—she would walk into the building and know everyone by name, no matter their position. Employees would yell down the hall, "Hi, Myrna!" then would notice her husband standing beside her and would follow with a "Hello, Mr. Snider." Between the two of them, the entire organization knew they were in the safe hands of a family who treated each of them like an extended branch. Snider took care of the players, while Myrna made sure the wives were happy. She would host events for them, throw numerous parties, and often presented them with gifts from the team. Myrna would give gold jewelry out on behalf of her and her husband, making sure they were happy and supportive of their Flyers family. She helped the Flyers become one of the first organizations that regularly gave holiday gifts to the players' families. While this is taken for granted in modern professional sports, at the time it was unusual, yet incredibly appreciated. Snider may have been the soul of the organization, but more often than not, Myrna was its heart.

To further this sense of community among the players' wives, Myrna created a private lounge within the Spectrum where they could gather and relax. It gave them privacy from the fans, along with places to take care of their children, breast-feed, and not worry about what was going on elsewhere in the arena. Myrna was like a mother to them and they all loved her just as much as the rest of the employees did. Her priority each day was looking out for all of the families. If they were happy, she knew the players would be happy—and if the players were happy, they would perform to her husband's liking.

Snider would also regularly help players out in a way that few owners did at the time. When Flyers captain Bob Clarke came into financial struggles stemming from a legal issue with his agent, Snider bailed him out and fixed the problem. When goaltender Bruce Gamble had to retire unexpectedly after suffering a heart attack, Snider continued paying him his salary and even reportedly paid for his children's college tuition. At a time when player salaries did not always cover a year's worth of personal expenses, Snider would connect them with friends and colleagues so that they had suitable summer jobs to make ends meet.

With both Sniders working endless hours trying to make sure the business was thriving, it was typical for neither of them to be home waiting when their children came home from school each day. Nonetheless, they always made sure to find time for family dinners in the directors' lounge in the Spectrum, where the many executives and their families would congregate before each home game. The Snider children would do their homework in the offices before joining their parents for dinner and a game. Daughters Lindy and Tina would, against their father's wishes, feed the cats roaming around the Spectrum basement (which were put there to hunt down rats). Sons Craig and Jay would play floor hockey outside the dressing rooms.

When the game started, the family was as raucous as the fans. Snider quickly made a name for himself among the Flyers faithful with his demonstrative and emotional game-watching tendencies. When the Flyers scored, he would jump up and high-five everyone around him. When they were scored upon, he would stay seated, squint his eyes in silence, and give his now predictable scowl toward the ice, unhappy that anyone dare embarrass his team by putting a puck into their net. When there was a perceived poor officiating call against the Flyers, he would jump up onto the ledge outside his superbox and gesticulate wildly toward the ice, screaming at the top of his lungs. Fans would see this and go crazy, turning toward their fearless leader, applauding, and yelling in agreement. Snider quickly learned that Philadelphia fans loved having an owner who cared even more about the team's success than they did—and in Philadelphia, that was a pretty lofty task.

Myrna, although not quite as center stage as her husband, was just as invested. She would mutter under her breath throughout the entire game, with an occasional "Hit him!" slipping out. When Ed went on one of his trademark tirades, she would be right behind him, cheering him on. The family never looked at it as a "game." The organization never felt like a "business." To them, they were the Flyers and the Flyers were them. It was all simply a part of their lives, and it was their right, if not duty, to be more emotionally invested than anyone else, win or lose. But above all, Snider insisted that the organization feel as familial as his superbox did night after night. The players, the staff, and his own family were all in this together, working as one to do what the pundits said couldn't be done—make NHL hockey a success in Philadelphia.

The 1968–69 season was one of on-ice struggles yet organizational promise. With the Phillies missing the playoffs and the Eagles losing their first 11 games en route to a 2–12 record, the Flyers saw an extraordinary opportunity in the city and gave Snider a chance to put his franchise front and center. Attendance improved more than 15 percent from the previous season, and by the end of the campaign they were still drawing close to 15,000 fans at the Spectrum when Original Six teams came to town. Again, though, they not only lost in the first round of the playoffs to St. Louis but were pushed around for its duration. Their two home playoff games each drew over 15,000 fans, but the Flyers scored just three goals in four games and were swept by their expansion rival.

For Snider, it was personal. His fists would clench as he recalled all those times he was bullied growing up, his glasses broken, the anti-Semitic chants. To be defeated in a hockey game was one thing, but to be pushed around and embarrassed was something he would not tolerate. The Flyers were banking on needing a few years to truly hit their mark on the ice, but in the meantime, the Blues, under legendary coach Scotty Bowman, had figured out how to bully their way to the Stanley Cup Finals each year. The Flyers may not have been talented enough to win every game, but they did not have to be embarrassed in the process. Snider gathered Poile and Allen in his office after the playoffs and made a promise to them that would define the franchise for eternity: "This will never happen again." When he was younger, Snider surrounded himself with tough guys to make sure he was never picked on. He would utilize the same strategy in building the Flyers toward success.

In Snider's eyes, it was a matter of adjusting the organization's draft philosophy. The Flyers' three centers at that time all stood 5'10" or under, and none were over 175 pounds. Heavily involved in the NFL Draft when he was with the Eagles, Snider was far from a hockey aficionado, nor did he, admittedly, have much eye for athletic talent at that point in his young life. But he understood the strategy and philosophy required to run a successful draft, and he wanted to impart that wisdom to his own executives. "We decided on the later rounds we would go for size," Snider told the *Philadelphia Inquirer* a few years later. "In our scouting program, if we have two players of equal ability, we take the bigger guy." The team would not ignore talent, by any means. Any team needs talented players to succeed—pucks still need to be put in the net in order to win games. But they also needed to be able to protect each other and the honor of Philadelphia.

That summer, at the 1969 draft, the Flyers drafted in a way that would change the face of the organization. After selecting highly touted Bob Currier with their first-round pick, Snider forced Poile and Allen to hear out scout Marcel Pelletier, who wanted to use the team's second-round pick to take a chance on a young star from Flin Flon, Manitoba, that other teams passed on due to his diabetes. Pelletier promised that he had done the research and was told that, with proper care and attention, it would not affect his play. The organization agreed and selected Bobby Clarke. In that same draft, the team selected Dave Schultz and Don Saleski, two talented players who would develop a needed knack for toughness and intimidation on the ice. With each draft over the next few years, they would continue to acquire the key cogs that would anchor the team for the next decade.

As their third season got underway, Snider began butting heads with general manager Bud Poile. The hard-headed manager came up through the old boys' hockey world, where managers and owners said how it would be, and that was the end of the discussion. Historically, NHL managers acted as tyrants. Players were expected to play every game they were asked, even if they were sick or injured. If they dared to claim they couldn't suit up one night, the odds were that they would end up on a train to the minor leagues the very next day. At the end of each season, players would sit in the manager's office and have another one-year contract slid across the desk to them, usually for the same amount of money or a negligible raise. There was no discussion—either sign it and keep playing in the NHL or be replaced.

Although Poile was not quite at that level, his mindset still lived in that era. He was an intimidator and wanted players to know that the leash was short. He felt owners should be seen, not heard, and was not too keen on Snider asking him questions about how the team was being run. Snider, on the other hand, came from football, and while he knew management, he was admittedly not an expert on his newfound love. Yet, when he approached Poile with a question, the answer was often dismissive, even borderline disrespectful. Nonetheless, Putnam assured Snider that Poile was the man for the job. With so much else on his plate, who was Snider to second-guess his team's president? He had hired Putnam to do a job and wanted to let him do it.

Privately, Putnam and Poile both saw Snider as an overly dressed, grandiose dandy, though publicly Putnam showed much more respect for his boss. Yet Snider was annoyed that they held their noses so high in the air. While they were managing the hockey team, Snider was working endlessly trying to ensure that the business was operating properly. One night when there was a mix-up in the ticket office, Snider, Scott, and Myrna spent all night fixing it so everything was prepared for the following day's Flyers game. "I didn't see Putnam in there sorting tickets," Scott recalled in Jay Greenberg's *Full Spectrum*.

Rumors continued to make their way back to Snider that Poile was badmouthing him to anyone who would listen, but Snider paid no mind. He did not do gossip, and frankly did not care anyway. But a week before Christmas 1969, Poile's emotions erupted, this time toward the team's television director, Harland Singer. Unhappy about Snider's constant television interviews between periods on the broadcast, he demanded to know why Singer continued to have his boss on the air. "Well, he's the owner," Singer said, perplexed as to what the issue was.

Poile got right up in Singer's face and said, "If you ever have that son of a bitch on again, you're fired." Unbeknownst to Poile, other team executives and even a few reporters were within earshot, and the story quickly made its way back to Snider. After making some calls late at night and confirming the facts from multiple sources, Snider decided it was the final straw. Not only was it insubordinate and disrespectful, but Poile did not have any management authority over Singer, who was not a member of the hockey team. Snider called his manager and told him he was fired, but Poile did not care. He felt his direct boss was Putnam, and informed Snider he would be in the office the next morning—which, of course, did not happen.

Snider immediately called Keith Allen and asked him to meet for a drink at the Philadelphia Marriott. Informed of the new developments within the organization, Snider offered Allen the general manager's position. Allen felt uncomfortable at first, not wanting to make it seem like he pushed his way to the top, but after thinking it through, he accepted and became the team's front-office leader.

When Putnam found out, he was extremely unhappy and felt Snider had overstepped him as team president. At that point, without Snider's knowledge, he began secretly shopping his 25 percent share of the team. When he eventually found a buyer in local philanthropist F. Eugene Dixon, Snider told Putnam he was no longer welcome in his organization and replaced him with Scott. In less than two years, the owner had dumped both his president and general manager— not exactly the turnover rate he was hoping to achieve. And his now ex-manager was not too happy with the move. When Snider publicly announced the move as a differing of opinions, Poile took a shot at his former boss. "He doesn't like some of my friends," he told the *Philadelphia Inquirer*. "I don't like some of his. I don't like bell-bottoms and big, flashy rings. He does."

Snider remained quiet, refusing to engage publicly. With Allen in place as the team's general manager and a young roster that had endless potential, the owner was confident that his organization was moving in the right direction. With attendance gradually rising and fan interest increasing by the week, he felt it was only a matter of time until his fledgling hockey franchise reached the top of the mountain.

Saving the Spectrum and Creating a Dynasty

WHILE SNIDER'S STAR was quickly rising in Philadelphia, Jerry Wolman's was crashing. Stuck in bankruptcy court, the Eagles' owner was desperately trying to save his assets. One of those assets, the Spectrum, posed a slight problem for Snider. The Flyers were reliant on the building in order to play, but with the structure in hock, there was a big unknown staring Snider in the face. He already foresaw the Spectrum's potential in just its first year, but without control of the building, all he had was its top-drawing tenant. The Flyers would get first choice of game nights, but past that, they had no flexibility. If they wanted to schedule a practice, they had to use the Cherry Hill Arena, since Snider did not control the Spectrum's schedule. It became an inconvenience that he believed was affecting their on-ice play. He wanted the team to have the flexibility to be on their home ice anytime they wanted. Perhaps more dire, with multiple banks holding mortgages on the building, if either or both of them decided to foreclose on the loan, the Flyers could be left without a place to play.

With the rest of the region in the dark regarding these internal issues, however, it was curious when Snider and Earl Foreman began showing up to every bankruptcy court hearing at the United States District Court for the Eastern District of Pennsylvania. These cases were led by Judge A. Leon Higginbotham, who would one day go on to become the first Black chief justice of the Pennsylvania Supreme Court, but for now was simply in charge of determining Wolman's fate. Publicly, Snider claimed that he and Foreman were attending the sessions because Foreman still held ownership in the Eagles, while Snider had his 7 percent option. Both wanted their interests cashed out for a market value of $5 million. On top of that, Snider was still owed money by the Eagles based on his termination agreement. SEC filings made by Wolman showed Snider was paid $287,996 by the Eagles between 1967 and 1968, as well as being provided with a new car. Snider regularly sat in the back row of the courtroom with Foreman. Now well-known as the owner of the Flyers, he wore a crisp, Glen Plaid Edwardian suit, listening carefully to each word uttered in court. At one point, when Wolman answered a question by referencing the shares of the Spectrum he got from Snider, his attorney asked, "Who is Ed Snider?" to which the courtroom burst out in laughter.

But no one was laughing when Higginbotham revealed information that few but Snider and Foreman knew. The reason the Spectrum had so many debtors, despite its early success, was because Wolman had transferred money out of his various businesses to himself, rather than using the funds to pay down its debt. He was in dire need of bailing himself out of his financial troubles stemming from the John Hancock Tower project. Between August 1966 and November 1967, Wolman took the $1 million he received from ARA and the $1 million he received from Fidelity Bank and moved it over to his and others' accounts. Throughout 1967, nearly 10 months during which Snider was running the Eagles, Wolman transferred $443,776.65 of funds from the football club to the Spectrum, and another $1.4 million to himself and others. Wolman was moving money around in ways that today would probably earn jail time, all in an attempt to keep his head above water.

It was at that point that Foreman and Snider decided to act. The city owned the land, and as the landlord they took back control of the building and sought a buyer for the leasehold improvement deal. Foreman was in a position of power, already holding a mortgage of just under $1.5 million on the Spectrum and having guaranteed the construction contract with McCloskey to build the arena in 1967. When McCloskey came to him to collect on the debt, he took a third mortgage out on the Spectrum—behind Fidelity and ARA, who had the first two options on the building. With Snider having a vested interest in being able to control the arena in which his team played, the two began working on a plan to take full ownership of the building. In total, the Spectrum owed $8,115,000 to all creditors and had just $1,785,000 in cash and accounts receivable. Battling against two other plans, the duo dug deep and unveiled what was referred to as the Foreman-Snider plan. In it, the brothers-in-law proposed how, with $7 million in capital from First Pennsylvania Bank (they presented a commitment letter to the court for a $6.5 million mortgage and a $500,000 line of credit), they would eventually repay every Spectrum creditor in full. Foreman agreed not to take a cent of payment on his mortgage until the rest of the creditors were paid off in full. It was 1971 at this point, and Snider knew full well the financial potential of the now successful Spectrum.*

From its opening event in 1967 through 1970, the building had taken in more than $13 million in gross receipts. With the Flyers' stature rising and the roster beginning to form the core that would eventually make deep playoff runs (which would bring with it higher

---

* An interesting gem of Philadelphia sports history was that, in 1968, Snider and Foreman were very close to actually purchasing the Eagles from Wolman. They even got as far as securing a loan from First Pennsylvania Bank for $7.5 million, according to financial documents from Snider's personal archive, which would have purchased Wolman's 52 percent share to add to Foreman's 48. At that point, though, Wolman was convinced that he would be able to keep ownership of his football team. Eventually, Wolman purchased the rest of the shares from Foreman (and paid Snider $491,400 for his option) in order to sell the team to local trucking magnate Leonard Tose.

gate receipts), the owner knew that, with enough time, they would be able to generate plenty of cash flow to pay off the building's debts. Higginbotham was overwhelmed by the ingenuity of the plan and wholeheartedly approved it. At once, Snider and Foreman became the beneficiaries of, at that time, the largest bankruptcy in Pennsylvania history where creditors got repaid in full.

Now owning the Flyers and the Spectrum, Snider began planting the seeds of what would eventually become a sports business empire. The Flyers' worth was already more than double what it was in 1967 (Putnam sold his 25 percent share for at least $1.25 million, valuing the entire team at over $5 million). The Spectrum was drawing about 2 million patrons a year to its various events, including Flyers games. By 1971, the Flyers sold out 26 of its 39 games and averaged over 14,000 fans per game. The 76ers' lease was coming up for renewal, and they were currently paying significantly less rent than the Flyers, opening the door for increased Spectrum revenue in the coming years. In fact, as the 1971–72 season ended, with nearly every game a sellout, Snider began plans to embark on a $1 million Spectrum expansion by adding a third deck of seats, which would add an additional capacity of 2,000. Perhaps for the first time, Snider had no doubt that those extra seats would immediately fill up. By the 1973–74 season, the Spectrum was sold out for every Flyers home game—17,007 fans filling the air with Philadelphia passion for the hottest team in town.

The team was hot for two main reasons: talent and fire. The talent was quite apparent—the 1973–74 roster consisted of three future members of the Hockey Hall of Fame: forwards Bobby Clarke and Bill Barber, and goaltender Bernie Parent; not to mention coach Fred Shero, who would also be awarded the same honor posthumously. Five players surpassed the 20-goal mark that season, while Parent finished second in the vote for the Hart Memorial Trophy, the league's most valuable player award. There was no doubt that the Flyers were among the most talented teams in the league.

But the draw was the team's fire. From the drop of the puck in fall 1972, the Flyers were demonstrably an improved team. They would find ways to beat their opponents any way they could—scoring goals, tight defense, or intimidating the other team out of the building with their fists and their bruising style of play. In a December game against Vancouver, an on-ice brawl spilled into the stands, and Flyers players went after rowdy Canucks fans sitting behind their bench. In a game at the Montreal Forum that same season, both teams brawled. And against Pittsburgh on the road, the Flyers traded major penalties and game misconducts en route to another crucial win. Once, they were escorted out of Detroit's Olympia by police. And in December 1973 multiple players got into a stick-swinging brawl against the California Golden Seals. These constant battles earned the Flyers the eternal nickname the "Broad Street Bullies," coined by *Evening Bulletin* writer Jack Chevalier, as well as the paper's headline writer.

Part of that fire surely came from above. The team's penchant for fury and intimidation stemmed from Snider's own annoyance at anyone who would possibly look at his team with disrespect, whether it was an opposing player, an opposing fan, a reporter, or a referee. As early as 1972, Snider was making waves in the media for his temper, often ignited by an officiating call that he felt was unwarranted. In the midst of a Rangers game at the Spectrum on November 5, Snider watched joyfully as his Flyers established a 2–0 lead on their regional rival. But his mood quickly soured when referee Wally Harris called two penalties in two minutes on the Flyers in the second period, leading to two Ranger power-play goals. When the Rangers took the momentum and scored a third goal in the same period to clinch the 3–2 win, Snider's face turned beet red and the owner was irate. He stormed out of his superbox and headed downstairs to confront Harris and, in the process, marched past Rangers coach Emile Francis, who wasn't happy that it took nearly two full periods for Harris to even call a penalty against the Flyers. "Say hello to that damn referee for me, too, while you're there," Francis said, half-sarcastically. Snider snapped back with an expletive before barging into the officials' room.

While nobody heard exactly what he said to the officials, he was not shy about sharing his opinions with the press shortly thereafter. "That's the worst monstrosity I've ever seen!" Snider yelled to the *Philadelphia Inquirer*. "It's damn disgraceful. It's not consistent.... We go ahead 2–0 by hard work. That fucking Harris turns it around all by himself. All by himself! He wasn't calling anything. All of a sudden he makes two chicken calls against us. I can't stand it!"

Even later that season, as they lost in the semifinal to Montreal, Snider publicly called referee Dave Newell a donkey in a *Philadelphia Daily News* piece, claiming he was the league's sixth-ranked referee and had no business officiating a crucial playoff game. He blamed NHL referee-in-chief Scotty Morrison, claiming, "This game doesn't mean anything to [him]." Whether accurate or not, the fire spread to the coaches, players, and fans as Snider fought on their behalf. This would become a habit of Snider's, both publicly during games and privately in the bowels of the Spectrum after games. And the players loved it, too. "It was great," Bob Clarke said years later, laughing at the memory. "It was support for us. He was the owner supporting his team, his players. He cared. We knew he cared about us, but he cared about us winning."

Snider's passion proved to be an exemplary representation of Philadelphia attitude at its best, and the Washington, D.C., native was proud to already adopt the city as his own. No one insults Philadelphia. No one disrespects Philadelphia. And, surely, no one dares to mess with his Flyers or any of the city's other sports teams. Snider was more Philadelphian than even some who had lived there for decades. He exemplified all of the qualities that gave the region its unique reputation. The fans took notice and grew to love him and the team he ran.

The Flyers had already become arguably the most popular team in town. Philadelphia had been a football city and a college basketball city. But it was also now a Flyers city. The 20 Canadian transplants wearing the orange and black jerseys personified the never-give-up attitude of the city's blue-collar population. And Snider was the one leading the way from the top. A favorite expression of his was, "A fish stinks from the head." If there were problems in the organization, he was ultimately to blame. He had to make sure he led them properly and personified the passion and fight that he wanted in his players.

So it was no surprise when, as the 1973–74 season progressed and the Flyers entered the playoffs as the division's top seed, the city was buzzing. Philadelphia had just one major league championship to its name since 1960 (a 76ers NBA title in '67), and the city was starving for a winner. After dispatching the Rangers in a hard-fought seven-game series, Snider, in the locker room, held a drink in the air and toasted, "To the best team in all hockey!" They had now earned the right to face the high-powered Boston Bruins for the Stanley Cup. But as the series with Boston progressed, the tension in the Snider household grew. With each Flyers win, the family knew they were one step closer to their dream. With each loss, they felt the anguish of potentially missing out after getting so close. The house was quieter than normal, not much needed to be said. The atmosphere permeated the workdays as well. Office chatter was now a hushed affair, with most of the hours spent in silence, lest anyone say something that might jinx their chances. Even those who were not as superstitious as Snider went along with his tendencies, so as not to be the reason the winds blew against the Flyers.

The potential for a championship win had taken on a new meaning a few months earlier when, on March 3, 1974, Sol Snider passed away. With diabetes and heart disease contributing to his death, the loss hit Snider especially hard. Having learned his entrepreneurial tendencies and work ethic from his father, he was always cognizant of trying to make Sol proud. Sol was generally a supportive parent, but he certainly was confused by the business Snider had entered—as was his mother. In fact, in one of the early years, Snider brought Lil to a Flyers game to show off his new pride and joy. As her head whipped back and forth, attempting to follow the action, she was a bit confused about what drew customers to this sport. When two players dropped their gloves and fought on the ice, she turned to her son and said, "Eddie, what kind of business is this?"

Similarly, Sol was unsure how a professional hockey club would become the kind of success he knew his son doggedly desired. Snider spent the 1973–74 season praying he could share a championship with his father and have Sol witness the frenzy that Philadelphia would find itself in when he finally achieved that goal. When Sol passed just two months before the Stanley Cup final, it left a gaping hole in Snider's heart, which stuck with him for many years.

Even before eventually winning the Stanley Cup, Snider had already proven himself and his organization as the cream of the crop. He was named hockey's top executive by *The Hockey News*, and Shero was named coach of the year in the same article. Even more surprising, the publication said Keith Allen was their runner-up to Snider's award. The Flyers brass had stunned the hockey world even before winning a championship. In just seven years, they went from throwaway expansion club to hockey's elite. Those accolades were proven accurate when the Flyers were up three games to two over the powerful Bruins and came home on May 19, 1974, to try and finish them off in Game 6 and clinch a title. Kate Smith, their perpetual good luck charm, was brought to the Spectrum to sing her rendition of "God Bless America" in an attempt to inspire the team to victory.

Parent shut the door on the Bruins, refusing to allow a single goal, and Rick MacLeish's single tally was enough to give the Flyers the 1–0 win, eliciting a raucous, never-before-seen celebration in Philadelphia (and perhaps not seen since). In typical, superstitious Snider fashion, he had refused to send security down to ice level in preparation for a celebration, not wanting to tempt fate against the mighty

Bruins, who with one shot could have tied the game and ended all hope. So, when the clock hit zero, hundreds of fans tumbled over the glass and onto the ice, crowding the celebration and essentially preventing Clarke and Parent from properly parading the Stanley Cup around the Spectrum ice.

Nonetheless, nothing could sour the mood that night. Even the term "euphoria" would not do justice to the celebration in the Flyers dressing room deep on the event level of the Spectrum. As the press waited to be allowed inside the room, Myrna led the Flyers wives to the door, where the security guard prevented her from going in. With a stern glare, she looked him in the eye and said, "I think the wives should come in first, then the press." The guard opened the door, letting the players' families, including Snider's kids, join them in their ecstasy.

Snider was in the middle of the celebration, surrounded by cheering players. At just 41 years old, he was not much older than the guys who played for him. Snider was younger than his coach, his general manager, and a good chunk of the staff. He was closest in age to the players and was often treated like one of the boys. Unlike most modern sports owners, who are off to the side with other executives during a championship celebration, Snider was right in the thick of it. Standing on a table, Snider held an inverted bottle of champagne over the Stanley Cup and filled the bowl with liquid gold, ready to be emptied quickly by the many players taking turns tipping the trophy toward their mouths. Drenched and half-unaware of anything else going on around him, Snider was picked up in celebration by Don Saleski, Terry Crisp, and Tom Bladon and thrown into the shower. Players kept calling out for more champagne as an excessive number of people continued piling into the room—including Pennsylvania Governor Milton Shapp and Philadelphia Mayor Frank Rizzo.

Two days later, on May 21, Snider and the rest of the organization sat in convertibles and paraded the Stanley Cup through Philadelphia.

Seven years earlier, just a few dozen people showed up for a parade celebrating the city's new hockey team. Now they were the pride of the city, the darlings of a region. Over 2 million people lined the streets, hung out of windows, and otherwise turned the city into one massive party. And this time, the mayor elected to show up, eliciting jokes from the few players who were there for the lackluster inaugural parade in 1967.

But as much as Philadelphia loved their Flyers, no one expressed it more so than Snider himself. Overwhelmed at the accomplishment of his organization, Snider threw a raucous party at his Radnor home on May 23 for all of the players and their families. With the Stanley Cup sitting on a table in the middle of the family's backyard and a band entertaining the guests, the players let loose and partied through the night. Dave Schultz got on stage and began singing, honoring them with an impression of Elvis Presley. Meanwhile, hundreds of prying eyes peeked over the wall surrounding the backyard, as Philadelphians from all over the city tried to get a glimpse of their newfound heroes. It was like a giant family picnic, with players pushing each other into the pool, hooting and hollering, and of course, drinking anything and everything out of the Cup. A couple players even tried to steal the Stanley Cup as a joke, but to no avail.

After the party was over, Snider heard people sneaking into his backyard. He peered out the back window to observe a bunch of his players tiptoeing across the property with some of the waitresses from the party, stripping down and diving into the pool to skinny dip with their newfound partners. The owner watched from his kitchen, laughing heartily at his players having a good time. Nonetheless, the entire week was a culmination of perhaps the pinnacle of his career. For the Snider family, it felt less like a team that won a championship and more like a family member accomplished something seemingly impossible.

As the 1974–75 season got underway, Snider purchased Foreman's 50 percent stake in the Spectrum, making him the sole owner of perhaps the hottest arena in the country. Meanwhile, the Flyers had so many people on the season ticket waiting list that Snider agreed to return everyone's $50 deposits, knowing that no space was going to open up anytime soon. It was reported that nearly 70,000 fans requested season tickets, while only two canceled their previous year's subscription. Business was great, and the only thing that could make it better in Snider's eyes was to remain atop the NHL pinnacle.

As always, it was a family affair to do everything possible to win. In the 1975 playoffs, before Game 7 of the semifinals against the New York Islanders at the Spectrum, according to the *Philadelphia Inquirer*, Kate Smith returned to sing "God Bless America" as she had before Game 6 against Boston the previous year. When she arrived, her dress, packed carefully in her suitcase, was completely wrinkled, with just hours to go before puck drop. When Smith's bodyguard began searching desperately for someone to help, he came across Myrna, who ran to her husband's office, which was offered to Smith for the night for her convenience. "Don't worry," Myrna said, "I'll have our wardrobe mistress take care of it. We'll have it back in minutes."

Just moments after she grabbed the dress and ran out of the office, it hit her that the team didn't have a wardrobe mistress—there was no such thing. She ran to the Spectrum's head usherette and asked for help, whereupon the employee called her aunt, who lived two blocks away on 13th Street, and asked if they could bring it over. And so it was that Myrna ran down Broad Street, got Smith's dress pressed and ironed, and returned it to the star just in time for her to walk the red carpet onto the Spectrum ice yet again.

When, just a week later, the Flyers defeated the Buffalo Sabres on the road to clinch their second consecutive championship, it was Snider, again, who led the celebration. Soaked with champagne and heading toward the team plane, he pointed at the Stanley Cup and said to the United Airlines workers, "Don't put it in the baggage compartment. Bring it up. Bring it inside." Snider lifted the trophy out of its case, walked onto the plane, and paraded it to the back, where a score of Canadian players sang out the words to "God Bless America," as Philadelphia again partied in the streets, proud to remain on top of the hockey world.

Over the course of those first few years, Snider developed intensely close relationships with the players. His passion was evident, and he always had their backs. He was extraordinarily protective of them, both privately and publicly, and everyone in the dressing room knew he would do anything for them. That attitude, coming from the top, led the players to fight for each other as well. They would go out for drinks together after games, sometimes bringing their young owner along as well. The mutual respect Snider had for his players was a trademark of his personality that made playing for the Flyers something to be proud of for the rest of a player's career, starting as far back as the 1960s.

But while wins and Stanley Cups left Snider feeling exuberant, there was one part of the world that consistently made him narrow his eyes and filled him with hatred: the Soviet Union. Not only did he hate their communist way of life, but their treatment of their citizens, specifically his Jewish brethren, got his blood boiling. Having grown up during World War II and the Holocaust, and knowing what his own ancestors went through just to survive and escape their persecution, he had no tolerance for the Soviets' actions. In fact, when Valery and Galina Panov, two Soviet ballet stars, defected to the United States and began a national tour, the Spectrum was the first arena to welcome them with open arms.

When Snider heard about the event his employees booked, he immediately called Joe and Connie Smukler, two Philadelphians who were at the head of the movement to bring attention to the plight of *refuseniks*—the term coined for Soviet citizens, mostly Jews, who were denied permission to emigrate to other countries. The Smuklers would regularly organize protests and pickets throughout the city to draw attention to the travesty that was occurring in the Soviet Union, imploring their fellow citizens to help support the cause. Snider called Joe Smukler ahead of the Panov performance and, wanting to help, offered to split the net proceeds of the event with him to help finance their efforts. (Though it was definitely possible that Snider wanted to ensure that there were no protests outside his arena.)

The next year, with the Soviet Red Army hockey team scheduled to play the Flyers in January 1976 as part of their North American tour of NHL clubs, Snider had another opportunity to make waves across the world. The entire hockey world was, for the first time ever, rooting for the Flyers. Through three games, no NHL squad had beaten the Soviets. But for Snider, the game was personal. His familial history with the Russian Empire was messy and ran deep within his veins. He wanted his team to beat them badly and show that the Flyers and the NHL were the best in the world. At the same time, however, Snider had the chance to subtly showcase his support of Soviet Jewry and efforts to help them escape to Israel and the United States.

He called Smukler ahead of the game and, perhaps in another attempt to avoid protests, asked what he could do for them. Smukler requested that signs be hung around the second deck of the Spectrum blasting the Soviets and their treatment of Jews. Snider agreed, and signs reading FREE THE JEWS, LET MY PEOPLE GO, GET SOVIET JEWS OUT OF THE PENALTY BOX, and many more were brought into the Spectrum the morning of the game, where staff hung them across the balcony. When the Soviet team came onto the ice to warm up for the game, Soviet coach Konstantin Loktev refused to play until the signs were removed. Snider ran outside the building to Smukler and told him of the issue. "What do you want me to do?" he asked. Smukler thought about it for a moment and replied, "Just let the media film the signs, and then take them down."

Snider sprinted back to his superbox, where he made sure the television cameras, broadcasting the game across the world, got a good look

at the signs, and then he instructed that the banners be removed—
thereby satisfying the Soviets without them even knowing that the
Smuklers had already accomplished what they wanted. Soviet Jews
across Russia, for the first time ever, saw proof of the United States
movement to support them and were given hope. The Smuklers
would forever call Snider their guardian angel because of his willingness to risk a portion of his business and take a stand for something
righteous. The game against the Soviets raised over $17,000 for the
cause, as Snider happily handed a check to Smukler during a photo-op
days later.

Yet, despite his animosity toward his opponent, Snider remained
a gracious host. As part of the event, the Flyers welcomed the Soviet
team and their players to a roast beef luncheon reception at the Spectrum the Friday afternoon before the game. With Snider expected
to give a speech, he spent the entire week trying to come up with a
Russian phrase to add some extra pizzazz. Running into broadcaster
Gene Hart in the Spectrum hallway one day, he asked the Russian aficionado for advice (Hart had studied Russian during his Army days).
Hart, in an anecdote told in his autobiography, told Snider how to say,
"Good luck to all on Sunday." All week, he continued practicing the
phrase out loud each time he passed Hart in the hallway. But when it
came time to deliver his speech, Snider ended it by saying, "Thank
you very much," and sat down. After the luncheon, Snider grabbed
Hart by the lapel and said, "I want to tell you, Gene, I appreciate what
you did, and I wanted you to know that I didn't forget it. It's just that I
looked at those cold sons of bitches and I couldn't say to them, 'Good
luck on Sunday.'"

The bad blood went in both directions. The Soviet players hated
Bob Clarke with a passion, perhaps as much as Snider hated them.
In the 1972 Canada Cup series (an international tournament), Clarke
had delivered a vicious, two-handed slash to the heel of Soviet star
Valeri Kharlamov, breaking his ankle and sidelining him for the series.

They called Clarke "the dirtiest player in the world," to which Clarke smirked and said to the Associated Press, "That doesn't bother me."

When the game started, it was clear the Soviets would be facing a different kind of team this time. While the likes of the Montreal Canadiens tried to go toe to toe with talent, the Flyers were clearly aiming to intimidate the Red Army squad out of the building. With hit after hit, Soviet players were knocked to the ice with regularity, and the Philadelphia faithful were on their feet, perhaps the loudest the Spectrum had been to that point. When Ed Van Impe put an elbow into Kharlamov's chin as he skated into the Flyers zone, the Soviet star lay motionless on the ice while the crowd roared and the Red Army bench objected. With no penalty forthcoming on the Flyers, Loktev told his players not to go on the ice in protest. When the referee called a delay-of-game penalty on the Soviets, Loktev brushed off the official, then led his players off the ice and back to the locker room.

Up in his superbox watching the festivities, Snider jumped up and sprinted to the event level of the Spectrum, eager to find out what was going on. Huddled with Campbell and other league executives, Campbell pleaded with the Soviet delegation to return their players to the ice. When they refused, Snider spoke the only language he knew they would understand. "You understand if your players do not resume the game," Snider said through an interpreter, according to United Press International, "we're going to have to refund the money to all the people here." When there was no immediate reply, he continued. "That means you fellows won't get the $25,000 for this game." After the Soviets exchanged a few words to each other in Russian, they agreed to return to the ice, with Snider grinning at the irony of the communists responding to a capitalistic pitch.

Seventeen seconds after play resumed, Reggie Leach deflected a Bill Barber shot to give the Flyers a 1–0 lead, and the Spectrum erupted. The Flyers controlled the entirety of the contest, winning 4–1, becoming the only NHL squad during the series to defeat the

Soviet Red Army. In the midst of Shero's postgame press conference, Snider burst in with a wide smile on his face and announced, "That's the greatest coaching job ever!" The following day, the Soviet newspapers printed a cartoon in which giants on skates with Flyers logos on their shirts held big wooden clubs to signify their style of play that the Soviets felt was despicable. It had the opposite effect on their American counterparts: Snider printed the cartoon and hung it in his office as a makeshift trophy for his team's accomplishment.

At the same time, the Spectrum was becoming the envy of the sports and entertainment world. In the 12-month span between March 1975 and March 1976, the building booked 400 events, including hockey, basketball, rock concerts, the circus, and more. Around that time, F. Eugene Dixon sold his shares of the Flyers to Snider, who now owned 85 percent of the team (with Scott still holding his 15 percent share).

With the Flyers riding the wave at the top of the hockey world, the Spectrum dominating the local entertainment industry, and Snider increasing his control of the entire empire, the still young businessman had established himself as one of the most dominant personalities in the sports business world. But even that was not enough—for Snider, there was always room for expansion.

8

The Start of a Business Empire

WHILE AT AN NHL Board of Governors meeting in the mid-1970s, Snider was seated next to then Washington Capitals president Peter O'Malley. Disgusted at the results of some of the discussions and votes regarding the World Hockey Association (more on the WHA in chapter 9), which had taken place over the previous few years at these meetings, he leaned over to O'Malley and asked why the owners continued to vote against their own self-interest. O'Malley chuckled, then wrote something on a piece of paper and handed it Snider. "Read this," O'Malley said. Snider opened the note, which simply read, "Atlas Shrugged."

Snider bought a copy of the famous Ayn Rand novel and, over the course of the following weeks, devoured it. Describing the experience to *Philadelphia Magazine* as "gazing into a mirror," he took a piece of paper and began writing a letter to the controversial author. "I have recently read *Atlas Shrugged*," he wrote. "It is, without question, the finest book that I have ever read. It clarified fully the principles that guide my life, and I became more aware, as well as more articulate, in expressing my views. I have, in discussing these views, been shocked to learn just how little our young people know about our system. I feel it is important that those of us who firmly believe in capitalism and the free enterprise system create a fully funded organization that would work to set up a course on 'Capitalism: The Unknown Ideal' in every college and university in the United States. This course, if I have my way, will be completely created and designed by you. I am fully prepared to devote considerable time and money to this project. I feel this must be [done] if we are to reverse the present trend in our country."

Even early in his success at the sports business level, Snider was bothered by his view of the country's academic state. With two sons in college, he was constantly hearing them regurgitate their opinions, shaped on campus, that capitalism was evil. In the midst of a family vacation in the Bahamas, Snider was bombarded with questions from Jay and Craig, forcing him to defend the business model that allowed the family to be taking that very vacation. Enraged at what he perceived as lies and misnomers being taught to his own children funded by his tuition dollars, he dropped his copy of *Atlas Shrugged* on the table and demanded that both read it. Weeks later, when they each completed it, they understood their father's way of thinking. "The results were even greater than I had possibly hoped," he said in his initial letter to Rand. "They now understand completely."

Despite the fact that Rand rarely made any public appearances or responded to any correspondence, she was deeply touched by Snider's words. For what may have been the first time in a while, she picked up a pen and responded, inviting him to meet her in New York. Bringing Jay and Craig with him, he was pleasantly surprised at the experience. For multiple days, Snider and his sons sat with Rand in restaurants, cafes, and her apartment to discuss their views on capitalism and the state of the country.

"Ayn was warm and charming, the strongest, most brilliant person I've ever met," Snider recalled. "She could see things instantly." Their viewpoints synced up, and Snider had a deep love of Rand's fiery personality. "I felt like a little boy around her because I felt if I said the wrong thing, I was going to get yelled at," he said. "And many times that happened."

Rand had a deep respect for self-made men such as Snider, while Snider shared her view that the point of capitalism was to give everybody the free and equal opportunity to chase success—something that he felt was endangered by the United States entering what he perceived as a "welfare state." "Who gave anybody the right to take money from one group of people and give it to another?" he once asked *Philadelphia Magazine.* "The Declaration of Independence says people have the right to the *pursuit* of happiness. It doesn't say they have the right to happiness. There's a difference. It doesn't guarantee a chicken in every pot. It says you have the right to go out and *earn* that chicken." He firmly believed that, freed from the burden of taxation and government regulation, those who achieved a level of financial success would voluntarily utilize their monetary reward to care for the sick, the poor, and involve themselves in charitable work, as he already had. Perhaps it was an overly optimistic, utopian view of society, but it fully explained Snider's beliefs of what capitalism was supposed to be.

Snider's politics could easily be described as both conservative and libertarian. He rarely voted, if ever, and was not interested in being involved in politics at all. He felt that capitalism was at its strongest when the government and private entity had nothing to do with one another. But he also understood the world in which he lived. Despite his lifelong protests against government regulations, he knew that the squeaky wheel got the grease. His conservative viewpoints were strongest when it came to economic and fiscal policies. Outside of the government's treatment of businesses and entrepreneurs, he rarely involved himself in politics.

One of the tenets of Rand's philosophies is that successful people should have "selfish egotism," which allowed for successful people to spend their own money as they wished, with no guilt for doing so. Snider certainly gave his fair share back, in how he provided for his employees, his extended family, and the numerous charities he regularly supported. But for the first time in his life, his business success was noticeably tangible. Even his children did not realize quite how much wealth he had accrued until they read it in a Philadelphia newspaper headline in the late '70s.

The family lived comfortably, with a beautiful ranch house outside Philadelphia, and had all of the amenities that came with being the owner of a successful major league sports team—driver, housekeeper, fancy dinners—but there was a difference between being quite comfortable and being massively wealthy. With an income that freed him from many of his early struggles, Snider was finally comfortable spending more on himself and his family.

The Snider household was an interesting place, to say the least. Myrna and her twin sister, Dobbie, were still as close as ever, and their children (four each) were often inseparable. Add in two children from Myrna's second sister, and you ended up with a clan of kids that were constantly running around the neighborhood together. As if their own children were not enough, there were up to 10 together on any given day. Friends would often call them the "Jewish Kennedys," with so many members of each generation always at each other's side.

And while family played a crucial role in Snider's life, work always came first for him. Still at a point where he was trying to build the business and spending many hours doing so, he never bothered to learn the names of his children's best friends. He was not home much, and certainly not on the night of a home game. When the team was on the road, he would be home for dinner, but the meal was often served on a tray in front of the television so that he and Myrna could take in the game. Some of the kids would join the festivities, but no one dared sit within striking distance of their parents' flailing and pumping fists, be it from excitement or anger.

As parents, the couple enjoyed giving their children their independence. There was oversight and strict boundaries, but no one watched over them like a hawk. The children were often left to make their own mistakes and face the consequences if they broke a rule. "It was kind of up to you," is how one of the children described their upbringing. Study hard and get good grades, or don't and their marks would suffer. The choice was theirs to make.

But just as he could be in the office, Snider was an intimidating presence at home, whether he was physically there or not. Myrna would constantly use her husband's fierce personality as a deterrent to any bad behavior. She would use the popular phrase, "Do you want to wait until your father gets home?" along with the threats of spankings (though there is only one recalled instance of Snider actually acting on that threat). The children, well aware of their father's capricious nature, were often reluctant to step out of line after such a threat.

Coming of age in the '50s and '60s, perhaps the simplest description of Snider is as a character out of *Mad Men*—fancy clothes, slicked back hair, booze, infidelity, chain smoking—the couple fit the stereotype, though Snider certainly gave in to those vices more often than his wife. They had their clubs and their circle of friends and would constantly be running around the city partaking in the latest craze. As young parents, still in their thirties when their children were going into high school, they wanted to have fun and did so, even at the expense of their family.

Snider also skipped many family functions because there was a Flyers game, often missing one of his sons' hockey games, his daughters' sports games or recitals, and even a graduation. One could easily say his priorities were out of order, but at the same time, there is no denying that his commitment to his work allowed him and his children the opportunities later in life that most never have.

But he tried very hard to be a good father when he was not at work. In the late '60s, he and Myrna had already invested some of the little money they had in a home in Monmouth, Maine, on Cobbossee Lake. They were sending their children to camp in the region and wanted a place of their own to stay in the summers. Although it started as a casual vacation spot, it quickly turned into a deeply important part of the Snider family's life. It acted as a getaway from the spotlight in which Snider consistently found himself. The months they would spend there became something they looked forward to every year. He taught his kids how to water ski during the day and manned the grill at night. In the winter, the family would go snowmobiling and play hockey on the frozen lake. On the drives up, they would pack the station wagon with all of the kids, and Snider would drive up I-95 with the windows open, both he and Myrna blowing their smoke out the window, and the family singing old camp and college fight songs. He would invite his sister, Phyllis, and her family, along with Myrna's family. Maine became a spot where all parts of the family from around the country could convene throughout each year, and it held deep meaning for Snider, as he always tried his best to keep family as the priority, no matter what else was going on in their lives. All the while, he and Myrna would continue to show their outward affection for each other, whether it was holding hands by the fire, sharing hugs in front of the family, or simply expressing themselves verbally for all to hear.

While making his second home up north, Snider, as always, felt the urge to find a way to make a business out of it. When he discovered that Portland was building a new ice arena to be ready for the 1977–78 season, he realized that he could put the Flyers' American League farm team up there so that, whether in Philadelphia or Maine, he could supervise a part of his business empire. After a brief bidding war among a few professional organizations, Portland announced their preference for Snider's idea of making the city the Flyers' sole top-level farm team, and the Maine Mariners were born.

With the Flyers one of the top teams in the NHL, the Mariners instantly became a contender for the AHL's Calder Cup by way of gaining the Flyers' second-tier and young, up-and-coming players. Snider wouldn't have it any other way. A man with two Stanley Cup rings on his fingers, he would never think to create a hockey team whose focus was anything less than winning its league championship. More importantly, though, it gave him an additional hockey team he could wildly cheer for any time he was in Maine with Myrna.

He and Keith Allen used their marketing genius yet again to ensure that the club would be successful at the gate. With the help of new Flyers president Gil Stein and Canadiens general manager Sam Pollock (who owed Stein a favor), the team brought hockey legend Jean Beliveau down from Canada and brought Bernie Parent and Bob Clarke up from Philadelphia. The two Frenchmen and Clarke traveled through the French areas of Maine—Saco, Biddeford, Lewiston—talking up the new team and involving themselves in the community. The move helped push initial ticket sales to a lofty level, drawing fans from miles away to the new arena in Portland.*

But a few weeks into their inaugural season, the team was a pathetic 4–8–3. With Snider perpetually unhappy to own a losing team, he instructed Allen to spend whatever was necessary to turn the team around. In 10 days, Allen made four deals that set the Mariners on the right path—and in doing so, garnered a call from an AHL rival with the snarky remark, "I didn't know the Calder Cup was for sale." The team still had a long way to go, but if it was for sale, Snider would outbid everybody.

Weeks later, the Mariners were challenging for first place, and Snider breathed a sigh of relief. As part of an international cultural exchange, the traveling Moscow Dynamo team arrived stateside to play a series of professional teams, including the Mariners, at the end of December 1977. With the Flyers having defeated a similar collection of Soviet players nearly two years prior, the organization understood the style of play and how to properly counter it. In an extremely

---

* One of the initial hires the organization made was a young broadcaster named Mike "Doc" Emrick, who would one day go on to national fame in the NHL

tight game that featured Soviet players skating in circles but failing to penetrate the Mariners zone, the Flyers farm team scored just one goal and defeated their Russian counterparts by a 1–0 score, an exhilarating repeat for Snider, whose hatred of the Soviet Union continued for years.

After the game, the Russian delegation gathered in the Mariners office, along with the Flyers staff, to make some informal speeches. The Russian representative got up and, through an interpreter, spoke about the interchange of ideas, the interchange of athletic methods, and how everyone learns from one another when you play a game like the one just played. When he was done, Snider got up to give a brief speech of his own. After a few minutes, he prepared to conclude. "I agree very much about the benefits of international play," he said with a smirk, "but we are very glad to have won."

The winning continued for quite some time, as the Mariners won the 1978 Calder Cup, becoming the first AHL team to win the trophy in their inaugural season. When they won again the following year, they became the only team to start their history by winning two consecutive Calder Cups—a record that still stands today. Snider was in attendance for the first win—which was clinched on home ice—and was nearly as ecstatic as when the Flyers won the Stanley Cup a few years prior. He beamed with pride for his players and salivated at the thought of those players representing the Flyers in the NHL soon. In fact, many of those players would lead the Flyers to the Stanley Cup Finals in 1980.

The night of the 1978 Calder Cup victory, Snider was actually somewhat disappointed when the trophy was presented. When it was handed to Mariners captain Dennis Patterson, he held it aloft with one hand and skated it around the ice. Snider was stunned to see how small and insignificant the trophy was. He felt that, in the second-best hockey league in North America, the trophy should be substantial enough to require two hands to raise, just like the Stanley Cup.

During the locker room celebration, he pulled AHL president Jack Butterfield aside and mentioned his unhappiness with the size of the trophy. Within a few years, the trophy was enlarged to the current size of two feet tall and 25 pounds. Simply winning was not always enough for Snider—he wanted the world to know it.

Throughout the Flyers ownership of the Mariners (which lasted until 1984), Snider and Myrna would consistently travel to Portland to keep an eye on their new asset. The small office staff would be thrilled to see the now-powerful NHL owner walk into the building a half dozen times per year—it was extremely unusual but very much appreciated. Snider would make the rounds, chatting at length with each of the workers at their cubicles and thanking them for the work they were doing. The Sniders were prominent when they attended games, taking their usual seats against the glass, so everyone could see that they were in attendance. Snider did not necessarily like the spotlight, but he did want the Mariners players and staff to know how much he cared for them, and it was evident.

The minor leagues were a tough place for anyone, be it a player, coach, or office worker. To have someone as famous as Snider not only show up for games, but treat each of them with the same respect and with the same importance as someone who worked for the Flyers, was touching to each of them. The team greatly appreciated when the Sniders were in town—and won nearly every game they attended. It was a continuation of his philosophy of treating every employee like a member of his family. He treated them with love and respect, and in return they gave everything they had to him and his company.

That company was beginning to grow well past the Flyers and the Spectrum by the late '70s. Snider had created a parent company, Spectacor, in 1976 to house the executives who oversaw the Flyers, the Spectrum, and every other branch of the company. With the Spectrum now the cream of the crop when it came to arena management and scheduling, arenas around the continent took notice and began paying close attention to Snider's business model. Many of them, unsure why their own arenas were less successful, simply called Spectacor and said, "How do you guys do it?" That led to the Nassau Coliseum on Long Island skipping the pleasantries and outright asking Spectacor to manage their arena for them. After discussion, Snider and his executives did not believe it was a worthwhile endeavor and politely declined. Two years later, the same people came back again, and again Spectacor rejected their overtures.

But Snider's entrepreneurial instincts kicked in: perhaps it was time to expand to other regions of North America. That would potentially provide two incredible benefits to the company as a whole: first, and most importantly for the short-term, it would provide a new revenue stream at a period when NHL player salaries were skyrocketing, yet ticket prices could not be raised quickly enough to cover the cost. Second, and most importantly for the long-term, by stretching his roots into all parts of the United States and Canada, it would provide him with the contacts needed to continue expanding his business into other segments.

From the early '70s, Snider had discussed various ideas that could complement his Flyers and the Spectrum: pay-television, sports-talk radio, arena management, food services, marketing services, ticketing companies, movies, and more. Those visions were now ready to become reality. The more famous the Spectrum and the Spectacor names became, the easier it would be to reach out to these new segments to try new ideas. That led to the creation of Spectacor Management Group (SMG), which would shortly become one of the largest segments of the entire company.

Another segment of the company formed during that time was Ovations, a food services company that would supply the Spectrum with their concessions, manage the arena's restaurants, and of course, provide the same services to those arenas being managed by SMG. They also created a network of ticket and sports memorabilia stores to go along with the rest of the sports entertainment assets. And in 1980, separately from Spectacor, Snider's son Jay partnered with ex–U.S. Secret Service agents to form Spectaguard, which would provide security for Spectrum events and, eventually, events across the country.

But perhaps the most progressive portion of Snider's new empire was his devotion to sports broadcasting. At a time when any radio or television contracts were signed with generic networks that would otherwise not broadcast sports, Snider wanted to create places for sports fans to get their fix at any time of day. In the midst of the Stanley Cup years, the Flyers had a wonderful problem: every game was sold out. The issue with that was twofold. Not only was demand completely outstripping supply for hockey tickets in Philadelphia, but that meant the Flyers were potentially at the limit for how much revenue they could generate. In addition, with few newcomers able to get to a game, Snider wondered aloud how they could create the next generation of fans. He went to his top executives and asked why they couldn't put the Flyers on television in South Philadelphia so that every fan had the ability to watch a game.

Philadelphia is one of those places that must be visited to fully understand the culture. When outsiders stereotype Philadelphia sports fans, they are referring, of course, to the sometimes vicious nature of those cheering on their team. The attitude of a New Yorker, but with an underdog mentality, Philadelphians are extremely protective of their families, lifestyles, and sports teams. If you show love and respect for the city and its culture, they welcome you with open arms. If you speak ill of it, they will make sure you feel their disapproval. Despite growing up on the streets of D.C., rather than Philadelphia, Snider acted in the same way. In return, the city's natives treated him as one of their own.

The area around the Spectrum was filled with Flyers fans. Just because they couldn't shell out money for a ticket, or didn't have access to a ticket, didn't mean the team should shut them out of the sport entirely. That was the old-school NHL, the pre-expansion years when owners were satisfied with only gate receipts and raising ticket prices every year. Snider, however, didn't like that business model. "Why should our fans have to finance our budget every year?" he would ask. Ticket prices could increase slightly to match inflation, but with salaries on the rise due to the rival WHA, he wasn't happy passing that extra cost onto his fan base. He remembered a time not too long ago when he could barely afford tickets to a sporting event. He wasn't going to allow himself to sit atop the pyramid so long that he lost touch with the average Philadelphian. At the time in South Philadelphia, there was only one small cable TV company. In the early '70s, Snider sold packages of 25 Flyers games to South Philadelphia cable customers for $100 each, which proved remarkably successful. But for him, it was not enough.

At one point during that time period, HBO had offered $200,000 for a package of Flyers games to be broadcast on their channel, but being low-priority on a dominant channel was not appealing to Snider. He wanted to have control over the distribution of his product. The only way to accomplish that was to start his own television network. That was the start of PRISM, the premier South Philadelphia television network and the only place, at the time, to find Flyers games.

PRISM's programming began as a mix of movies and sports, mostly because there were simply not enough sports to cover an entire day's worth of air time. They would sign deals for old movies that could be shown during the day, and at night the network would broadcast a Flyers or 76ers game from the Spectrum. Early on, the company was struggling to turn a profit and bring in the revenue that they expected. Snider called on an old business associate, Jack Williams, a representative of a similar network in Houston, whom Snider knew from early PRISM meetings with movie studios.

Williams was a typical Oklahoman, a no-bullshit kind of guy. He had deep respect for Snider but did not have the fear that many others exhibited. Initially, he did not even want the job, but when Snider called him personally, Williams was convinced to at least give Snider the benefit of an interview. Once the two sat down in Snider's Philadelphia office, the chairman laid on his charm and convinced the tough-minded Williams by promising that he would report directly to Snider and no one else. The early years of their relationship proved to be fairly tough, with Williams often unhappy about the way things were being run, but ultimately, any time he approached his boss about an issue, Snider ceded and allowed his manager to run it the way he wanted. Snider was always one to ask questions and point someone in the right direction, but he was rarely one to outright meddle. Hire the right people and let them do their jobs remained his mantra.

Snider liked those who stood up to him and stood by their beliefs. He always claimed he had no time for "yes men," nor did he have time for an executive who tried to answer a question based on how they believed Snider wanted it answered. "He could smell a bullshitter a mile away," said one of his top executives—a notion that was mirrored by many others who worked for him over the years.* Even more importantly, Snider was a fantastic listener. He was not one to bloviate or desire to hear himself talk. All he was interested in was solutions to problems and ideas for success. When an employee came to him, he would focus deeply on whatever it was they were speaking about, before engaging in a lengthy conversation about the topic. When it came to PRISM, he simply wanted to see it succeed. It didn't matter who got the credit for its success. He wasn't in it for the fame. He was in it to build something successful with lasting power.

One of the ways Snider prodded PRISM in the right direction, as he did with each of his businesses, was with the many questions he

---

* Though there is no doubt that Snider surrounded himself with like-minded people, perhaps creating an illusion of people disagreeing with him, even though they mostly saw eye-to-eye.

would ask about what could be done to bolster its prospects. As was typical at the time, PRISM would go off the air around midnight and not come back on until the next afternoon. When Snider asked why, he was told that they simply did not have enough programming. He scoured through the movie contracts and realized that they paid for the rights by the day—not per viewing. So, when he suggested they replay the day's movies and sports games through the night, knowing that a different genre of viewer is watching at 2:00 in the morning versus 3:00 in the afternoon, Williams was intrigued and agreed wholeheartedly. They would also add a postgame wrap-up or a small sports talk show to the programming to give the network a bit more pizzazz. PRISM then became one of the first 24-hour networks in the country and had near exclusivity on anyone in the region watching TV during the night.

By 1977, just a year after its start, PRISM had grown to 60,000 paid subscribers in the region. By 1981, the number had ballooned to 240,000. That number nearly doubled by the end of the '80s. Years before regional sports networks were a commonplace source of revenue for sports teams, Snider was having immense success, drawing an eight-figure income from this one portion of his empire, a portion that eventually led to the NHL's modern-day business model.

At the same time, Spectacor formed WIOQ-FM in partnership with Dick Butera, who owned the Philadelphia Freedoms tennis team. Within a year, the radio network was bringing in over $2 million of revenue, while PRISM's popularity continued to skyrocket—in fact, the cable company could not lay lines fast enough to fulfill the demand from across the region. WIOQ was sold just two years after its creation for a whopping $6 million, setting the stage for Snider's eventual ownership of WIP as a 24-hour sports talk radio network—which Williams also ran for some time.

By 1981, Spectacor was drawing $60 million per year in revenue, $32 million of which was attributable to PRISM. The network shortly reached 265,000 subscribers and was the fastest-growing regional pay-TV network in the country. By 1985, Spectacor was an $84 million-per-year empire—the Spectrum parking lots alone generated over $1 million per year of revenue. Snider was quickly becoming known around the sports world as an entrepreneur who was bringing the industry into the future, doing things well before his time that are now typical and mainstream.*

The companies formed under the Spectacor umbrella all worked in tandem. The Flyers and the Spectrum were the basis of the company, and every other business either fed that core or generated its success from the core. The Spectrum was managed by SMG, which also managed other buildings around the continent. Those buildings needed food supply, so they utilized Ovations as their food service company. They needed security, so they utilized Spectaguard. They needed software to process tickets, so they used Spectacor's services. The companies became successful because of each segment's reliance on the other segments. Like the spokes of a wheel, they created an empire that kept turning, day after day.

While he continued to make a name for himself nationally through the expansion of his businesses, what kept him in the news locally was his continued passion for and commitment to the Flyers. Even winning two Stanley Cups and two Calder Cups did nothing but make him hungrier for more championships. That passion was on full display every night as he sat in his Spectrum superbox with friends, family, or other team executives—even if it manifested itself in silent, but deadly anger.

One new executive, who grew up a fan of the Canadiens, sat at one of his first Flyers games a section over from Snider's box. When the Canadiens scored, he instinctively yelled, "Yeah!" before suddenly

---

* Snider would sell PRISM in 1983 and go on to establish a very similar business model with Comcast SportsNet in the 1990s. He not only created an exorbitantly successful regional television network from scratch—he did it twice.

realizing his egregious error. He shot a glance toward Snider, hoping the chairman had not noticed, but it was much too late. Snider was staring daggers at his new hire, refusing to break for what felt like an hour. The executive quickly learned that you never cheer against Snider and his team, especially when you were a member of the organization. "If you're in Philadelphia," the employee recalled, "you root for the guy who butters your bread."

His employees were far from the only ones subject to his wrath. At a game in Minnesota in the 1970s, Jack Williams was sitting next to Keith Allen. Suddenly, Allen tapped Williams on the shoulder and said, "Come on, let's go." Williams was confused. "Boss is in a fight," Allen said, running down the aisle. Williams turned and, sure enough, Snider was causing a ruckus with some unruly Minnesota fans, who were chiding his team.

"Does this happen often?" Williams yelled to Allen as they were racing toward the situation.

"Sometimes," Allen replied with a smile.

Snider's love of success and fanatical need to win was surpassed only by his intense hatred of losing. While his children knew that you only asked for a raise in their allowance or a favor after a Flyers win, everyone in his orbit knew, or learned quickly, that you never, ever approached him with bad news after a Flyers loss. Even the following day, everyone tiptoed around him. And those who did not quickly discovered their mistake.

Early in the tenure of Sandy Lipstein, who would eventually become the company's chief financial officer, he called Snider the day after a Flyers loss with a bit of minor bad news. Snider jumped down his throat. "I thought he was gonna tear my tonsils out over the phone," Lipstein recalled.

Confused (and unaware of Snider's mood swings dependent on the Flyers' performance), Lipstein said, "Ed, what's the matter? What I just told you did not merit the reaction I just got."

Snider immediately paused, took a breath, and said, "I'm sorry. I'm just really upset with the way the team is playing." As their relationship evolved, Lipstein, like most everyone who worked for the organization, began to understand Snider when it came to observing games. "If we were winning, he was in a good mood," Lipstein said. "If we were losing, the period would end, you'd be sitting there, and he'd have a look on his face. It would just kill you."

Another tic that affected the game-day experience for those close to Snider was his devout superstitious tendencies. It ranged from typical to completely unreasonable. Snider would refuse to walk under ladders and insisted that everyone walk on the same side of an arena column (as opposed to one walking on each side simultaneously). Black cats would drive him up the wall. If he came upon a black cat while driving, he would turn around and find a different route, even if it took him on a 20-mile detour. In fact, when his daughter, Lindy, owned a black cat years later as an adult, Snider was beside himself and consistently questioned why she would do such a thing.

Snider's superstitions during Flyers games were even more legendary, if not ridiculous. If you were sitting in a certain spot and the Flyers scored, you absolutely were not allowed to move for the rest of the game. If you moved or did something unusual shortly before the Flyers gave up a goal, you received the Snider glare. One family member even remembers being forced to stay in the bathroom for an extended period after the Flyers scored when they went to relieve themselves. In typical Snider style, he did anything to gain an edge— even if it was irrational.

One piece of his viewing experience that was less superstition and more perceived slight was his reaction to the officials and his subsequent treatment of them. While opposing players visiting the Spectrum were at risk of a bruising body check or a hostile crowd, referees and linesmen visiting Philadelphia were at risk of Snider himself. He found himself consistently in the news for his antics toward the officials—and despite what some would claim, it was not a conscious effort to be a sideshow. Snider legitimately got so angry when he felt his team was subject to an officiating mistake (which was just about every game, in his opinion) that he would begin steaming, his face turning beet red and the Spectrum crowd turning to see what would transpire next.

As early as 1973, he was already making a name for himself with the officials. The sentiments often trickled down to the staff and the players, as Snider's coaches were regularly encouraged to challenge the officiating publicly if they felt they were victim. During a December 1981 matchup against the Buffalo Sabres at the Spectrum, with the Flyers up 2–1 late in the third period, referee Bruce Hood gave Bob Clarke a 10-minute misconduct for swearing in the face-off circle. Clarke, enraged at the call, gave Hood a "choke" signal, earning him a game misconduct and ejection. With the crowd irate, Snider was predictably fuming in his superbox. It was typical of him to stand on the ledge of his box, screaming and gesturing wildly at the officials, who often couldn't hear him or simply ignored him. This time, Snider jumped over the ledge, into the back row of the lower level, ran down the stairs to the glass behind the penalty box, and put both hands to his throat in his own "choking" signal toward Hood. The crowd went ballistic, cheering on their fearless, albeit impulsive, leader as he defended the team's honor. Snider's executives up in the superbox were laughing hysterically and shaking their heads in a "there he goes again" sort of way. They were used to his in-game antics and were entertained by them.

Perhaps most notably, after the 1980 Stanley Cup Finals in which the Islanders scored on a play that was very clearly offside, Snider went off on the linesmen, but saved his biggest and most dishonorable complaint for his regular sparring partner, referee-in-chief Scotty Morrison. "It was an absolute, total, fucking disgrace," he screamed through the hallway of the Spectrum after the final horn sounded, deliberately in earshot of the Flyers reporters, according to *Full Spectrum*. "Anybody who's impartial knows we took a screwing today. I believe the [officials] who come out of Montreal and Toronto don't want [us] to win. I believe that right down to the pit of my stomach.... The problem with this league is Scotty Morrison. He should be shot."

The comment drew incredible pushback from the NHL and Morrison himself, who suggested he would take legal action against Snider for the public threat. As was typical, the following day Snider "apologized" for his action, despite acknowledging that he was still just as angry. "Haven't you ever said things like that and didn't mean them?" he asked pointedly at a *Philadelphia Daily News* reporter who challenged his previous day's sentiment. The league ultimately fined Snider $5,000 for the statement.

Snider's temper became notorious throughout the company, but it was a unique type of emotional outburst. In the decades that he ran the organization, you would be hard-pressed to find anyone who received a tirade directed at them personally. His sole care when he was at the office was the work at hand. He was a perfectionist and often demanded those who worked for him be the same—often to a fault. Failures were acceptable, so long as the effort was honest and the process was sound. But if he felt someone was giving anything less than 100 percent, he could drill you into the ground with a single look, accompanying words of displeasure being unnecessary. Those around him knew when he was unhappy. Those who understood, fixed the issues that arose. Those who didn't, generally did not last long with the company.

Part of what may have contributed to Snider's regular blow ups was his sheer brilliance when it came to numbers and seeing situations from a different angle. With his CPA training, he could decipher a situation as quickly and efficiently as anyone. Those he worked with were often stunned when he would sit down in a meeting with a stack of financial documents, flip through them extraordinarily quickly, and then pinpoint one spot in the middle where a number did not make sense. Sure enough, there was either a mistake or something simply didn't add up.

Similarly, he would insist that his financial people provide him with a printed stock market update three times a week so he could analyze his investments and make decisions about how and where his money was placed. If even one cell of a spreadsheet was mislabeled or incorrect, Snider would catch it and insist it be fixed immediately. (And God help his employees on a day after the Flyers lost *and* the market went down.) He constantly saw every part of a situation and was frustrated when others did not see the same. It is plausible and possible that this intelligence he always exuded was part of the reason he would consistently be frustrated by the work of certain employees.

But minutes after berating someone's work or giving them the Snider stare, he was just as likely to say, "Hey, let's get a beer." He would head down to Frank Clements Tavern, the joint next door to the Spectacor offices in the '80s, and he and his executives, and sometimes his family, would engage in games of pinball, which became one of his favorite activities to cool down from work. His love of pinball became just like everything else in his life: he needed to win. No matter what he was doing, whether it was building a world-class hockey organization or playing a game with friends, he had to be the best. His friends would joke that he was always the most competitive at whatever it was he was doing at that moment.

Socially, he could be just as intense as he was at work, but work was always left in the office. Snider had a unique laser focus no matter what he was doing. If he was working, every ounce of his being was devoted to the task at hand. As the business evolved, he did not always work long hours, but the hours he did work, he would be more productive than anyone else in the same amount of time. When he was in a social activity, such as pinball, every fiber of him was focused on that. In conversation, he could captivate an entire room. He had a magnetism that consistently drew people to him from all realms of the business and social world.

But while one side of that magnet would invite some in, the other side would just as quickly repel them out of his life. Too often he would drop friends or even family members from his mind for any perceived slight against him. And, in the late '70s, when Myrna finally had had enough of his womanizing and extracurricular activities, the two delved into a messy and adversarial end to their relationship. Snider often told friends a story of him discovering, while on a rented boat, that Myrna was having an affair with the captain. As he told it, he grabbed his wallet, dove off the back of the boat, swam to shore and never saw her again.

Of course, it is important to remember that Snider often exaggerated his anecdotes—he was always the hero of any story he told. Others have suggested the true story involved him getting into the dinghy on the back of the boat, calling for a valet to bring him his bags, and leaving the trip. The latter does sound more likely, yet the point is the same. The two had grown progressively apart over the previous decade, and it was now time for each to go their separate ways. Anecdotally, Myrna ended up marrying the boat captain, remaining happily married to him until her death in 2014.

As she quickly learned, it was extremely dangerous to be on the other side of a fight with Ed Snider. Instead of drawing in, she stepped away, opting to protect her children from what could have become a public divorce played out in the media. Snider, admittedly, treated her quite poorly in those final years, leading to a strain between him and the mother of his children, along with some of his children themselves. For Snider, though, his business was always the priority. And in the '70s and early '80s, he had plenty to keep him occupied and distracted from the mess that he had made of his personal life.

9

At the Forefront of NHL Progress

NOT LONG AFTER the Flyers started in 1967, Snider was consistently looking for ways to grow hockey in the United States. He was well aware that, no matter how successful his team became in Philadelphia, it would be limited by hockey's national footprint, which at the time was not significant. It was still Canada's sport, and even with six new teams in his own country, Snider was not okay with moving at a snail's pace. He wanted to see hockey become the most popular sport—a lofty goal, indeed, but one in which he fervently believed.

Even as the Flyers were struggling to battle for supremacy among the new teams, Snider continued to vote for additional expansion throughout the continent. The league added teams in Buffalo and Vancouver in 1970 and in Atlanta and New York (Long Island) in 1972. Proceeds of the expansion fees of those four teams netted the Flyers $1.5 million, which essentially covered their own expansion fee paid in 1967, just by continuing to exist.

But in the early 1970s, the NHL was the only major league for the sport. Salaries were stagnant, and if players wanted to showcase their talents at the highest level, they generally had no choice but to concede to their owners' demands. The doubling of the league in 1967 helped to an extent, but the sport was still run by team owners—the players had little to no say in the matter. The NHL Players' Association was created in the 1960s but had almost no power or influence, a far cry from what it's become in the 21st century.

So it should not have surprised the NHL when Gary Davidson and Dennis Murphy created the World Hockey Association in 1971 to compete directly in major league hockey. Two persistent "disrupters," they had previously established the American Basketball Association to compete with the NBA. Subsequently, they turned their attention to hockey. Philadelphia was not initially awarded one of fourteen WHA franchises to play in the inaugural season, but when the owner of the conditional Miami franchise could not come up with the funds for the league fee, it was transferred to Jim Cooper, a lawyer, and Bernie Brown, a trucking magnate, who announced their plan to relocate the new franchise to Philadelphia.

At the time, Philadelphia sports did not have a great reputation, even within the city limits. There was a perpetual feeling of hopelessness among the fans and the media, always annoyed with their teams finding new, creative ways to lose. "This is the town with a baseball team that blew a six-and-a-half-game lead with 12 games to go," wrote Frank Dolson in the *Philadelphia Inquirer*, "a football team that has had one winning season in the last 10, a National Hockey League team that blew a playoff berth in the last four seconds of the season, a coachless pro basketball team whose star might spend more time in court than on court next season."

The presence of this new team, eventually named the Blazers, presented serious potential problems for Snider. The rival league was going to be an NHL competitor in the first place, just by giving players an alternate league where they could play for more money. But now that there would be a franchise in the city, it potentially would create a business issue for Snider, since Philadelphia hockey fans now had a second choice of team to follow and support. Publicly, he showcased his confidence and bravado, confident that the Flyers would always come out on top. But privately, he recalled his earlier days fighting with the American Football League as an executive of the Eagles. He knew the damage that a rival league could cause. The new league had filed multiple lawsuits against the NHL and their "reserve clause," which allowed franchises to keep perpetual ownership of a player, even when their contract expired. The WHA claimed it was an anti-trust violation, and the courts would eventually agree.

At the end of their first season, the Blazers made claims to the Spectrum and their ability to become a tenant. Spectacor begrudgingly "obliged," though in a way that was transparently passive-aggressive. They offered the Blazers 41 subpar dates (such as holidays, Eagles game days, and other dates no one wanted) and said to pick 39 of them. The issue became moot when the Blazers were sold and relocated to Vancouver a month later, yet the WHA remained and continued to thumb its nose at the NHL.

From a Flyers standpoint, Snider protected his most valuable assets by offering them lucrative contracts that did not quite rival the WHA's frivolous spending, but was generous enough to convince his players to stick around for a while. Fortunately for him, some of his players showed the same generosity and loyalty in return. When Snider and Bob Clarke were negotiating a contract renewal in the summer of 1972, they had agreed on a five-year deal worth $500,000, to be paid over 20 years. The young Flyers star flew to Philadelphia and stayed in a hotel for a night, expecting to sign the contract the following day.

Having a drink by himself in the hotel's bar, in walked a member of the Blazers who had previously worked for the Flyers. Recognizing the Philadelphia stalwart, he approached Clarke and struck up a friendly conversation. When he realized that Clarke was technically not yet signed, he ran to the pay phone for a brief conversation. Returning, he said that the Blazers were willing to pay him $1 million a year for five years if he joined the team. Clarke politely declined, then signed his contract with the Flyers the following day.

A few weeks later, back in his hometown of Flin Flon, Clarke received a call from Snider. Expecting to be told he had been traded, he walked nervously to the phone and picked up the phone from his mother.

"There's a story in the paper today," Snider said, referencing the Blazers' offer.

"Yeah, but we'd shaken hands on a deal," Clarke replied.

Snider was dumbfounded. "You didn't think of using it to get more out of us?"

"No, we shook hands on a deal."

Snider paused for a moment and simply said, "I'll never forget this." Clarke's $100,000-per-year contract still ultimately infuriated those in the NHL's front office, both at its length and high dollar amount—even though it prevented one of the game's top stars from jumping to the rival league. And of course, Snider treated Clarke like a son for the remainder of his life, taking care of him every step of the way. Express loyalty to Snider, and he gave it back tenfold.

But from the perspective of the sport's health, Snider went even further than simple loyalty to his own players. Partnering with Bill Jennings, the progressive Rangers president who first convinced the NHL to pursue expansion in the 1960s, the two sat down with the WHA in the summer of 1972 and offered peace between the two leagues. In exchange for the new league dropping all of their lawsuits against the NHL, they would take in every one of the WHA teams and add them to the circuit, so long as they paid a $4 million expansion fee. The move would have nearly doubled the size of the NHL for the second time in five years. And while there was keen interest from the WHA, not unsurprisingly, Snider and Jennings faced significant pushback from their NHL brethren.

At the next Board of Governors meeting, Snider was excoriated by NHL president Clarence Campbell for both Clarke's contract and for making an offer to the WHA without having the support of the other owners. At the same meeting, those owners approved a resolution that prohibited any contact by NHL team owners with the WHA regarding any merger between the two leagues. Snider's blood boiled at what he considered the incredible short-sightedness of the conservative, hard-headed owners. He had already been through this with the NFL-AFL merger in the 1960s. His attempts to impart that experience on his new NHL colleagues was failing.

"I don't believe in war," he told the *Philadelphia Inquirer*, "because everybody in hockey would be hurt. Look what has happened to pro basketball. That has been ruined, and hockey could suffer the same fate." After the first Stanley Cup win, Flyers coach Fred Shero was reportedly offered a $100,000 salary to jump to the WHA's Minnesota Fighting Saints. Snider quickly gave his Hall of Fame coach a raise to $80,000 per season—enough to keep the loyal Shero in Philadelphia. Snider consistently found himself in a pickle. As the owner of the defending Stanley Cup champions, it was even more in his interest to keep a tight grip on his roster. Other owners allowed their players to depart at will, but Snider was watching his team sell out every game and win championships. He couldn't personally afford to let anything happen to a business still finding its proper footing. Yet, when he paid his players or staff more, he would consistently be reprimanded by his colleagues across the league. And when he suggested making peace with the WHA, he was similarly laughed out of the room.

At the time, the NHL Board of Governors was akin to anarchy. The league president was extremely weak and his only job was doing the direct bidding of the majority of the owners, most of whom were from the old guard and did not care for change. It did not matter how well thought-out an idea was—if a few powerful people at the top disagreed, that was the direction the league would go. "Merger wouldn't solve a thing," Campbell said to the *Philadelphia Inquirer* in 1975, before the Flyers second Cup win. "It would only cause more trouble. It won't reduce your salaries one dollar. What's causing our problem is excessively high, long-term contracts. I made representations to the owners as far back as 1972. I told them to play it cool. But some of them wanted to have a perfect sleep potion, to have everybody signed up for a good long term." Campbell's fury at anything progressive echoed his sentiments on expansion until he finally conceded in 1965. But his constant shots at Snider, both subtle and flagrant, did not sit well with the Flyers' owner, who knew he was arguing for the right cause. As far back as 1972, Campbell assured the owners that the WHA would not even last through their first season. Now, three years later, the league was still chugging along and the NHL was taking a big financial hit. Merging would not lower the existing salaries, but it would surely stop them from skyrocketing.

Around this time, Snider pulled one of the few power moves of his career. With Red Wings owner Bruce Norris's two-year term as chairman of the board expiring, Snider decided to make a run for the position, in the hopes that he could help control the direction of the league. Not wanting to see the arrogant, young Flyers owner succeed, Black Hawks owner Bill Wirtz decided to oppose him in the election. The league's owners immediately split their support behind each of them, with the newer, younger owners supporting Snider and the old guard throwing their weight behind Wirtz.*

With 18 clubs in existence at the time, Snider needed at least nine votes. He made it clear that he wanted to move the league away from their hardline approach to the WHA, resolve the war at once, and even hinted at removing Campbell from the president's position. Snider was nominated by the Pittsburgh Penguins' Thayer Potter and the motion was seconded by Montreal Canadiens legend Jean Beliveau. On the other side, Toronto Maple Leafs owner Harold Ballard nominated Wirtz.

---

* Snider's group was called the Young Turks, after the early 20th-century political group that favored overthrowing Turkey's monarchy—a fitting metaphor for the NHL of the 1970s.

Ballard was a constant thorn in Snider's side. From day one, the two did not get along, which was predictable based on their personalities and business views. Referred to by the *Montreal Gazette* as "Harold the Terrible," he joined the Toronto Maple Leafs organization in 1940, became a part-owner in 1961, and the majority owner in 1972. He was known for his hot temper and his ability to find any reason to hold a grudge. A man who refused to attend the weddings of two of his children because he disapproved of their spouses, he would regularly spurn sportswriters who wrote negatively about his team and even throw a homophobic slur or a sexist comment around every once in a while. When a female sportswriter requested entrance to the Leafs locker room for a story, he told her she was welcome, as long as she was also naked. Ballard was also known to have suggested that the only position women were at their best was on their backs. In addition, he threatened and was abusive toward European players who came across the pond to play in the NHL. He was accused of being a racist, a sexist, a homophobe, an anti-Semite, and a bully.

But more to the point, Ballard was as cheap as could be, willing to do anything for an easy buck. For years he refused to agree to put player names on the back of Leafs jerseys because he did not want his program sales to take a hit. He once asked his building manager how many pickles could be stuffed into the arena's 30,000-gallon brine tank so that he could sell them at the concession stands. In the '60s, he booked the Beatles for a show on a hot summer day, then turned off the air-conditioning, disconnected the drinking fountains, and tripled the price of the soft drinks at the concession stands. In the '70s, he charged an astronomical sum for a Maple Leaf Gardens tenant, then when the tenant arrived to a dark rink, Ballard said he would turn the lights on for an additional $3,500 per game. And, of course, he refused to even consider treating his players with respect, instead demanding they either sign his piddly contract offers or walk.

The dishonest and tyrannical tactics he utilized in running his hockey team rubbed Snider the wrong way. For years, Snider worked endlessly to create a family-like atmosphere throughout his organization, and he prided himself on caring for the players and their families. Then there was Ballard, constantly making ridiculous statements to the press that gave hockey owners the public persona of dictators who cared solely about lining their own pockets.

After hours of politicking and attempts at smoky, back-room deals, the vote was tallied and Snider fell one vote short, losing in a 9–8 decision—the ballots were secret, leaving only our imagination to determine who cast the deciding vote. When Wirtz took over the board, his first course of action was to remove Snider as head of the league's finance committee and further refuse to appoint him to any of the league's standing committees. In a power struggle between the old guard and the Young Turks, it was Campbell and his cronies who came out on top—and they wanted to be absolutely sure Snider knew it.

Despite his disagreements and battles with some of his colleagues, Snider was still respected as one of the faces of the league. He was invited, along with Campbell, Bruce Norris, and Walter Bush to represent the NHL, with Howard Baldwin and Harrison Vickers representing the WHA, to speak to Congress at the 1976 House Select Committee on Professional Sports. That day gave Snider the opportunity to make known his feelings about government regulations that he felt were preventing him from properly exercising his rights as a business owner and as a representative of his league.

"From the point of view of merger…that we would want to talk, regardless of what an individual club or an individual owner's views might be, we are prevented legally by anti-trust from discussing merger," Snider said. "From what I gather…the end result of the basketball situation was that they couldn't talk until the [American Basketball Association] could show that they were about to go out of business. So that it appears that the only time you can discuss any type of an accommodation is after you attempt to put another league out of business, which I think is not the intent of the anti-trust laws."

While being cross-examined by multiple congressmembers, Snider claimed that government regulation was the cause of the massive increase in ticket prices—one of the biggest reasons the owners were called to testify in the first place. "The anti-trust laws are there to protect the consumer, and what they are doing to us is killing the consumer," he explained. "Our ticket price keeps going up. We have no television revenue of any significance nationally, and the only way we can hope to survive is through our ticket revenues." By preventing the two leagues from communicating, Snider explained, it was actually perpetuating the war. This war, while in principle supposed to help consumers by lowering prices, actually worked in the opposite direction. When two clothing companies are in competition with each other, they each have to lower their prices to garner the sale, and they can afford to do so because the cost of their product remains the same. But in hockey, the cost of their product (player salaries) continued to increase as the two entities competed for the same exact product. Therefore, the war between the two leagues caused salaries to rise, which in turn caused ticket prices to skyrocket. Snider's point makes logical business sense, though he was often questioned and challenged by opposing congressmembers who disagreed with his thesis.

The years of the WHA have, for decades since, been an example of how player salaries rose to a level that predicated the massive contracts we often see today. And while that's true, Snider saw it differently than most of his peers. While other owners worked on keeping their player salaries as low as possible, even to the extent of making life quite difficult for their players, Snider did not view business the same way. He fervently believed in a capitalistic society in which business owners are the ones who provide the greater good to their employees and society as a whole. It explains why, despite his desire to keep his team payroll low enough to remain profitable, he never ruled his players with an iron fist. Once he found players who were loyal to his Flyers, he paid them well, treated them well, and kept them involved. More than anything, he hated that some of his fellow owners did not do the same, thereby creating the perception that all owners were cruel, greedy money-grubbers.

As the WHA battles continued through the '70s, the tide seemed to turn in Snider's favor when, in 1977, Campbell stepped down from the league presidency, to be replaced by John Ziegler, who had served time on the Board of Governors as a member of the Detroit Red Wings. With the change in leadership came an opportunity for Snider to again try his hand at diplomacy between the two leagues. Ziegler did not hold quite as hard a line as his predecessor, though there were still many on the Board of Governors who refused to make peace with the rival league. Snider still failed to understand this mindset.

"From the very beginning, I've been convinced that the WHA is a very viable entity," he told the *Philadelphia Inquirer*. "They are a fact of life. They exist. We can't just wish them away.... Anyone who has a brain, and Harold Ballard has none, can analyze that hockey in the United States is on the decline, despite the promise we shared in the early 1970s." The next day, Ballard had to evacuate his hotel room due to a minor fire, and with an opportunity to take a return shot at his rival, did so with a smile.

"Too bad that goddamn Snider wasn't in it," Ballard said to the *Gazette*. "I could have thrown a little gas on him."

That week, the NHL voted 16–2 to allow for the exploration of peace with the WHA. Snider was ecstatic, though he kept his expectations in check. The league required a three-quarters vote in order to approve any deal, which in 1977 was 14 of its 18 teams. Ballard, against the move from the start, made it his duty to gather four other teams to join him in vetoing any agreement Snider might make. "A lot of owners look only one year ahead," Snider said to the *Philadelphia Daily*

News. "I'm trying to look at the long haul.... I wouldn't be serving on this fact-finding committee if I thought it was hopeless."

Along with some of his fellow owners, Snider worked nonstop to come to an agreement with the WHA that would satisfy 13 of his colleagues. He even met with Judge Higginbotham, who Snider knew from the days of Spectrum bankruptcy, to ensure that the agreement would not raise any anti-trust flags in the U.S. Justice Department. By the end of June, there was a consensus between the two leagues that seemed able to pass any legal hurdles. Snider's job now was to sell it to the Board of Governors. He publicly pegged his chances at 50–50, but privately was more confident. He firmly believed the deal was in the best interest of both leagues and would help solidify the sport across North America.

But, when the group met in New York in August, Snider had clearly underestimated his fiercest opponent. Ballard had gotten the support of at least four other teams and when the final vote was tallied, Toronto, Boston, Los Angeles, Chicago, and Colorado were firmly on the "no" side of the ballot (it is possible that Vancouver voted no as well). "I won," Ballard bragged to the *Edmonton Journal.* "It was always in the bag. It was very easy."

Snider was mortified and dejected. "All I know is it is a disaster for our league," he said to the *Philadelphia Daily News.* "The threats the WHA is making about renewing the war are very real." Within months, the NHL was again in talks with the rival league to set aside their differences, but Snider had enough. He put years into his efforts and was thwarted by a bully who cared nothing about the health of the league—only being able to prove that he could win in a fight against Snider himself.

Even the WHA was irate at what they perceived was the NHL toying with their business. "We were used," said Indianapolis Racers owner Nelson Skalbania to the *Edmonton Journal.* "They took a peek at everything...from our player contracts to financial statements. We agreed to their every demand…even when they seemed excessively harsh. Obviously, we were talking to a blank wall. They must have selfish reasons for rejecting us…because there was no doubt about our financial capabilities."

For the remainder of the WHA's existence, Snider continued to vote in favor of merger agreements, but never again took part in the nitty-gritty negotiations. (It would take until the 1990s for him to legitimately have an influential leadership role in the NHL front office.) In fact, in January 1979 he appointed as Flyers president Bob Butera, the former Republican leader of the Pennsylvania House of Representatives. This allowed Snider to shift some duties and focus more on the parts of his business that did not frustrate him quite as much. He continued to be disappointed in the league's treatment of the negotiations and berated the league's policy of requiring a three-quarters vote. "Even though the majority wants something to go through, they are stopped by a minority," he said at the beginning of 1979, according to the *Canadian Press*. "Collectively speaking, we have mostly progressive owners. But there are a few negative people in the NHL not interested in the best interests of the league—people who are happy to see teams in trouble financially, people who would prefer to see others go out of the business.… If I was involved in anything like this on a social basis, I would get out."

Snider was a staunch believer that a group of businesspeople were only as strong as their weakest link. By refusing to help those weak links, you were not making the league stronger but, in actuality, weaker. For the decades that he was involved, he always sought to bolster the league's weaker, smaller-market teams, even if it came at the expense of his own Flyers. To him, the only thing in business more important than the Flyers was the health of the sport. Without it, his team could not succeed in the long run.

And so it was, in March 1979, that Snider finally got his wish, albeit much too late in his opinion. After rejecting a merger on March 8, the league finally achieved the required vote on March 30, with just Toronto, Boston, and Los Angeles voting against the measure. The NHL and WHA ended their war, and it was decided that four new expansion teams would be added to the NHL for the 1979–80 season. For the rest of his life, Snider would resent that he could not get the job done in 1973 when he first met with the rival league and came to an off-the-record agreement. "We were shot down by a group of selfish owners who said the new league wouldn't last until Christmas," he said, according to the Associated Press. "At the time, we had our nice little television contract with CBS and adding the WHA then would have given us a solid geographical base around North America…that would have encouraged CBS to continue. Not taking in the WHA at that time cost us hundreds of millions of dollars."

Even a few years after the deal was done, Ballard and Snider continued to take shots at each other across the border. "I don't like Snider because he's arrogant," Ballard said in 1982. "I don't think he's the type that should be in hockey. He's the kind of guy that tries to take over. That Clarke has been the sparkplug of the Philadelphia team and he's been quite an asset to the game, but he's too good for Snider. If Snider has had any success, it's because of Keith Allen—he's a helluva guy."

Snider, not taking the bait, said in reply to the *Philadelphia Daily News*, "The only thing I can say good about Harold is, he's not sneaky. You always know where he stands.… He would do anything to help his hockey team. But he makes no bones about his anti-Semitism, and I find that disgusting. We haven't talked for 10 years."

The era of fighting with the WHA proved something else that Snider had been pleading for years: the NHL was not keeping up with the times. He had been through this before during his time with the Eagles. His involvement in the NFL-AFL merger years earlier helped him understand the damage that fighting with a rival league could inflict. He knew that, at the end of the day, the leagues would need to make peace, or even merge, in order for teams to survive economically.

Furthermore, he felt it was time for the NHL to update their own front office and modernize so they could keep up with the other sports leagues. With no central planning from the league, there was no way to market the game, properly monitor the financial health of each organization, or create any semblance of publicity for their players. He wanted to see a development of international hockey, to create ancillary sources of revenue for the teams to help bolster those that were weaker. He wanted to see merchandising deals so that the teams' logos would be seen on apparel and knick-knacks across the country—even a film department that could create NHL-sponsored productions to whet the fans' appetites. "In the U.S., we are considered a fringe operation," he said to the *National Post*. "We've done all the wrong things and none of the right things." He may have been years ahead of his time, but he foresaw the need for an NHL front office that extended its reach throughout every aspect of the sport—something that is typical, if not required, in present-day sports. At the time, Campbell and perhaps a few assistants were the only league employees. Once Ziegler was made president, with Snider's influence and help, the league expanded its operations drastically.

His messy history trying to make peace with the WHA was one of the more prominent examples of Snider's ability to see years ahead of his fellow owners. Despite his conservative social and political views, he was perhaps one of the most progressive owners the NHL saw in the 20th century. While that trait would remain quite prominent for the balance of his time leading the Flyers, to have been so in the '70s and '80s was even more remarkable. Even as far back as his first year in the NHL, he was extolling the virtues of national television, even if it technically hurt his team. At the time, the Flyers garnered more revenue from their regional television contract than they did from the NHL's national contract. Yet he thought it crucial to continue fighting for national airtime because it would help provide the league with more exposure, thereby increasing consumer demand for hockey.

Even if national television did not provide the proper revenue now, Snider was more interested in what it could provide years or even decades later.

"It is a basic fact that hockey is not successful on national television because hockey has been, and to a great extent still is, a regional sport," Snider said to the Associated Press in 1980. "Ratings are arrived at on a national basis, that is, the number of sets throughout the country that are tuned into the game. Please tell me how people in Dallas, Texas, can watch a hockey game if the Dallas station has not been carrying it? From the outset hockey cleared fewer stations than any other sport. That is not to say I am against a network television package; I am for it. I think we need it. But on terms that would be beneficial to the National Hockey League, not detrimental—not ratings that can be laughed at by so-called experts who do not care to understand the facts."

His strong feelings about how and where the game should be shown tracks with his business mindset. His understanding of marketing, going all the way back to his days in his father's grocery store, was legendary. During a 1980 game against the Winnipeg Jets, the Flyers were dominating the score and making the game a bit of a snooze-fest. Yet, just a few hundred miles north, the United States Olympic hockey team was playing Czechoslovakia in a matchup that was garnering national attention due to the team's potential to challenge for a medal. During intermission, when Snider saw the Americans were winning 4–2, he went into his Spectrum superbox and picked up the phone to make a call to the scoreboard operator. After a moment, he hung up and returned to his seat. A few seconds later, the scoreboard showed that the United States was winning 3–2 against the Czechs, considered at that time to be the second-best team in the world behind the Soviets. The crowd cheered, albeit nervously, for the young college-aged team that would soon inspire a nation. A minute later, at the next stoppage of play, the scoreboard showed a scoring update: 4–2.

The crowd went wild, buzzing at the potential of their national pride defeating the tough opponent. Snider turned and smiled. "It's not fun if you put them up all at once," he said to the *Philadelphia Inquirer.* Why make the crowd go nuts once, he figured, when you can make them go nuts twice?

Snider's views on improving his sport continued throughout the following years, whether it was preaching the need for instant-replay review in 1990 or discussing the benefits of legalizing sports betting in 1992. But by the time the '80s rolled around, he was exhausted. He wanted to find a way to take a step back and enjoy his life more, rather than battling in the NHL boardroom. His wealth had grown to a level he had never before seen, and with his children coming of age, he finally saw an opportunity to shift his focus to the other parts of his life.

10

Passing It to the Next Generation

AT A PARTY in the early 1980s, the recently divorced Snider's eyes locked with a young woman named Martha McGeary. Tall, blonde, and stunning from every angle, she was 25 to Snider's 49—an enormous age difference that bothered neither of them as they exchanged pleasantries and hit it off. Martha knew little of sports and was new to Philadelphia. She had heard of Snider, but knew nothing about him beyond his involvement with the Flyers. At the end of the party, Snider asked if he could call her, but she politely declined, having arrived at the party with someone else.

About a year later, the two reconnected, and their memories of the night they met were still fresh. They began spending each day together and quickly fell in love. Just three weeks after they started dating, Snider sat with her in his backyard under his favorite magnolia tree and in the midst of conversation stated that they would get married. While it was not an official proposal, nor did it merit an official response from Martha, the intention of sharing their lives together was solidified. After the 1982–83 hockey season, they spent the summer in Maine, windsurfing, barbecuing, sitting on the dock, and staring at the stars. Snider's family was stunned at how madly the two seemed to have fallen for each other, with one member describing their windsurf sails moving in tandem with each other as they coasted through the lake.

Martha's father, on the other hand, was less than pleased with the relationship. Only a few years Snider's senior, he struggled with the unconventional partner his daughter had chosen. A talented charmer, Snider invited Martha's mother to join the couple in New York City for dinner and a show in order to make a good impression. Once his future mother-in-law was on board, he invited both parents to his home for a summer pool day. With Martha's father sitting across the backyard refusing to engage, the other three chatted casually about the future. When her father jumped in the pool to cool down, Snider quickly followed suit and swam over to the hard-nosed man. "I understand you're having a tough time with this," Snider said. "But I need you to know that I really love your daughter and I'm going to take care of her. You don't have anything to worry about."

Although it took some time, Snider finally received the approval of both parents, eventually developing a close, loving relationship with his future father-in-law. With that box checked off, he took Martha to Mrs. J's Sacred Cow, a fancy New York restaurant on West 72nd Street and prepared to propose. Choosing the classic route, he had the waiter drop the diamond ring into the bottom of Martha's glass. When it arrived at the table, Martha looked down and burst into tears. The two had done nearly everything together from the minute they started dating, and neither one wanted it to end. Excited about this new stage of his life, he phoned his mother from New York to inform her that he was now engaged to Martha.

"Martha," Lilian mused. "Is she Jewish?"

"No, Mom."

"I might as well die," she snapped as she hung up the phone.

Despite the ruminations of a stereotypical Jewish mother, the two married in 1984 in an elaborate ceremony and reception, held at the Bellevue Stratford Hotel in Philadelphia. With Martha's sisters and Snider's daughters attending to the bride and Jay and Craig as their father's best men, the couple celebrated the next phase of their lives with all of their closest friends and family—including Snider's mother. The 250-plus guest list included a who's-who of the hockey world: Bob and Sandy Clarke, Joe and Pat Scott, Bernie and Carol Parent, Keith and Joyce Allen, NHL President John Ziegler, Blackhawks owner Bill Wirtz, and many more. The couple honeymooned in the Caribbean, sailing between islands in a chartered yacht.

Perhaps one of the best stories to properly characterize Snider and his priorities in life was that of his wedding ring. At the time, he wore the Flyers Stanley Cup ring on his left ring finger. Martha, understanding the man she was marrying, looked him in the eye and assured him that she would never ask him to take it off. Instead, they agreed to repurpose a family heirloom from the Snider family into a pinky ring that he would wear as his wedding ring. For the remainder of his life, the Flyers ring remained on that finger. One could joke that the Flyers were his mistress through multiple marriages, but in reality, his first vows were always to his team.

But regardless of his passion for the team, Snider was ready for a change in the management of his businesses. It was a shocking revelation to the Philadelphia media and fans when, in 1984, he named his 24-year-old son Jay as the team's president. But to Snider, it was the most logical decision. Jay was not someone who grew up with a silver spoon in his mouth. Rather, he had worked his way up through the various businesses that the family operated, from sweeping the floors in the Spectrum and cleaning out old closets in rickety JFK Stadium, to working as a ticket seller, helping in the accounting department, learning the art of settling shows, and eventually becoming the vice president of marketing.

Jay had also already started the private security company, SpectaGuard, which was separate from the family business but, with the Snider name behind it, successful in its own right. He had never outwardly considered following in his dad's footsteps in leading the Flyers, nor were there ever many serious conversations about it among the family. At one point, Snider sat his children down and welcomed them to work in the business, but he advised that they would be judged and promoted based on their abilities, rather than their last name. He also had an in-depth conversation with both Jay and Craig during a long walk on the beach in Florida in the late 1970s, as he discussed with each of them an opening to join the company if they so desired. Nearly every child spent at least some time working for Snider, but none more than Jay.

So, when Flyers president Bob Butera resigned to join the New Jersey Devils in 1984, Snider repeatedly offered his son the position, which Jay declined multiple times. But, as was his hallmark, Snider wore his son down, and Jay finally accepted. The move allowed Snider to spend more time with his new wife to plan the next stage of their lives together. The father-son duo had a unique relationship that Snider did not necessarily have with the rest of his children. Few words needed to be spoken between them—they were cut from a similar cloth and often understood exactly what the other wanted with just a sentence or two spoken. When Snider decided he wanted to elevate himself to the chairman's role and name Jay as president, even those closest to him were skeptical. When he confirmed that Jay would indeed be the ultimate decision-maker for the team, many simply looked at him and said, "Yeah, right."

Even though his name was not in the newspapers nearly as much at this time, as expected, Snider was still greatly involved in the running of the organization. While he was not necessarily the one hiring the general manager or the coach, he was certainly on the phone with Jay regularly, listening to the happenings and offering his opinion and advice, whether it was requested or not. Perhaps the only move during this time span specifically made by Snider was appointing the recently retired Bob Clarke as the team's general manager. But future ownership decisions were subsequently made by Jay. Everyone in the organization knew that the buck still stopped at Snider's desk, but as in any family business that passes to the next generation, Jay would constantly be in touch with his father, getting opinions and approvals for any major business decision. Pretty soon, though, the nature of their working relationship became evident. Snider would approve a decision Jay made, but more often than not, as soon as Jay executed it, his father would be on the phone furious about how it was done. Sometimes he felt his son was executing a slightly different version of the decision they had previously made, while other times he simply could not help but second-guess. Nonetheless, from a public perspective, Jay was calling the shots, whether those in the region believed it or not.

Snider was still working, to be certain. He could throw around the term "retirement" all he wanted, but those close to him knew he was always involved. No major decision was ever made in the Flyers office without his knowledge or approval. At the same time, he was getting involved in Spectacor Films and even had an office in West Hollywood for a short time. That led to him becoming friendly with many stars and celebrities who called California home, eventually leading to his own move to the state.

One of the celebrities Snider befriended while living in California was Wayne Gretzky, the NHL superstar who had married a Hollywood actress and become a fixture in the region. When he was traded to the Los Angeles Kings in 1988, it gave the two of them an opportunity to spend more time together. They would regularly go to dinner, either by themselves or with their wives, and would spend certain holidays with each other's family and friends. Because of their love of hockey and deep desire to better the game, they became very close, despite the vast age difference. As would be expected after spending so much time together, they often would find themselves in humorous situations.

At a Christmas party at Canadian musician David Foster's house, a mutual friend of Gretzky and Snider's, Foster separated the group into men and women for a Christmas carol singing competition. With Gretzky, Snider, and others on one side, they looked across the room and saw many celebrity singers, including Barbra Streisand. Gretzky turned to Snider and said, "Are you going to carry us or am I?" The duo laughed hysterically and continued to giggle about the absurdity of the episode for the rest of the night. Snider was known for his love of singing and dancing and was always comfortable at these enjoyable gatherings.

But Snider was as intense with Gretzky as he was with any of his friends or business colleagues. Shortly after Gretzky retired in 1999, Snider took him to lunch to catch up. One of the reasons the two hit it off so well in the first place was because they consistently put the game above either of their own self-interests. Gretzky would always say, "The game is bigger than any individual," and Snider felt the same way—perhaps replacing the word "individual" with "team." No matter how passionate Snider was about his Flyers, the health and success of the sport was always more important. That's why he so desperately wanted to meet up with Gretzky at this moment.

"You should be *in* hockey," Snider said to his counterpart, trying to convince him to get back in the game at some level, be it coaching, management, or ambassadorial. "You should be involved with the league."

Gretzky, having already heard the pitch, smiled, knowing it was tough to ever disagree with Snider. "You know," he replied, "the league's been great to me, everything I have is because of hockey. But there's no race, there's no rush. I'm always going to be around hockey."

The two went back and forth, with Snider making his case, but Gretzky holding his ground. No matter how stern and strong Snider could be, it was impossible to convince someone to do something for which they simply weren't ready. But it didn't stop Snider from continuing to push for the Great One to be visible in the sport. Eventually,

Snider was successful in drawing Gretzky back into the game, as he was eventually named an ambassador to the NHL, representing the sport across the world.

While the elder Snider was creating his new life out west, Jay was working on building the Flyers back to their previous championship form. His first coaching hire was Mike Keenan, a young upstart who had just won an American League championship in 1983. Snider was not involved in the interview process, but he did make sure to be present for the introductory press conference. It was still his team and he wanted to be sure he showed support for those running it. The day of the conference, Snider pulled Keenan aside. The Flyers were losing some top players to retirement and trades. They were in a rebuilding mode for the first time since their early years. Keenan had exuded confidence that the young Flyers squad could make the playoffs, a laughable suggestion to the chairman, who, despite his fervent desire to win every year, also recognized when that demand was unrealistic. He pulled Keenan close to him and said, "If you make the playoffs, I'll kiss your ass at center ice."

Months later, amid the race for the playoffs, Snider was steaming after the squad blew a lead at home and lost. He came charging through the Spectrum hallway toward the dressing room. Keenan stood outside, waiting for his boss to arrive. Snider exploded, screaming, "This team's not ready for the playoffs!" Keenan, confident in his club's ability to pull it all together and make the postseason, let his boss rant, then said, "Ed, do you want to kiss my ass now or later at center ice?" Snider was immediately disarmed, laughed, and said, "You're right, I'm sorry."

Snider's confidence in his re-shaped team quickly skyrocketed, especially with the addition of goaltender Pelle Lindbergh, who was becoming known as the best young goalie in the league. After the Flyers' run to the Stanley Cup Finals in 1985, Lindberg won the league's award for the best goaltender that season. Philadelphia was buzzing with excitement. On November 9, just a few weeks into the 1985–86 season, the team threw a party for players, coaches, and management. After seeing the camaraderie surrounding Lindbergh (and witnessing his play, of course), Snider had seen enough. Lifelong superstitions went by the wayside as he drove home with a smile on his face. He turned to Martha in the passenger seat and said, "He's the one. He's the one that is finally going to bring us the Cup."

A few hours later, he was awoken by the phone—when it rang that early in the morning, Snider knew it was never good. After hearing the news on the other end, he buried his head in his hands and simply said, "Has the family been notified?" An intoxicated Lindbergh had crashed his Porsche into a wall driving home from the party, rendering him brain-dead almost instantly. As the Sniders arrived at the hospital to see their star goalie on life support, Snider shook his head, tears welling in his eyes, and muttered, "I shouldn't have said that."

The pain of the loss was ever so slightly muted by the physical distance he now kept from the team. With Jay running the organization, Snider found an opportunity to bond with Martha. They purchased a beautiful new home in Bryn Mawr, Pennsylvania, and the two began spending more time together than Snider had ever spent with Myrna. With his companies running smoothly and having enough executives to essentially operate with only his oversight, he jumped at the opportunity to do what he loved most: enjoy life. He took his family to California, which he had grown to love, where they rented homes each summer before finally purchasing a second home in Malibu on the Pacific Coast Highway. They soon would spend more time in California than they did in Pennsylvania.

While he enjoyed relaxing in his second home, he still had a burning passion for his team in Philadelphia. Snider often felt pulled between the worlds. With the team not only making the playoffs, but also advancing to the Stanley Cup Finals that year, Snider also welcomed his fifth child, Sarena, to the world. He was ecstatic about his second round of fatherhood, passing out cigars to his executives in the director's lounge the next game, imploring them to celebrate with him.

Snider was still involved with the team—he always attended the home opener and all playoff games by flying back and forth between Philadelphia and California. But his focus, perhaps for the first time in his life, was more on his new family than anything else. That focus was as intense as anything he had ever done. He dove head-first into fatherhood with the financial backing and time to devote to his young children that he didn't have the first time around.

His older children were surprised at his behavioral change. When they were growing up, he was constantly working and sometimes struggling to make ends meet. Despite how much he wanted to be with his family, often times that simply was not an option, as anyone with a full-time job and mortgage might understand. But by the 1980s, his wealth had grown to a point that he could relax and focus on what was truly important to him: his family. Young Sarena became daddy's little girl, playing with him, running around their property, and laughing wildly together. She would bring him his orange juice and vitamins in the morning and sat with him while he read his papers—a daily pile of the *Wall Street Journal, Philadelphia Inquirer,* and *Philadelphia Daily News.* He would take her to kids' shows at arenas that Spectacor managed in California, where she would sit on his lap with a big smile.

Their new Malibu home also had a pool and a tennis court, combining two activities that Snider loved dearly, stemming all the way back to his youth and his summers at Camp Cody. While Sarena was young, he would get in the pool with her and throw her around as she laughed and screamed. It was during this time that he realized he was struggling physically to do so. As a new father in his fifties, he was far from physically fit, having spent most of his life in offices and boardrooms trying to progress in the business world. But now, with a young daughter who needed him around, he felt it was time to take control of his physical health and commit to getting in shape. First, he quit smoking, something he had done regularly since he was a teenager. Then he hired a personal trainer to get him on the right track.

He spent hours on the tennis court with Sarena, building up her confidence and trying to impart to her his penchant for laser focus and hard work on whatever task was at hand. He introduced her to soccer, and they would regularly practice together. When the family went to Maine in the summers, he would water-ski and teach his children how to do the same. All the while, he would show extreme passion and adoration for his daughter in a way he had never done before. He would pick her up and throw her over his shoulder, something that people around him noticed as unusual for him. He had reached an acceptable level of success and now wanted to focus on being a father.

At this point in his life, fatherhood was one of the greatest experiences Snider had. He loved to be there as a role model for his young children. He was always the one they went to for help writing papers and with math homework. His penchant for dealing with numbers was legendary and he was always willing to impart some of that talent to his kids. And he had always been a fantastic writer—one of the talents that was apparent to those who worked with him was his ability to take complex situations and issues and simplify them quite easily. When it came to thesis papers and clarifying complex thoughts, he could run with the best of them, giving his kids a valuable resource for their schoolwork.

But even schoolwork was not something he was wont to take too seriously. A mediocre student himself, he wanted his children to focus on enjoying their lives and finding something they loved to do. He didn't care what college they went to—he was surely not a snob when it came to that part of life. He had attended a state school, cherished his time there, and turned out just fine. When one of the kids was up late struggling with an assignment, he implored them to go to sleep.

Getting a full night's sleep was much more important than whatever grade they would receive. He cared deeply about them succeeding in school, but also wanted them to do so without the levels of stress often involved in perfectionist students—ironic, considering his own perfectionist tendencies.

Amid the travails of parenting, he also wanted to find ways to spend quality time with his children. If he wasn't watching *60 Minutes* or an investigative show, it was Flyers games from the comfort of California. He never missed a game if he could help it, and the events became a regular note on the calendar for him and Sarena. Grabbing a glass emblazoned with the Flyers logo, and filling it with some ice and vodka—"hockey water," they would call it—Snider would sit alongside Sarena, the game in front of them. His superstitions didn't subside with the cross-country move, either. If the team had won the last game, they would watch the next game in the same spot, sitting in the same positions, perhaps wearing the same clothing. If they lost the previous game, they would change it up. In his mind, anything he could do to give the team an edge.

The Flyers were just one small portion of the work he continued to do from his perch in California. At a time when Spectacor was continuing to expand rapidly across the country, Snider utilized his contacts in California to help bring new business in for the company. At the same time, the organization continued pursuing contracts with other arenas and even looked to purchase other franchises. They explored building a stadium in Jacksonville for a new NFL expansion franchise and worked out a deal to manage the Pittsburgh Penguins arena. It was reported that they were also bidding for the team itself, but that rumor was quickly quashed by the family. They bid against Donald Trump for management rights to the Atlantic City Convention Center. One deal that never happened was the bid to purchase the Dallas Cowboys and Texas Stadium. The bid was higher than the one businessman Jerry Jones had made, and Cowboys owner H.R. Bright was willing to take it. But upon further review, Jay and his executives did not believe their bid was properly organized, and after discussing it with his father, they decided to drop it and move on.

But perhaps the most ambitious project Snider worked on during this time was in 1985, when he attempted to purchase the Philadelphia Eagles. By now he had achieved financial success, creating numerous rumors of his interest to buy his way back into his first love. Perhaps it was nostalgia. Perhaps it was a subtle reminder that he was a rising superstar, while Jerry Wolman was nowhere to be found. Most likely, though, it was that Snider saw a financial windfall from owning an NFL team. The league was on strong economic footing, and the value of professional football teams was skyrocketing each year.

Snider formed an investment group that put together an eight-figure offer to purchase the team from Leonard Tose, who had purchased it from Wolman in 1969. The group publicly backed out of the deal, and shortly thereafter, it was announced that auto dealer magnate Norman Braman was purchasing the organization for over $60 million. Many in Philadelphia were disappointed, preferring that Snider take control of the football club. There was an NFL regulation at the time that prevented someone from owning another major league sports team—but there were multiple NFL owners who came out and said they had no problem with Snider and that they would welcome him with open arms.

But with that NFL regulation, the socialistic tenets of the NFL's revenue-sharing program, as well as a sizable potential tax liability in purchasing the team,* Snider was getting uncomfortable. Unbeknownst to Philadelphia, he was exorbitantly close to actually closing

---

* Courts at the time had found that the NFL's television deal was an intangible asset without an end date, due to the near-certainty that it would renew upon its expiration. Therefore, new owners could not amortize that value, creating potential tax implications relating to increased net income for anyone purchasing a team.

on the deal and becoming the owner of the Eagles. It was months of work, enormous attorney fees, and numerous headaches. But for the duration of the pursuit, he went after the team like a man on a mission. He never articulated it, but it was evident that he was chasing after something he never previously had and which he could now afford. The pain of his firing from the Eagles stung for the last two decades and continued to do so right up until his death. Now he finally had the financial backing and ability to take control of the team that he believed he could bring to unparalleled success.

There was one major problem, however—deep down, he did not actually want the team. There came a point when he had the ability to pull the trigger and complete the deal. That day, he returned home and immediately began feeling sick. He was sweating profusely, so much so that his bedsheets needed changing. He was shaking uncontrollably and was white as a ghost. He even mentioned to Martha that he thought he was having a heart attack. Pregnant with Sarena at the time, she became as uptight as he was. At one point he was pacing nervously through the house. Minutes later he would be sitting on the bathroom floor, clenching his stomach. He finally looked up at his wife and said, "I don't even fucking like football. I'm a hockey man. What am I doing? I can't even remember the last time I was at a game."

It was typical for Snider to have second thoughts about a major deal, but this breakdown was something Martha had never seen. She tried to comfort him by joking that there are only eight home games per year, and that it would not take up that much of his time—he could fit it into his Flyers schedule fairly easily. He wasn't willing to do that. If he couldn't be all-in on a deal, if he was unable to put 100 percent of his entire being into a venture, then it was not for him. Subconsciously, he was very clearly coming full circle on all of his battles with Jerry Wolman. Perhaps he was trying to prove something to himself, perhaps he was trying to prove something to the world.

One could plausibly argue that he truly knew what he was doing. Snider was not one to make business decisions on emotion. But it is also possible that in his fire to "get back" at Wolman, his competitive drive was so strong that it blinded him to the reality. The bottom line was that, for perhaps the only time in his life, he pursued a major deal for mostly selfish reasons, even if he did not identify it as such at the time. That was not Snider's style, and when it hit him, he became nearly incapacitated. Like securing the homecoming queen and then later realizing you don't actually like her, Snider had just about secured the Eagles, but then immediately realized it wasn't what he wanted. The next morning, he called his attorney and said he was out. At that point, with only one bidder remaining, Tose and Braman agreed to terms, and the rest is history. Braman's presence ultimately bailed Snider out of the stress of owning a team in which, at the end of the day, he did not have the requisite interest or passion.

The only business for which he had that fiery passion was the Flyers. That passion was unexpectedly rewarded when, in 1988, he received a call from Brian O'Neill, the chairman of the Hockey Hall of Fame, informing him that he would be inducted into the hallowed Hall later that year. Snider was seldom emotional, but this call was one that triggered a deep reaction. He informed Martha when he got home from the office, and tears filled his eyes as he realized he was being recognized for his life's work.

The family decided to pull out all the stops for the ceremony, inviting all of the children, Snider's mother, and anyone from the team's history who could attend. Bob and Sandy Clarke had a pair of diamond-encrusted cuff links made with the Hockey Hall of Fame logo in the center and gifted them to the boss. Snider received his Hall of Fame ring, had it sized down, and gave it to Martha to wear to Flyers games. Lillian attended the ceremony and, despite not quite understanding why her son was being honored, was still as proud as a mother could be that all of this hubbub was for her Eddie. A photo from the event shows an ecstatic Snider and Martha, surrounded by all five of his children, two daughters-in-law, Martha's parents, and Lillian.

Year after year, Snider continued to see the Flyers as the crown jewel of his business empire. He still tried to manage it as a family business, regardless of how much it had grown. When he and Martha attended games in their superbox at the Spectrum, they would hold their hands out below the box as fans walked by and high-fived each of them. In the ultimate show of love for the average fan, Snider would quite literally reach out and touch them, both owner and fans showing resounding respect for each other.

But that deep love for Snider was possibly the spark behind a deeper issue within the organization. The fans always looked to the elder Snider as their true leader, no matter how much the family tried to convey that Jay was in charge. So, when in the late '80s a power struggle brewed between Clarke and Jay, there were very few people on Jay's side. Publicly, there were all sorts of musings in the press that Clarke did not respect Jay's authority and that Jay did not understand the running of an NHL organization. While the truths were greatly exaggerated, what is indisputable was that the two had working issues with one another that ultimately led to Jay deciding to make a change. Whether it was an attempt to put his own stamp on the team or move the organization past the Broad Street Bullies era, it did not make a difference. Over the course of months, he continuously called his father to hint that there were issues between him and Clarke. Although Jay never outright told Snider that he was going to pull the trigger, it was certainly not a decision that stunned his father.

The firing created enormous blowback from Philadelphia fans, who were shocked that the best player in team history was now unemployed at the doing of Snider's son. When the reporters called, Snider defended his son vociferously and expressed his sadness that it had even come to this. But privately, he was furious. The situation put an enormous amount of pressure on Snider, who now had to deal with picking sides between his biological son and a man who had been as close as one. Later in life, Clarke would often suggest that he was in a better position than Jay, because while he was like a son, he never had to be disciplined. Jay had the unfortunate position of receiving his father's wrath anytime the elder Snider was upset. When Snider, who was in Malibu at the time, found out about the firing, he called Jay and laid into him—those within earshot described the conversation as "explosive." He was furious at the way it was handled and the public relations debacle it caused. He viewed the entire situation as simply a mess, about which he was not afraid to let Jay know.

Snider was often inconsistent when it came to his method for managing those beneath him, but that inconsistency was sometimes intentional. He was a huge fan of the Ralph Waldo Emerson quote, "A foolish consistency is the hobgoblin of little minds, adored by little statesmen and philosophers and divines." He felt it was more important to take each situation and make a decision based on the facts at hand, rather than use any overarching rules or principles to make absolute rulings. That inconsistency possibly contributed to the struggles that he and his son shared in establishing a proper balance between their job duties.

As the years progressed following Clarke's firing, the Flyers performed horribly. Amid the team's woes, a slow breakdown began to happen in the business relationship between Snider and his son. While it was true that Snider rarely, if ever, explicitly told any of his employees what to do or what decision to make, he was a world-class second-guesser. That went double for Jay, whom Snider arguably had even higher expectations for as a member of the family. Ever since Jay took over, the two would regularly chat after each game, as Snider was always looking to talk Flyers hockey. As the on-ice product suffered and the team missed the playoffs the first of what would be five consecutive years, the calls between the father and son duo became less about business and more about frustration.

Snider, who was three hours earlier on the West Coast, would watch the team lose, call Jay, air his frustrations, hang up, go to dinner, and cool down for the rest of the night. Jay, meanwhile, would take both his father's and his own critiques and go home, tossing in bed in anger at the team's performance. With so little good news during the late '80s and early '90s, Jay began experiencing a Pavlovian response when his phone rang and he heard it was his father. He would tense up, something that troubled him. With the team's performance, mixed with the stresses of trying to build a new arena (more on this in chapter 11), Snider simply was not in a good mood most days. It put a strain on the relationship with his son, who in turn yearned to return to his SpectaGuard business that was growing and in dire need of more supervision. Jay felt it was not healthy to have a father-son relationship so predicated on the ups and downs and the stresses of the business and the team's performance.

In the meantime, a frustrated fan base and press corps began seething at the lack of progress in the Flyers rebuild. As it was, on March 29, 1991, when the Flyers were shut out by the Washington Capitals to officially eliminate them from playoff contention, the crowd began chanting, "Jay Must Go." Across the country, Snider watched with rage, his face beet red and his eyes narrowed, as usual. Painful memories of Eagles fans chanting, "Joe Must Go," decades earlier rang in his head as he tried to wrap his brain around what was happening to his team. As a boss, he was enraged. As a father, he was beside himself. When he and Martha attended games, the chant would be louder, as fans would literally turn around and chant it toward them. He was furious but also unsure of what to do. But, at the same time, he also was unaware that his son was losing the passion for his job.

Jay refused to abandon the Flyers in their time of need, instead wanting to steer them in the right direction before he inevitably departed. It looked as if that plan could get accelerated when Eric Lindros became available. Lindros was the most highly touted prospect the NHL had seen since Wayne Gretzky. When he refused to sign with the Quebec Nordiques, who had drafted him in 1991, he was publicly put up for sale to the highest bidder. Years earlier, when the Indianapolis Racers put a teenage Gretzky up for sale, it was Myrna who tried to convince Snider to pursue him and submit an offer they couldn't refuse. At the forefront of the movement trying to make peace with the rival WHA, Snider refused, saying it was against NHL rules. "They're gonna do it," Myrna responded, "so you ought to do it." At the end of the discussion, Snider concluded that he had to put the league ahead of his own team. The family then watched as Gretzky was traded to the Oilers and subsequently led them to four Stanley Cups throughout the '80s—two of them won against the Flyers.

With the knowledge that his family had missed out on potentially the greatest player in NHL history years earlier, Jay felt it was the right time to make a move. In discussions with his father, Jay decided that pursuing a stalwart offensive forward who could be the foundation of the team for over a decade was the best move. Over the course of 1992, Jay negotiated with Quebec owner Marcel Aubut, keeping in touch with Snider the entire way. Although Jay ran nearly every step of the negotiations, Snider did get involved when Jay threatened to remove the $15 million of cash from the deal when he felt Aubut was playing games. At one point, Snider received a call from Aubut begging him to tell his son to put the money back in the deal. Snider demurred, stating that Jay had the authority to build the deal as he wanted—but, of course, the father and son were on the same page the entire time. Hours before the draft, the Flyers came to an agreement to acquire Lindros, and the family was ecstatic.

At this point, Snider, who was at Memorial Sloan Kettering in New York for thyroid cancer surgery, had to shut his phone off to go into the operating room. He went into the room optimistic, with the knowledge that his team had secured Lindros for themselves. But shortly thereafter, it became clear that Aubut had also agreed to a deal with the New

York Rangers, claiming that the deal with the Flyers was never consummated. As Snider was rolled out of surgery and brought into the recovery room, Martha was in the waiting room, an emotional wreck. She had been waiting for many hours—no one had updated her on his condition, nor was she even aware that the surgery was successful. With warnings from the doctor that complications could include the loss of his voice or worse, Martha crept through the hospital, desiring to find out on her own whether her husband was okay.

When she turned the corner toward the recovery room, she heard (but could not see) her raspy husband screaming and cursing, using the word "Lindros" multiple times. Snider had not only snuck his phone into the operating room by storing it under his body, he was waving off any nurse or doctor that came in trying to check on him. By the time he hung up the phone, both his and Jay's internals were at a full boil. It prompted Jay to march up to Aubut at the draft and say his now-famous line: "Bullshit, we had a deal." After days of arbitration hearings arranged by the league, Lindros was awarded to Philadelphia, where he would spend the next decade of his Hall of Fame career.

By that point, Jay had realized that running the Flyers was not what he wanted to do in the long run. With the private security industry booming, SpectaGuard needed their leader, and Jay wanted to return to his first love—running his own business. With Lindros in hand, the rest of the roster slowly coming into focus, and plans for a new, state-of-the-art arena in the works, the Flyers were finally on the right track. It was time for Jay to make the difficult choice. At 5:00 o'clock one morning, while Snider and Martha dozed in their home, they were awakened by the fax machine kicking on. When Snider grabbed the single paper, he sat down next to Martha, read his son's resignation letter out loud, and placed it down while the two sat in silence.

The era of Jay running the Flyers was one of great contradictions for Snider. He legitimately wanted his son to succeed and firmly believed he put him in a position to do so. But his second-guessing and his anger toward certain decisions were debilitating. When he was furious about something personally, Snider would often use the phrase, "I'll be nicer if you'll be smarter." With that mindset, it would be impossible for any of his children to run his organization, whether they were doing it well or not.

Snider lived and breathed the Flyers. He felt whoever ran the team should do so as well, and it was evident that, despite how much he loved them, Jay would never look at the team the same way. It is difficult for anyone to develop that kind of passion toward something, for Snider had built the organization from scratch—it was in his blood. How could anyone ever meet that same level of love for the Flyers? There is no doubt that Snider put his son in a no-win situation, and it had finally come to a head. If Jay was going to leave, it was perfectly acceptable, and Snider would support him 100 percent. But it left a gaping hole at the top of the organization, one that Snider knew, at the time, could only be filled by him. After a few quiet seconds, he looked up at his wife and said, "I need you to help me build an arena."

11

Battling for Philadelphia

IN THE MIDST of his faux-retirement, Snider got a rude awakening when the Spectrum's largest tenant dropped a bomb. In 1988, 76ers owner Harold Katz began working with the New Jersey Sports and Exposition Authority (NJSEA) to see if he could get his team out of Philadelphia and into a new home in Camden, New Jersey. At the time, Spectacor was charging the basketball team over $1.5 million per year in management and rental fees for the use of the Spectrum, and Katz was tired of the exorbitant expense. The Flyers owner was extremely uncomfortable with this possibility—losing a large tenant would cost the organization a lot of revenue that he couldn't afford. To retain that revenue, he knew both teams needed a new, state-of-the-art arena.

At a May 1989 event held by the Philadelphia Police Athletic League honoring him, Snider sat next to Philadelphia mayor Wilson Goode on the dais. He leaned over to his companion and expressed his concern. "He said we'd have a deal for a new arena in the city in five days," Snider recalled in *Full Spectrum*. Snider called Katz and proposed to work together to determine what was best for both teams. In June, Snider and Jay visited Katz at his home in Huntingdon Valley, Pennsylvania, where they shook hands and agreed to collaborate. The project became known publicly as "Spectrum II."

But in July 1989, Katz, who had historically butted heads with the Flyers owner, changed his tune and announced publicly that he was considering moving the team across the Delaware River to Camden when his lease expired in 1999, causing an uproar in Philadelphia. Negotiations between the two parties had stalled, leading Katz to approach New Jersey to request financial assistance to erect a state-of-the-art arena on the river, adjacent to the Ben Franklin Bridge.

The NJSEA was working on an ambitious plan to stimulate the Camden economy, including a $42 million aquarium and Campbell Soup's new corporate headquarters, which would be constructed in the same area. Those, along with a 23,000-seat arena, covering 40 acres, would give New Jersey an area to rival the South Philadelphia Sports Complex. As part of the initially reported deal, Katz would receive a share of the parking revenue, a share of concert revenue, tax abatements, and development rights on the land adjacent to the proposed arena location. Simultaneously, Katz was negotiating with Spectacor and Snider for new terms on his lease. It was reasonable to assume that the entire Camden plan was just a ploy to garner Katz a better bargaining position with Snider.

Although the idea initially seemed like a lofty goal, the region was astonished when, in September, Snider joined Katz for a tour of the proposed Camden site, suggesting that the Flyers were also interested in potentially moving the hockey club across the river. For most of the summer, Snider was negotiating with the city of Philadelphia for a new building. Within the Flyers offices, he and his executives had been saying that the team needed to either renovate the Spectrum or construct a new home for the Flyers. When they agreed that a new building was more plausible, he entered talks to tear down decrepit JFK Stadium, located just to the south of the Spectrum, and erect a new state-of-the-art arena to house both the Flyers and 76ers.

The negotiations with the city were crucial to Snider's ability to afford the project. From the start, he planned on privately financing the building, as opposed to using taxpayer money—a prospect his libertarian viewpoint despised—yet he still needed the local government's help with the tax breaks that allowed the Spectrum to be so successful. From the time he and Earl Foreman took the building out of bankruptcy in the '70s, Spectacor had saved nearly $250,000 per year in real estate taxes, allowing it to put that capital back into the growing business. If he was going to sink nine figures into an arena nearly 30 years later, he needed even greater help from the city.

Just a few weeks after the tour of the Camden site, Mayor Goode proposed a 60-year lease that would keep both teams in Pennsylvania. When both Snider and Katz demurred and continued meeting with Camden, Pennsylvania governor Bob Casey got involved as well. In November, Snider denied reports that there was a deal to keep both parties in Philadelphia, whereupon New Jersey upped their offer. Philadelphia did the same a few weeks later. The bulk of the 1989–90 season was overshadowed by constant negotiations, lines set in the sand, and an eventual devolution of the relationship between Katz and Snider. Each continually blamed the other whenever a potential deal was delayed, causing a major rift between two owners who should otherwise have been partners.

Katz and Snider had a strikingly similar upbringing. Katz also grew up the son of a grocer, also worked in his father's corner store, and also had no desire to take over the family business when he got older. Instead, he worked his way up through various companies before starting NutriSystem, the well-known weight-loss firm. When he purchased the 76ers in 1981 for $12 million, it began an ongoing difficult relationship with his landlord, who was charging him one of the highest rents in the NBA. Unlike the Flyers, the basketball team still did not even have their own dedicated locker room.

When Katz first expressed serious concerns about his lease to Spectacor years earlier, Snider pulled out the original architectural plans for the Spectrum and began scheming with Katz on a way they could expand the building and make it work for both sides. Ultimately, Katz had little interest in it—he wanted a brand-new arena, and if Snider was not going to provide it at terms he felt were favorable, he would find his own way to do so.

As 1990 progressed, talks see-sawed wildly between Camden and Philadelphia. By September, the local papers were reporting a new 30-year lease that would keep both teams where they were—but the deal was never signed. Confusion reigned, and Snider began working on plans for a new arena, whether Katz was a part of it or not. The entirety of 1991 saw progress move at a snail's pace, frustrating Snider and creating incredible anxiety as he found himself nearly as stressed as he was decades earlier when he first thought he may lose the Flyers' home.

As 1993 came around, he was still struggling to come to a deal with all of the parties involved. By this point, Snider was frustrated and burning out. "I don't think I would have gotten started on it if I had known [it would take two years to get the financing]," he told the *Philadelphia Daily News*. "It's taken more energy out of me and our organization than I would have liked." Later in the year, Spectacor came to an agreement with PNC Bank: they would provide $134 million, Snider would contribute $50 million, and a combined $15 million would come from Pennsylvania and Philadelphia.

But the deal was still not signed. Katz continued to muse publicly if it was feasible for him and the 76ers, while Snider stood next to a now-empty lot, after the state had paid $4 million to raze JFK Stadium. He had agreed to PNC's collateral demands, but without the guarantee of the 76ers as a second major tenant, the bank would not sign off on the loan. There was even a rumor that the Eagles were looking to build a new stadium on the same lot, but Philadelphia mayor Ed Rendell immediately quashed that. "The only time we would even begin to consider a stadium on the Spectrum II site," he said to the *Philadelphia Daily News*, "is when Ed Snider announces publicly he's not going ahead with Spectrum II."

When the deal with PNC fell apart, Katz continued negotiating with New Jersey, but Snider was clearly unwilling to go along with the plan. He wanted to stay in Philadelphia, even if it pained him to do so. He was suddenly forced to adjust his strategy. Having spent the last four years trying to woo Katz into teaming up with him, he came to the realization that, in order to beat his new competitor, he would simply need to crush any potential for a new arena in Camden.

Snider rarely made business decisions based on personal feelings. It was always about his companies and his desire to see them progress. But, even if it was not personal, he could still be ruthless in his attempts to emerge on top in a serious negotiation. In the battle between two professional sports team owners, he was just that. At the end of 1993, Snider hired a Trenton lobbyist to make the case to New Jersey voters that the proposed Camden project would not be beneficial to the region. When he was accused of meddling by the *Philadelphia Daily News*, his reply was simply, "We're trying to get the truth out. If anybody wants to dispute our facts, let them. We'd like to hear it." Snider also had members of his staff lurk through the Spectrum during 76ers games to make sure Katz behaved himself, and to inform him if anything out of the ordinary was occurring—if he was meeting with anyone he should know about, if he was saying anything unusual. As always, Snider simply needed to have the information. Only then could he pick the proper strategy.

The decision Snider made was to simply guarantee that the Spectrum and any potential new arena would be so successful in the coming years that a competing arena across the river would be foolish. He directed his top executives to begin snatching up all of the available events for Philadelphia to show New Jersey that any new Camden arena would not be able to fill its schedule enough to be profitable. Over the final months of 1993 and the beginning of 1994, Peter Luukko, the executive in charge of booking the Spectrum at the time, established regionally exclusive, long-term deals with the Harlem Globetrotters,

Sesame Street Live, Disney on Ice, the Electric Factory, and the Ringling Brothers circus. By committing scores of additional event nights per year to Philadelphia and thereby preventing them from going to Camden, Spectacor was essentially able to turn toward the New Jersey politicians negotiating the deal and say, "I don't know what kind of numbers they're giving you, but all of those shows are already booked here."

Just days later, when incoming New Jersey governor Christine Whitman announced that she was rejecting the plan for the new Camden arena, Snider claimed victory and told Katz publicly that he was welcome to come back to Philadelphia to work with him. By the end of January, the two had gone through intense, final-hour negotiations—a four-hour meeting at the Conshohocken Marriott with all of their advisors, as well as Prudential, who was willing to help finance the new arena. The next morning, they announced an agreement had been reached to keep both teams in Philadelphia and to construct a new arena in the empty lot next to the Spectrum. "I started this deal when I was 19 years old," Katz joked. "Now I'm going on 66." When asked how they finally reached an agreement, Katz again reached for humor. "I took Snider outside, I beat the crap out of him, and then we made a deal."

Snider wasn't amused. With a mischievous smile, he leaned over the microphone and said, "Anytime you want to step outside, Harold."

Snider was still annoyed with the stress that was involved over the previous few years. So when he was presented with the opportunity for an unusual radio ad featuring him and Katz, making fun of the entire feud, he was not initially a fan. His daughter, Lindy, showed him the final script, and he was incensed. He looked at Lindy like she was out of her mind, but she knew how to appeal to his lighter side. "This is funny, Dad," she pleaded, according to the *Philadelphia Inquirer*. "Just think about it." After the press conference announcing the deal, Lindy again pushed him. She told him that Katz was laughing over the whole ordeal and thought the ad would work great to help market the new arena.

Snider relented. They spent the next couple of hours in the director's lounge recording the spot, as Jack Williams narrated. By the end of the final take, dozens of people were watching from the corner, cheering when they finally completed it. The 60-second radio spot featured the two bickering on everything—what activity to do, who would pay for the snacks at the movies—with the goal to help sell the luxury suites that would be crucial to financing the building. Within a few days, the staff was overwhelmed with the positive response from the business community. They had sold out all 22 of the most expensive luxury suites priced at $135,000 each; half of the 60 luxury suites priced at $125,000, and half of the $75,000 balcony suites.

With excitement building and the wind at his back, Snider again reverted to his normal, confident self. With Lindros on board and the Flyers roster taking shape for the coming decade, he promised a Stanley Cup would be coming back to Philadelphia within three years—perhaps in the new arena's inaugural season. The groundbreaking for Spectrum II was scheduled for May 1994, but more delays hit Snider like an arrow. His frustration was rising and he was about to blow a gasket. He had spent the previous five years on almost nothing but this project, and even when there were agreements from every party, he still could not seem to get it moving.

With Prudential working on completing the underwriting before Snider signed the final paperwork, they came to Spectacor CFO Sandy Lipstein with a demand. The incredible amount of collateral Snider had already agreed to put up was no longer enough. They needed a bit more in order to receive final approval for the loan—and the city would not officially approve the project until the loan was confirmed. Snider had already committed to $200 million of collateral—the total expected cost of the project—but Prudential wanted an additional $60 million completion guarantee, in case the project ended up costing more. Lipstein knew this would be unpopular in the chairman's office, yet had little choice but to walk upstairs to inform his boss. Snider was in his office with Philadelphia businessman and good friend Lewis Katz, catching up as they often did (more on their friendship in chapter 15). When Lipstein informed him the deal was not yet done, Snider became irate. His face turned bright red, he grabbed things from his desk and started throwing them across the office. "Go tell the lenders to go fuck themselves!" Snider screamed, continuing his rampage. "There's no deal. We're not building the building."

The organization's CFO had his marching orders. He began walking out of Snider's office to inform the lenders that the Flyers would not be constructing a new building, when he heard Lewis Katz behind him speak up in a way only he could to the chairman. The famous philanthropist grabbed Snider and put his face just inches away from his best friend's.

"Snider, what the fuck is wrong with you?" he said, loud enough for the entire outer office to here. "This is your guy, he's telling you what's going on, he's trying to protect you, and that's the way you treat him? You're really a schmuck."

Lipstein, recognizing what always came next in the sequence of Snider anger, returned to his office and did nothing. A few minutes later, Snider called him, apologetic. "I didn't mean it," he said. "I know you're trying to do the best job for me. I'm sorry." Later that night, with Lipstein still in the office trying to finalize the deal, Snider barged through the door, ran around the desk, grabbed Lipstein, kissed him on the cheek, said, "We're good," and walked out.

But despite his understanding that he essentially had no choice, Snider was extremely uncomfortable at the amount of collateral he was asked to commit to the loan, and at this point it began to strain his life at home. He struggled to sleep, up many nights fretting over the damage a failure might cause his family to endure. He had essentially put up every hard asset he owned in order to secure the loan: all of his

homes, his plane, his art collection, even Martha's engagement ring—
but not his Stanley Cup rings. He had confidence in the decision he
made, but always had the little voice reminding him what was on the
line.

When the city delayed the approval vote in June, Snider was furious—the *Daily News* even wrote an editorial a few weeks later essentially imploring city council to get on with it already and approve
the deal for which everyone had been jerked around plenty for one
lifetime. In July, the loan agreement was officially signed, the city
approved the deal, and everything was finally done—other than, of
course, constructing the actual building. Five years of endless frustrations were finally behind Snider. He was going to get his new arena
and a new opportunity to expand his empire.

"As long as we're around," said city council president John Street,
"some of us are going to look out for Ed Snider, because he looked out
for us." Through years of intense negotiations, Snider never once for-
got the city that gave him everything he had. Regardless of what was
said publicly, he never once truly intended for the Flyers to relocate.
Those close to him knew that his only desire was to find a solution in
Philadelphia—and that's exactly what he did.

"He never threatened to leave town," wrote Rich Hoffmann in the
Daily News. "He never attempted to [blackmail] the city into anything. Certainly, he negotiated. Certainly, he negotiated hard. But it
was always a fair fight."

"I know it got testy," Snider said to the *Courier Post*, partaking in
the press conference from a pay phone in Maine, where his daughter
Sarena was at camp. "And it took a lot of sweat."

The entire process rubbed Snider the wrong way for the rest of
his life. When the Spectrum was built in 1967, it cost $8 million, was
completed in 15 months, and was documented with an agreement that
was about a half-inch thick. In the '90s, the architect's fee alone was
$9 million. The entire project cost $210 million, including a refinance

of the Spectrum, took 26 months to build, and the paperwork filled an entire room.

The week the documents were ready to be signed, Lipstein and Spectacor general counsel Phil Weinberg brought printouts of the entire deal to Snider's home. For nearly 10 hours on a Sunday night, the three went over every detail to ensure the chairman understood each word on which he was affixing his name. When the deal was finally signed a few days later, Lipstein joked to his boss, "You know what, if you ever decide to build the next one, I don't want to be around, because if you extrapolate where this is going..." Five copies of each form needed to be signed. Snider did so, but laughed the entire time at how ludicrous the entire ordeal was. Needless to say, this was going to be the last time Snider would be willing to risk his financial future for such an ambitious project.

Jay and Lindy Snider started the arena process by working with the architects and designers for the initial plans. And though Snider and his executives were in charge of overseeing the legal and financial aspects of the construction, by the time he had ended his brief California "retirement," the chairman put Martha in charge of the continued design of the building. As soon as the two returned to Philadelphia, she realized that her budget would be much tighter than expected. She had previously designed and oversaw the construction of the couple's Bryn Mawr home, but this was a completely different beast. There was a strict limit to how much they could spend on this massive project. The price of steel was quickly increasing, lowering the amount of money they could spend on the nitty gritty details. Martha's job soon became figuring out the best method of designing the public-facing parts of the arena as beautifully, but as inexpensively, as possible.

Given a budget of just $3,000 per suite, she procured wallpaper that was on clearance from a Canadian manufacturer, then used both sides of the material to make it look like they had two different types of décor. She picked out the Zolatone paint that would be used on the

brick and the Fritztile that would be used for the floor of the concourse. She even went as far as picking out the specific fixtures that
would be placed in bathrooms throughout the building. She chose the
ceiling paint color from a swatch, then asked how many thousands
of gallons of it they could procure in a short time. No detail was too
small for a job that had the potential to make or break the Snider name.

Throughout the construction, Snider would drive his executives
crazy with his flip-flopping between micromanaging the contractors
and leaving them alone to do their jobs. Lipstein wanted to keep a
close eye on Dick Fox, the consultant who was helping to build the
new arena. But Snider, sticking to his mantra, told his CFO to let the
man do his job. "You're the finance guy, he's the construction guy,"
Snider would say. "He's the expert. Just leave him alone." Of course,
as Lipstein knew would come to pass, when the bills began arriving,
Snider ran down to his office yelling, "I can't keep paying these bills,
you've got to protect me!"

"Ed," Lipstein replied, "you told me to stay out and he's the expert.
If you want me to protect you, you have to let me get into it."

Snider thought about it for a moment and understood. "Yeah,
you're right," he said, before turning to walk out. Within days, Lipstein had the green light to do what he wanted in the first place.

Snider's executives were not the only ones with whom he butted
heads during this time. With Martha overseeing a majority of the project, she was often working even longer hours than he was. He would
often get annoyed when he came home at the end of the day and she
was nowhere to be found. More often than not, she was still with the
architect or one of the subcontractors, trying to fix the latest issue to
arise that day. But Snider was used to being pampered upon his arrival
home from work, having his wife by his side, and being served dinner.
Despite the fact that it was his initial request that put her in the position of working so hard, he struggled to handle the reversal in roles—
he was now home in the evening, while Martha often was not. The

couple remained in Philadelphia for most of this time, even though Snider wanted to be in California. He even suggested they build the arena from across the country, but was talked out of the idea by those close to him. Although he would never admit it, it is certainly possible that the entire period generated some resentment in his mind, even though it was nobody's fault. It began to create a small chasm between him and Martha that lay dormant for some time, but festered under the surface for many years.

The building progressed nicely and on budget, partially due to Lipstein's shrewd financial maneuvering. Because the draw schedule for the loan ended up being more backloaded than initially anticipated, Spectacor started saving significant amounts of money on interest that ended up not needing to be paid. Lipstein put all of those savings on the side, knowing there would always be adjustments that needed to be made over the course of a construction project. Anytime Snider wanted to change the building or add a feature, he would rush into Lipstein's office and say, "Do we have the money for it?" Lipstein would jokingly fish around in his pockets and say, "Yeah, I got it."

One of the changes was an upgrade to the lower-level seats that allowed for quicker changeovers between the hockey rink and basketball court. At the time, changeovers in many buildings around the NHL and NBA took as long as eight hours. Snider was not happy with that inefficiency. The quicker they could turn the building around for another event, the more events they could hold and the closer together they could schedule events with Flyers games. He went to his arena workers and canvassed them for ideas. They determined that if they could get all of the seats out of the way quicker, it would save a lot of time during a changeover. The organization created a change order with the contractor that put the end seats on risers and added hydraulics to allow them to move with just the press of a button. The change order cost $2 million (which was available in Lipstein's "secret" budget) and allowed the new arena to convert over in just two-and-a-half hours.

Throughout the construction, Snider remained as involved as possible. He brought a 10-year-old Sarena with him to the work site and was often toured around by a contractor or Martha to plan out the work for the coming weeks. But despite using the project as additional time to spend with his family, the stresses of the job did not dissipate. Money was always a concern, especially when the budget got pretty tight as the project neared completion. When it needed an extra $20–30 million that Snider did not have, he began searching for a means of added revenue. He signed a 25-year deal with Aramark to run the food services in the building in exchange for up-front cash that he needed to inject into the construction.

But the biggest splash he made was in making the decision to sell the naming rights to the new arena. While naming rights were not new, they were seldom used at that point for sports arenas. Only a few buildings existed across the country with corporate titles. Yet Snider foresaw an opportunity to give himself the cash needed to complete the project without needing to return to a bank that already had him over-leveraged. It pained Snider to put a corporate name on the arena, but he knew that without it, he would not be able to complete the project. The end goal was well worth the sacrifice. When decision time came, the choice was between CoreStates Bank and Verizon. With both financial offers being similar, it came down to Snider and Martha's personal feeling on the name. They agreed that CoreStates Center sounded better, and they signed on the dotted line. The deal gave Snider $40 million for 29 years of naming rights for both the Spectrum and the new arena. In exchange for the hefty amount of cash, Snider also agreed to an unusual clause that allowed CoreStates to change the name on the arena up to five times over the life of the contract in case of an acquisition or merger—foresight that proved quite valuable to the bank, as the name would change three times in the building's first 12 years due to bank mergers.*

At the groundbreaking itself, there were smiles all around, as Snider expressed joy and relief. On the other side, Mayor Rendell made sure everyone knew who truly deserved the credit for the project on which they were about to embark. "People should understand that there is one real hero in this," the mayor said, "and that is Ed Snider.... It was Ed Snider's dedication and commitment that made this possible."

When the building was finally completed in the summer of 1996, it had used over 7,000 tons of steel, 19,000 cubic yards of concrete, 32,500 square feet of glass, and 400,000 square feet of drywall. Not only would the building now house the entirety of the Flyers corporate staff, but it had plenty of room for company growth, in addition to having a sparkling new director's lounge for Snider and his executives. Snider even chose the suite closest to the lounge as his own—though he was forced to choose another suite when he realized that he would be facing the Flyers players' backs during games. Ultimately, he chose the suite at center ice across from the Flyers bench, even though it was the furthest one from his lounge.

As inconvenient as it was, the executives would parade down the stairs, up the stairs, and around to the other side of the arena. It became a beloved ritual. Snider would see various business associates and fans on the walk to his seat, enabling him to interact with those who chose to patronize his business and make his dream a reality.

Despite the end result being exactly what was needed, the multi-year period in which he fought for a new arena was one of the most stressful stretches of his life. There were days he woke up and struggled to build up the motivation to get out of bed. He often felt crushed,

---

* Between 1996 and the publication of this book, the building would, at various times, be known as the CoreStates Center, the First Union Center, the Wachovia Center, and the Wells Fargo Center. For the purpose of simplicity, henceforth the arena will be referred to as "the Center."

As the 1970s progressed, Snider expanded the Flyers and Spectrum into an empire, with various companies supporting one another like the spokes of a wheel. Here, he stands with longtime executive and friend Fred Shabel admiring the subsidiaries of Spectacor.

Two of the players that Snider always made time for were Bob Clarke (left) and Bernie Parent (right). He would regularly take them on trips with him and treat them like members of his own family.

Snider married Martha McGeary in 1983, and they immediately moved into a stunning new home, along with their dog, who of course was named Stanley.

Snider's friends joked that he was always the most competitive at whatever it was he was doing. Here he is after teaming up with Martha in a pinball tournament at Frank Clements Tavern— more often than not, he found a way to win.

When Snider named his son, Jay (right), as the Flyers president, he was looking forward to potentially passing the reins down a generation. Unfortunately, it ultimately ended with Jay leaving the organization after their relationship went downhill during multiple losing seasons.

Snider introduced his kids to various activities that he loved in order to spend quality time with them. Tennis was one of those activities that he and Sarena (left) regularly shared.

Being a father was the most important part of Snider's life, even if he sometimes prioritized incorrectly. In his second round with fatherhood, he tried extremely hard to be present for his kids. Here (at right), Snider plays on the floor with Sam.

Snider often took exotic vacations with his family and friends. But the one constant was his being on the phone at any hour, trying to put out whatever fire came his way.

When Snider was finally able to secure the financing to build the Center, he had three of his four older kids join him at the groundbreaking. Pictured (from left to right) are Craig, Martha, Ed, Lindy, and Jay Snider.

One of the biggest benefits of being acquired by Comcast in 1996 was the relationship Snider shared with Comcast CEO Brian Roberts. The two were each other's most important business confidants and often each one's last call before a major decision.

Despite admittedly not having the same passion for basketball as he did for hockey, Snider still fought fervently for his 76ers, especially when he felt an official was treating his team poorly.

Snider's closest friend in his later years was philanthropist Lewis Katz. The two became like family to each other and their families often traveled together. When Katz and his wife perished in a plane crash, Snider became a second father to Katz's two children.

When Snider was introduced to Rajshree Agarwal as a potential director for the Snider Center, he immediately was sold. At the center's opening, he said that when he speaks to Agarwal, it was like he was talking to Ayn Rand—a hefty compliment from Snider.

When Ron Hextall (at far right with Snider and Paul Holmgren) was named GM of the Flyers in 2014, he wanted to put the team through a full, multiyear rebuild. Snider was not a patient man, especially when he knew his health was going downhill. But when Hextall asked him outright, he accepted—perhaps one of the most selfless acts of his career.

Taking down the Spectrum was one of the more difficult decisions Snider had to make, but he couldn't put nostalgia above entrepreneurship. He certainly loved looking back at the history of the building over the course of its final months.

The Ed Snider Youth Hockey Foundation was Snider's greatest gift to Philadelphia. Always passionate about making his city a better place to live, the foundation became the chairman's legacy, of which he was always ecstatic.

When an ailing Snider was confined to his California home for the last few months of his life, a friend suggested that the Flyers visit him in Montecito. When his Flyers showed up at the door, it was the happiest day of his final year. The chairman sits at the center of the photo, alongside his fourth wife, Lin Spivak, and then coach Dave Hakstol.

In October 2017, Comcast-Spectacor unveiled a statue of Snider at the northwest corner of the Wells Fargo Center. Those who pass by rub his Stanley Cup ring for good luck.

defeated, and unsure of how he would make this all work. At one point, Martha hung a quote up in his dressing room to help keep him in the right mindset. The quote she chose was a famous one from Theodore Roosevelt, one which perhaps better describes Snider's mindset than anything else ever said:

> It is not the critic who counts; not the man who points out how the strong man stumbles, or where the doer of deeds could have done them better. The credit belongs to the man who is actually in the arena, whose face is marred by dust and sweat and blood; who strives valiantly; who errs, who comes short again and again, because there is no effort without error and shortcoming; but who does actually strive to do the deeds; who knows great enthusiasms, the great devotions; who spends himself in a worthy cause; who at the best knows in the end the triumph of high achievement, and who at the worst, if he fails, at least fails while daring greatly, so that his place shall never be with those cold and timid souls who neither know victory nor defeat.

Snider read the quote every morning while he got dressed and prepared to get back to work. It not only comforted him in difficult times, but motivated him and reminded him why he was working so hard. It was not just for himself, but for the people of Philadelphia. If he succeeded, he would be remembered forever. If he failed, at least he would have done so having valiantly chased a dream that he fervently believed was required to keep his team competitive. And, in typical Snider fashion, he did not stop at the Flyers—he wanted the entirety of the NHL's front office to match his own ambition.

An Unexpected Return

EVEN AMID HIS STRUGGLES with Katz and the city of Philadelphia in the early '90s, Snider simultaneously found himself back in the fray within the NHL. At the same time, his Flyers began experiencing on-ice struggles. Between 1989–90 and 1993–94, the Flyers embarked on a seemingly endless drought. When they missed the playoffs five seasons in a row and profits began to slip, Snider did the only thing he knew when a problem arose: he took charge. He was disappointed in how the team was performing and felt they would benefit from the return of his strong leadership. Right around the time construction was ready to begin, he had Martha and the kids (she had since given birth to their son, Sam, his sixth child) pack everything up and head back to Philadelphia, telling them that the Flyers needed help and he had to go fix it.

But the Flyers were not the only team struggling at that time. The league as a whole was floundering under inflated salaries and revenues that were not keeping up with the increased expenses. By 1992, the 24-team NHL was drawing about 13 million fans per year and selling their stadiums to 90 percent capacity. But the average player salary had jumped from $149,000 in 1984–85 to $369,000 in 1991–92—and the top players were now making more than triple what they were making during the same time span. The other leagues were pulling away: the NFL's teams were collectively worth $3.6 billion and MLB's were worth the same. The NBA's teams were worth nearly $2.2 bil-lion. The NHL's squads were worth only $1.42 billion.

The league's owners were waging a losing battle against them-selves, as they clamored for economic certainty, but then raced to out-bid each other for the game's biggest stars. Meanwhile, the players continued to win in their regular battles against a hard salary cap or a luxury tax each time the two sides met for collective bargaining. League president John Ziegler had helped push the league past the WHA battles of the '70s and through the '80s, but the game had stag-nated. Even interim president Gil Stein, who was promoted from his position with the Flyers, was unable to push the league forward the way the owners had hoped. Snider had attempted to involve himself in the boardroom battles of the '70s, but was constantly overruled by the old guard. This time around, though, he would not only have a seat at the table, but be one of the most influential voices in the room.

The executive board agreed that they needed to move in a different direction; they needed a new leader who could take them to the next level and develop the economic model that would keep the owners solvent while still rewarding the players appropriately for their ser-vices. The Board of Governors created a hiring committee to find a new head for their league, whose position would henceforth be known as "commissioner." The committee consisted of five influential own-ers: Los Angeles' Bruce McNall, Detroit's Mike Ilitch, Edmonton's Peter Pocklington, Montreal's Ronald Corey, and Snider.

The group interviewed a plethora of candidates, including a former Canadian prime minister, the CEO of a healthcare company, and the president of a major insurance company. All of them showed extreme intelligence, but Snider was concerned that the committee was on the wrong track. The biggest issue was labor negotiations, and these candidates had no experience. Why were they even on the list? The group had a crazy idea—perhaps with an enormous, offer-he-can't-refuse compensation package, they could lure NBA commissioner

David Stern away from his current position. But it was a non-starter with Stern, as were the requests to pursue his No. 2, Russ Granik. Stern did, however, recommend a young upstart in his league, a lawyer from New York who was the brains behind the NBA's recent labor talks. That's when the committee first reached out to Gary Bettman.

The 40-year-old was an outside-the-box option and was the fifth of five candidates, in terms of ranking by the owners. When he was first informed of the idea, Snider was not impressed. Bettman was not a hockey guy and he was extremely young relative to the others vying for the position. How was he going to wrangle and control a couple dozen egotistical, highfalutin sports moguls? During the initial interview with the committee, Snider, who was backing a different candidate, came in with his usual narrowed eyes and stern glare, certain he was going to stick to his guns. But within minutes, Snider was stunned at what he heard from across the table. "He blew me away," Snider said, according to *The Instigator*. "I just felt that he had to be the guy. He was so well-versed in league matters and what was necessary, and the kinds of things he could do with the experience he had at the NBA."

During the interview, one owner even blurted out, "He knows more about our business than we do." Bettman had not only done his homework, but knew exactly how to take the league out of its funk and bring it into the future. Within an hour after he left the interview, the owners had called him to offer a contract. Bettman was hired on February 1, 1993, and became the league's first commissioner. His initial goal was to help work on the league's collective bargaining agreement (CBA) with the players, which was set to expire at the end of the following season.

While Snider could certainly find himself as an antagonist to the league's higher-ups, when push came to shove they were on the same page. Along with the rest of the league, the biggest battle in front of Snider in the '90s was an inevitable clashing of the owners and players in perhaps the first seriously contentious CBA negotiation. With

Bettman running the show for the first time, he leaned heavily on feedback from his owners, perhaps no one more than Snider. He had been front and center in NHL labor talks since the early 1980s, when he was first put on the league's committee tasked with negotiating with the players. That was the first time that Snider had showed dedication to honest and open negotiations with the players, something that was not always the case with his colleagues.

Even the players recognized that Snider's method of negotiation was the best of any owner in the league. During the 1992 players' strike that threatened to cancel the Stanley Cup playoffs, Snider rolled his eyes as his fellow owners lobbed veiled shots at the players through the media. Instead, Snider sat down with his counterparts and opened up his financial statements to show them that what they were asking for was unaffordable. He showed them that each year since 1989, their profit margin was dwindling, culminating in a 1992 season where, when the Flyers missed the playoffs, they lost over $2 million. It was only Spectacor's other businesses that kept Snider in the black—a luxury most owners did not have at that time. His moves earned a rare compliment by NHLPA president Bryan Trottier. "If everybody was like Jay Snider and Ed Snider," he said to the *Philadelphia Daily News*, "I don't think we'd have a problem. But not everybody's opening their books."

That reputation earned Snider an influential position within the league, as he was eventually asked to be the only owner to sit on the players' competition committee when it was created in 2005. He also played an enormous role in the 1994 CBA negotiations that would ultimately see half of the schedule canceled when the two sides could not agree on a new deal by the start of the season. After attempting and failing to utilize his voice during the WHA battles of the 1970s, Snider was finally being recognized for what he was: one of the most influential executives in professional sports and a leader among NHL owners.

During the previous decade, Snider had complained publicly about various demands made by the players' association. The biggest one was unrestricted free agency*—in fact, there were multiple times in his first 25 years running the Flyers that he threatened to sell the team if the league ever implemented free agency in a way that forced him to overpay for players. But despite his many public threats and rants, deep down he truly understood the players' plight. His concern was not for maximizing his profits or any other sinister motive often suggested of owners during sports league labor negotiations: rather, he was always interested in finding an equitable agreement that preserved the economic business model of the league while also guaranteeing the players their deserved salaries and benefits. Previous negotiations were often stymied when representatives on either side drew lines in the sand for no reason. To Snider, you never made a claim in a negotiation that wasn't based on demonstrable facts. He ran a hard bargain and would easily blow his lid if something upset him—but he did so with honesty and without ever trying to trick the other side. Not only would that be dishonorable, but it certainly would also not be productive. His goal was only to improve the league.

The issues in the 1994 negotiations centered around cost certainty. Player salaries were rising, and with no limit on what owners could spend, teams did not know whether or not they would turn a profit until the end of the season. Players and the media made the typical claims against the owners—they were billionaires who wanted to squeeze their players for all they were worth, they were making plenty of money already—all of the typical arguments that arise during sports labor negotiations. But Snider was not willing to let those comments slide. It did not bother him when people tried to blame business

---

* Unrestricted free agency is the method in which a player, when their contract expires, is free to negotiate with any team in the league once they hit a certain age and number of years of experience. This is relative to restricted free agency, where the previous team retains the player's rights.

owners for issues that existed in the economy, but he surely was not going to accept factually incorrect statements, especially when he could prove otherwise.

"We have to have some sensible system that works," he said after the NHL nixed the last players' proposal before the owners began canceling games. "Forget the small markets. We're in a large market and we're losing money ourselves. If you can't pay your mortgage, you sell your house. I don't want to sell the team. I want to operate it without going broke. I can't eat off the value of this team."*

"They want a free market," Snider said to the *Courier Post*, correcting the definition of something the players continuously claimed they were after. "A free market means no guaranteed contracts, no option years, no arbitration. They want a free market? How about if they all get one-year contracts, and if they don't play up to their standards, they take a pay cut or they get fired? That's a free market. They want to have their cake and eat it too."

The back and forth that progressed very publicly in the media bothered Snider. His sole care was getting a deal done that worked for both sides. Frankly, he became enraged at those on either side of the table who were looking to muscle their way to the spotlight. "If the players really want to get a deal done, we can get it done in two weeks," he said to the *Philadelphia Inquirer*. "If not, I'm willing to throw out the season. I'm willing to throw out two seasons or three seasons. I don't want to stay in the game if I'm losing money.... I can't imagine me sticking around for this mess."

The first lockout in NHL history bothered Snider perhaps more than anything else that had happened throughout his tenure with the

---

* One of the practices that greatly bothered Snider through the years, both in labor negotiations and in corporate America, was when people utilized someone's net worth to claim they could afford to lose money, either via operations or taxes. A net worth is solely an estimate of the value of someone's assets, not necessarily how much money they have.

Flyers. To him, it was very simple. Yet all he saw were some players publicly berating the owners, and some owners publicly berating the players. He wasn't interested in gossip; he wasn't interested in posturing. He just wanted to run his sports businesses. Even at this point, he was one of the few owners whose entire livelihood was in his sports business. Many other owners had other companies that made them money while they toyed with a hockey franchise.

By December, Snider was publicly musing on ways the two sides could come to an agreement. From his perspective, he was simply looking for a way to keep salaries in check. He preferred a salary cap, which the players were vehemently against, but he recognized that there were potentially other ways in which that could be attained. He offered the players to drop the salary and rookie cap ideas in exchange for the players dropping their arbitration rights. In his mind, one of the reasons owners kept paying inflated salaries was because arbitration was an extremely painful process and they were willing to overpay in order to avoid it.

At the beginning of January 1995, the owners made a "final proposal" to the players, and the players rejected it, making Snider furious. Reportedly, the proposal was extremely similar to the one the players had submitted weeks earlier. It appeared to him that NHLPA executive director Bob Goodenow was simply looking to have the final say. In the players' next proposal, Snider was one of seven owners voting to accept it. However, his true anger came when the owners received the players' "final proposal" days later, which was essentially the same deal the owners presented earlier. One executive submitted a motion to the board to send the owners' final proposal back to the players with a message to accept it or else.

Snider was enraged, stating, "That's the dumbest motion I've ever heard," according to *The Instigator*. The offer was perfectly acceptable, but he felt his colleagues were simply catering to their overinflated egos. Snider could care less about the optics, he just wanted to get back to business. Nonetheless, the players' proposal was barely defeated in a vote, with Snider one of the 12 who voted to accept it, against 14 who rejected it.

The owners and players then got into a room for a last-minute attempt to break the impasse and salvage what remained of the season. "In my heart of hearts, I want to be optimistic," Snider said to the *Philadelphia Inquirer*. He wasn't one to ever give up. "What's already happened has been the biggest disappointment of my career." The meeting would end up being the turning point that saved the 1995 season.

With the potential half-season hanging in the balance, Snider couldn't hold his tongue any longer. He perceived the other owners as being nonchalant and casual with the lockout, since many of their teams were not their primary source of income. They were ready to give in to the players so they could move on and be done with it. But Snider knew the league's economics were not working for him. He agreed to shut down his entire business model, thereby putting himself, his family, and his employees at risk, all in the service of creating an economic system that would inure to everyone's benefit—yet he felt he was the only one willing to fully sacrifice for the greater good. The time for games was done—it was now time for them to take responsibility as business owners and fix the issue once and for all.

In the midst of a Board of Governors meeting, Snider stood up and became animated and irate. "Look," he said poignantly, "we've come this far, we need to have a system that makes sense." He pointed at Bettman and the league executives (though everyone in the room understood he was really talking to his fellow owners) and said, "You guys have to get this done." His passion and dedication to the league's health was apparent, and his outburst settled some of his colleagues in the room, creating the pathway to come to an agreement with the players at the last minute to save what remained of the season.

It was typical for Snider to be pointed and straightforward, even confronting fellow owners he felt were hurting the game. Bruins owner Jeremy Jacobs recalls Snider getting angry at him at a board meeting over the Bruins' ticket prices being too high. Snider called it "unconscionable." Yet, a few years later, when Flyers ticket prices went higher than their counterparts in Boston, Snider told him it was just part of the business model and keeping up with the economics of the game.

But his pointed statements were nothing if not coming from an honest place. He had a deep-rooted love of the game and cared profoundly about the players who made the game special. That care came through quite evidently to everyone around him. "There was a lot of compassion shown in that meeting," said Flyers coach Terry Murray, referring to the last-minute meeting that helped seal the agreement. "There was an understanding of where the players are from Mr. Snider. There was no talking down to the players."

"Mr. Snider really rallied them," Eric Lindros said of his owner, who continued to pay all of his full-time employees during the shutdown, according to the *Philadelphia Daily News*. "It makes me feel good."

Snider's calm under the pressure of labor negotiations earned him a spot close to Bettman, and eventually to David Stern, as Snider would represent the 76ers during the NBA's labor negotiations throughout the '90s. He and Bettman developed a very close relationship from the start. Just prior to a meeting during the 1994 lockout negotiations, Snider approached Bettman privately and warned him that, once the meeting started, he was going to oppose the new commissioner on an item on the agenda. Sure enough, when the meeting got underway, Snider passionately and fervently disagreed with the league's head in a way that, if he didn't know it was coming, would probably have made Bettman extremely nervous and uncomfortable. Instead, Bettman was prepared, fought his case as well, and the owners eventually sided with the commissioner. After the meeting, Snider shook Bettman's hand and told him he did a great job. From that moment on, Bettman always leaned on Snider as a helpful and passionate voice in the game.

The two would talk at least once per week, just to catch up, discuss league matters, or have a personal conversation. Snider would go to New York half a dozen times a year to have lunch with the commissioner. And, of course, Bettman would hear from the Flyers chairman anytime he was upset about an officials' call. Bettman would assure him that he'd pass along the message to the league's hockey operations department—though, of course, he never did. Snider was on the league's executive committee for almost his entire ownership tenure. He had Bettman's ear on every league matter, perhaps more so than any other owner during the same time period.

By the end of 1999, teams were already saving money for what they knew would be a potential lockout in 2004, when the current CBA would expire. The '90s had not proven successful for the owners as salaries continued to skyrocket and small-market teams were being left in the lurch. The health of individual franchises was falling, and even some of the larger-market teams were unprofitable.

This time around, the owners would not be directly involved in negotiations, instead leaving the job to Bettman and his staff—though of course the Board of Governors would be kept in the loop. Therefore, Snider spent much of the negotiations on the sideline but was a close confidant to Bettman during the course of the meetings that ultimately canceled the entire 2004–05 season. During the negotiations, Snider found himself with much more time, allowing him to focus newfound energy on the other segments of his business. But the lack of hockey, yet again, bothered him to no end.

He and the rest of the league staked their position on a salary cap, which would be linked to league revenues. If the game succeeded, the players would succeed. By knowing exactly how much they would be spending on player salaries each year, it gave teams economic certainty and the ability to plan more than a year ahead. But the negotiations were even more bombastic and personal at this point. Players were regularly calling guys like Snider, Jacobs, and Chicago's Bill Wirtz liars and cheats, while owners were sending the shots right back.

This time around, Snider's financial position was much stronger. Instead of having every penny on the line as majority owner of his businesses, he now had Comcast's financial resources behind him (more on this in chapter 13). And with the Center and Spectrum selling more non-sporting tickets than any other facility in the world, he had plenty of revenue to fall back on for as long as hockey needed to get their economic situation on track.

The players' union frustrated Snider much more during these labor talks. Goodenow took a significantly stronger position than he had in 1994, and it was creating incredible issues that could not be resolved. Snider was 100 percent behind Bettman and supported him throughout the entire endeavor, both publicly and privately. When Goodenow publicly mused that Snider should join the negotiations, since he had helped the last time, Snider flat-out rejected the idea. "I don't need aggravation from Bob Goodenow," he said matter-of-factly to the *Philadelphia Inquirer*. "I might jump over the table and choke him to death. That would not be good."

Though not directly involved with the eventual deal that shaped the modern NHL economy, Snider was instrumental in adding a piece to the agreement that bolstered the health of the league overnight. One of the biggest issues of the league economy in the 1990s and early 2000s was that the large-market teams ran roughshod over the small-market teams that could not afford to keep up. While that was beneficial for a handful of NHL cities like Philadelphia, New York, Toronto, Montreal, Chicago, and Detroit, it was not conducive to a healthy league. Instead, Snider went against a passionate capitalistic belief and jumped at the idea of revenue sharing—an idea he had spoken about as early as the 1960s, based on his experience with the much more successful NFL. That plan was adopted and has since created a much healthier collection of teams within the NHL family.

The NHL's version of the plan is, in essence, a socialistic tenet that takes a percentage of money from the top-10 earning franchises and redistributes it to the lower-earning franchises to help financially struggling teams in any given year. With the Flyers consistently near the top of the league in gross revenue, the plan meant that Snider's club would contribute to the pot nearly every year and rarely, if ever, receive anything from it. It is extremely ironic that perhaps Snider's crowning achievement as a leader in the NHL was something that so fervently went against his core principles in how he viewed the world. He knew that the league was only as strong as its weakest link. The Flyers could be bringing in hundreds of millions of dollars per year, but it did not matter, as long as even just one other franchise was bleeding. Snider knew that the league functioned best when it worked as a single unit, and when he got on board, the other owners had no choice but to follow someone who had previously seen it all.

But despite his acquiescence when it came to league matters, Snider was steadfast in his perception that the Flyers were continually treated poorly by league officials, including the referees. His fire and passion that presented itself for the first time in the '70s did not diminish with age. Rather, he always found a way to explode after a referee's decision cost his team a game, regardless of the rank someone had in the NHL front office.

One of the first hires Gary Bettman made was Brian Burke, the recently fired general manager of the Hartford Whalers. Burke was to be his confidant as the league's executive vice president and director of hockey operations, allowing Bettman more time to work on legal matters. Burke was someone who Snider loved and respected. The truculent, silver-haired executive had been around hockey his entire life and was even once an employee of Snider's. Prior to the 1977–78 season, Keith Allen signed Burke to a one-year, minor-league contract with a one-year option for $10,000. He spent his only full professional hockey season playing with the Maine Mariners that year, winning a Calder Cup with the organization. After playing the season with the Mariners, Burke made plans to leave hockey and go to Harvard Law School. He approached Allen and informed him of the decision and mentioned that he owed the Flyers $5,000, since he was not going to complete the contract. Allen rejected the offer, saying, "Keep it. Good luck with the rest of your career."

For several years afterward, the now-famous NHL executive was one of Snider's proudest disciples. Anytime he saw Burke at a league event, Snider would throw his arm around the much-larger Burke, pull him in close, and inevitably tell anyone within earshot, "This guy played for me *and* went to Harvard Law School!" Allen's management style was learned from Snider, in that you always take care of the players the best you can. And Snider, as usual, had immense pride in anyone who ever stepped on the ice for his organization—in this case, even if it was only in the minor leagues.

But even the closest of friends were not immune from Snider's wrath when he felt his team was given the short end of the stick. Since Burke oversaw the league's officials, part of his job was to travel around the country and attend games in each arena—something that often put him in Snider's firing line. And Bettman was often the recipient of Snider's regular phone calls each season, in which he gave his unfiltered opinion about the league's referees and where Bettman could shove them.

Sometimes Snider utilized his staff to send the message, though it was always clear the note originated from the top. A May 12, 1996, semifinal matchup between the Flyers and Panthers ended in double overtime, with the Panthers scoring the winning goal and securing themselves a 3–2 lead in the series, in which they would eventually emerge victorious. A rough matchup from the get-go, referee Don

Koharski put the whistle away and called no penalties in the last 27 minutes of regulation and both overtime periods. In that span, the Flyers felt the Panthers players took many liberties that went uncalled by Koharski. Burke, who was at the Spectrum for the game, was extremely proud of his referee's performance. Not that it mattered: when you were in Philadelphia, only one person's opinion was relevant.

Just a few seconds after retreating into the officials' room with his crew, a knock came on the door. Burke popped his head out and saw a security guard with a stern look on his face. "Mr. Clarke would like to see you," he said. Burke walked down the hallway to the Spectrum offices, where he found himself in front of GM Bob Clarke, coach Terry Murray, and Snider. Although Snider sat quietly for the entire meeting, it was clear he was as upset, if not more so, than the other two participants. Clarke began laying into Burke about the officiating. Burke listened politely, but was known for his tough exterior and refusal to take excuses from anyone. When Clarke was done reciting his list of transgressions, Burke replied, "You know, it's not officiating. Your team's just getting beat. As long as your players feel they have that excuse, that they're getting screwed, they're never going to win." Needless to say, the three men opposite him disagreed with his assessment.

Snider's run-ins with Burke were not always so polite, though. As was often the case, his emotions sometimes got the better of him when a poor referee's call was involved. Game 2 of the 1997 Eastern Conference Finals was on a Sunday afternoon against the Rangers. In the midst of a 5–4 loss, the two teams battled hard and took many cheap shots at each other, with referee Paul Devorski letting them go. In attendance with his kids and some of their friends, Burke felt his referee could probably have cooled the temperature of the game a bit by calling a few matching minor penalties, just to send a message to the teams without causing either one a disadvantage. Nonetheless, Burke was comfortable with the officiating and thought nothing of it. Snider inherently disagreed with that analysis. With Burke standing in the Center hallway outside the dressing rooms, with multiple children in tow, Snider walked by and muttered audibly, "What do you think of your fucking referees?"

As was typical when confronted by an angry owner or general manager, Burke ignored it—everybody always complained when their team lost. But a minute later or so, Snider returned, went right up to Burke's face, and started yelling at him, "You and your fucking referees!" He began bumping Burke chest to chest and ranting, like a baseball manager to an umpire after a faulty strike call. After about six seconds of this, Snider walked away. Burke's son, Patrick (who would later go on to work for the Flyers hockey operations department), asked his dad why he, a man much larger than Snider, didn't punch the Flyers owner. "I was counting to 10," Burke replied. "I was only at six."

The next morning, while sitting in his office at the NHL's headquarters in New York, Bettman barged in to Burke's office, seething from a story he had just heard through the grapevine. The two argued about whether or not Snider should be fined, with Burke defending his former boss. Burke prevailed, but, as was typical after a Snider blow-up, his phone rang a few hours later and a recognizable voice was on the other line, sounding remorseful. "I know you could have broken me in half," Snider said. "You're twice my size and half my age. I shouldn't have done it, but I was just upset."

Even Bettman was not immune from Snider's in-person confrontations. A playoff matchup against the Rangers featured two early, questionable penalty calls on the Flyers that led to two power-play goals and a Rangers lead. When they went on to win by one goal, tying the series at one game apiece, Bettman, who was in the crowd with his family for the contest, walked quickly back to his car and tried to get out of the parking lot as fast as possible.

As he was about to make the turn out of the lot, he saw a car blocking the exit, preventing him from leaving. A security guard got out and approached his driver-side window. "Mr. Snider wants to see you," he said. "Now." Bettman was escorted back to the main entrance of the building, already emptied of the nearly 20,000 fans that had witnessed what Snider believed was a travesty. When Bettman walked through the front door, Snider was standing in the foyer of the Center, waiting for the commissioner.

"Do you really want the games played like that?" Snider asked with his face beet red and his hands gesticulating wildly. Naturally, he did not even give Bettman a chance to answer, instead going on a tangent for about 20 minutes before finally allowing Bettman to speak—not that anything he said would change the chairman's opinion. Meanwhile, Bettman's wife and young children peered through the glass, watching the debacle unfold. The commissioner laughs about the story today, recalling with a big smile the passionate rage that Snider would unleash in order to protect his team. Those who felt his wrath were often able to see past it to the core of Snider's being. "He was always a builder," recalled Brian Burke. "He always wanted to leave the league in a better place than it was the day before.... He was viewed as a leader and a consensus builder by the other owners."

Snider's wrath toward anyone he believed short-changed his Flyers was both one of his greatest and worst personality traits. It gave those who loved him an extra reason to respect his love for the Flyers and those who worked for the club. It also gave those who disliked him a reason to roll their eyes at his continued off-ice charades. Nonetheless, it continued to reveal the passion he had for his organization and ensuring its future success, both on and off the ice. That passion was critical as he entered the next stage of his professional life, when one of the country's largest corporations came unexpectedly calling just a few years later.

The Comcast Deal

THE WAY IN WHICH Snider ended up partnering with Comcast is perhaps one of the most unusual business stories that ever occurred in sports. Not only did executives from three separate companies coincidentally align just perfectly and at the right time, but the structure of the resulting entity is one at which any competent corporate attorney would have laughed hysterically if you had approached one for advice. Nonetheless, its completion further cemented the legacy of Snider as one of the most brilliant businessmen to ever grace Philadelphia, if not the entire sports world.

The first of these pieces was the 76ers. Despite finally coming to an agreement on the construction of what would soon be known as the Center, Snider was still very nervous about Harold Katz. The basketball owner did not like the Flyers chairman, yet they were forced to get along as any lessor and lessee should. While the lack of control of his main tenant bothered Snider, there was no way around it. The easiest solution to the issue would simply be to purchase the 76ers, but there was no chance Katz would even consider speaking to his regular sparring partner about the possibility.

At this time, Snider was still struggling with the position into which he placed himself due to the construction of the new arena. His personal finances were stretched thin, and the stress Snider was putting his family under made him struggle to sleep at night. With a

$200 million arena under construction and uncertainty still surrounding other tenants, the strain was enormous. He had risked more than ever, and with a 20-year mortgage on the building, it was likely to last for the rest of his life.

The third, and potentially most important, piece was the major corporation that called Philadelphia its home—Comcast, run by the Roberts family. Ralph Roberts founded Comcast in 1969 after running a small, subscriber cable operator for six years in Mississippi called American Cable Systems. He saw an opportunity in Philadelphia to expand his cable business to a larger region and relocated his family to the area. His son, Brian, became interested in the cable business at a young age, often following his father into meetings to get a close, hands-on experience of the media empire. Brian would graduate from the Wharton School at the University of Pennsylvania and, upon graduation, immediately began working for the family business, including stringing cable at new subscribers' homes. Like Snider, he worked his way up from the most menial jobs to be named president of the company in 1991 at age 31. At that point, Comcast had $657 million in annual revenue and by 1995 had grown that figure to over $3 billion. But Brian had grand visions of creating a cable giant, the likes of which the world had never seen. Comcast had about 12,000 employees at that time and had the resources that could help Snider's entire company grow to previously unforeseen levels.

Comcast was always interested in the sports business. Not so much managing a team, but in garnering the distribution rights for their games. As the 1980s progressed, the consumer demand for sports programming was immense. ESPN had been founded in 1979 and, over the following decade, grown itself into an impressive business. The Robertses were interested in replicating that business, but catered specifically to a Philadelphia audience that was crazy about their teams.

That desire is what drew Ralph and Snider together for the first time in the '80s. As two of the most successful businessmen in the city, they had met multiple times and became friendly over the years. And, in the 1980s, they had convened a meeting between themselves and a few other bigshots in the cable industry to figure out how to make that dream a reality. With intense negotiations and incredible posturing on all sides, the meeting ended in a stalemate, each side claiming their asset was the most important piece of the deal. They all separated, though Snider and Ralph kept in touch and continued their light friendship.

A few years passed, and Comcast's business continued to grow. Yet Brian, now running the company, was continuously bothered by the result of that meeting he had witnessed years earlier. Comcast had spent the previous few years putting their money into major acquisitions, including a $1.4 billion deal to buy a majority stake in QVC (the home shopping network) and $1.59 billion to purchase a rival in the cable industry, E.W. Scripps. Other major competitors were beginning to enter the sports team business, including Turner Broadcasting and CableVision. But the one business in which Comcast had no presence was the regional sports network they had dreamed about.

That dream suddenly appeared within reach when Ralph came into the office one morning and mentioned to his son that there was an option to purchase one of the city's teams—Ralph thought it was the Eagles but could not remember for certain. The elder Roberts was far from a sports fan, but he knew an opportunity when he saw one. A visionary, he had a distinct ability to look years ahead to see where the business was heading. More than 20 years before his company would acquire NBC in one of the largest media deals up to that time (2011), Ralph turned Brian onto the possibility of utilizing Philadelphia's sports franchises for their own television network benefit.

As Brian examined the landscape, he realized that it was not the Eagles, but the 76ers who were potentially on the market for a new owner. Pat Croce, a former strength and conditioning coach with both the Flyers and 76ers, was leaning on his friend Katz to give him an option to purchase the team. Although Katz continuously insisted the basketball squad was not for sale, Croce wore him down, eventually allowing for the possibility that a deal could be struck. Croce, however, did not have the personal financing to even consider making the deal on his own. Instead, he got in touch with the Roberts family through an intermediary.

Croce's pitch to Comcast included purchasing the team, building a new basketball arena, and installing him as the head of the entire thing. The Robertses were not interested in building a new arena, but the pitch for the 76ers—valued at $125 million—intrigued them. Sports teams did not come on the market very often, and they were almost always an asset that appreciated quickly. But as a standalone squad, the 76ers were more of a risk. They did not own the building in which they played, making them subservient to their landlord—Ed Snider. With that in mind, Ralph decided to pay a visit to an old friend.

Although Comcast was preparing to enter the regional sports network industry, they realized that by owning the local sports teams, they could guarantee their first tenants on that network. After explaining the situation, Ralph sprung the question to Snider. How interested would he be in selling the company? Not just the Flyers, but the entire thing: the Spectrum, the new arena, the Flyers, and all of the related companies under Spectacor's management umbrella. He was surprised at the suggestion, but was not opposed to the idea in principle. "Jay had gone his own way, and my other children had gotten involved in other things," he said in Jay Greenberg's *Full Spectrum*. "I wanted to spend more time in California. For estate planning, for overall planning, I had already explored a few avenues."

With the Comcast offer hanging over him, Snider was unsure of what to do. He was nearly debilitated by the number of personal guarantees and collateral he had out on the building. He had already mortgaged his life once before, and though it worked out to his benefit, the situation was now different. It wasn't just a few million he had put up, nor was he in his early thirties. This time around, he was guaranteeing over $200 million and was 63 years old. He desperately wanted a way out from behind that shadow, even if it meant selling the asset he worked 30 years to develop—his beloved Flyers.

On the other hand, regardless of the money he would make by selling, he wasn't ready to retire. It was never about the money for him—it was about building companies, creating a future. Plus, he had no desire to leave. For years he was convinced that his own father met an early death because he retired, lost his life's meaning, and slowly descended into poor health. Snider was much too proud and much too ambitious to allow that to happen to himself. He wasn't ready to give it all up just yet.

He went to a meeting at the Comcast offices on February 24, willing to explore his options but also skeptical that he truly wanted to sell. After lengthy discussions between Snider, the Robertses, and a few advisors from each side, it was clear that Snider was amenable to selling his assets, but he was not interested in retiring. At that point, the Comcast guys excused themselves to discuss privately, while Snider and an advisor sat at the table, discussing their own possibilities. When the Robertses returned, Snider confessed, "Brian, I don't want to sell out."

"That's okay," they replied. "Because we don't want to buy you all out, either." Comcast was almost fully behind the deal, but had one concern: they had no clue how to run a hockey team, nor did they want to. For them, the value of the deal was in the media rights and the potential new sports network. They did not want the perception of a large, faceless corporation making the calls of whether or not to sign a star player. That was not a formula for fan satisfaction. "The only way we're going to do the deal is if you stay and run it," they said.

Snider was on board as soon as the suggestion was made. He had considered selling his beloved Flyers, but he would never have entered the meeting in the first place if he thought he was going to be asked to leave the organization. In this potential scenario, he could keep his job, keep his team—even if he didn't own the majority of it—while getting the financial support and organizational resources that Comcast could provide. Just maybe it could be a deal that satisfied both sides and allowed each to win in both the short- and long-term. "The only way we're going to do a deal is if I can stay and run it," Snider said.

The sides very quickly agreed on a plan. Comcast would create a new partnership called "Comcast-Spectacor." They would purchase the 76ers and contribute it to the entity. Snider would contribute the Flyers, the Spectrum, the new arena, and all of his subsidiaries. The entire package was worth about $500 million. Snider would lower his share of the company to 20 percent. Each of his kids cashed out their 5 percent shares, and with the Tobins' 12 percent* and Pat Croce purchasing 2 percent, Comcast would end up owning 66 percent of Comcast-Spectacor. Snider received his payout in Comcast stock, which was a mutual agreement: he wanted to avoid tax implications of a cash sale, while the Robertses wanted to ensure that their new business partner had a vested interest in the continued success of the company. The entire deal was done with just a few people in the room. It was only about a month from the first conversation to the handshake agreement.[†]

Most importantly, and most surprisingly to the business community, Snider would be the managing partner of the new entity, having full management rights despite his being a minority owner. In the

---

* Fran and Sylvan Tobin, local businesspeople and philanthropists, approached Snider about becoming minority partners in the team early in its existence. They remained quiet but fully supportive business partners for decades.

† By 2019, Comcast's revenue would balloon to nearly $110 billion. Though Comcast-Spectacor itself only accounted for a small percentage of that revenue, their regional sports network business accounted for an enormous piece of that success.

midst of final negotiations with Comcast, Phil Weinberg sat with then Comcast CFO Larry Smith. As Smith perused the terms of the deal, he looked up and said, "Let me see if I have this right. We're going to put all this money up and we're going to own 66 percent of the company, but we're not going to have any say about anything?" Weinberg matter-of-factly replied, "Yeah, that's right, Larry."

Comcast had never before agreed to this kind of deal, nor did they ever do so again. In the many acquisitions the company has made in its history, Snider was the only person who was given majority control of a subsidiary without owning the majority share. An astute observer would question why, but the answer is simple: the Roberts family had complete trust in Snider. Despite his being difficult to work with at times and being one of the tougher negotiators of his era, he was always honest when it came to business dealings. In addition, he valued his integrity over everything else. With a friendship that went back nearly a decade, and through the brief negotiations for this deal, the Robertses and Snider saw the same end goal and envisioned a similar road to travel. Ralph had passed down a saying to his son: always go into business with an expert. When Comcast purchased an existing business with the intention to continue operating it, they always made sure to hire someone to run it who was a specialist in that field. When you purchase the Philadelphia Flyers, there is only one person in the world proficient enough to run it to perfection.

But, of course, Comcast was a public corporation with millions of shareholders. The Robertses did not leave themselves without wiggle room. Instead, they placed mechanisms in the deal in which both sides could buy each other out at various points. It would be extremely unlikely for Snider to desire or have the financial backing to purchase Comcast's stake, so the clause essentially gave Comcast an exit ramp to their advantage. If there were problems, Snider could cash out the remainder of his ownership or Comcast could force him out. Each side was confident in their new business partner, but the future was always uncertain. The deal worked magically for both sides, a win-win that was evident almost immediately.

According to the SEC filing in 1996, Comcast distributed over 5 million shares of its stock to all seven members of the Snider family—Snider himself and each of his six children—to finalize the deal. It perhaps was the most brilliant business decision he ever made. In the 20 years between the transaction and Snider's death, Comcast's stock increased more than 13-fold, making the ultimate appreciation of his value more than it would have been had he simply held on to the majority ownership of the team. Yet, by holding a minority interest of the new entity for the remainder of his life, that value also appreciated, which would be cashed out upon his death.

On March 14, rumors began to leak of the impending deal. As a public company, any acquisition of this size required approval from Comcast shareholders. Once investors found out, the news quickly made its way to media outlets. The next morning, front-page stories were plastered all across Philadelphia and the investment world. A cable company was looking to invest $500 million in two sports arenas and a couple of professional sports teams. The deal was, at the time, the largest sports acquisition package in U.S. history. Investors scrambled, with a volume of Comcast shares traded that day of nearly 5 million, more than five times the previous day's volume. The stock dropped nearly 10 percent by the end of the day as Wall Street tried to figure out the angle.

But those who were a bit more astute understood the value of Comcast's new acquisition. The company was looking to get into the regional network business. Between the Spectrum and the new arena, there would be about 500 events per year that Comcast would have first choice to broadcast, including 82 76ers games and 82 Flyers games, plus any potential playoff games and special events. All of those eyes, which currently went to PRISM (which was sold by Spectacor in 1983) for Flyers and 76ers games, would suddenly be tuned to a potential new Comcast network. The acquisition would also allow them to test their business model in Philadelphia before expanding it to other major markets throughout the United States.

The next day, Philadelphia mayor Ed Rendell held an impromptu press conference to confirm the deal as reported. "It brings a Philadelphia company, a strong, stable, growth-oriented company, owning our two stadiums and our clubs, and that's great," he said to the *Philadelphia Daily News*. He also confirmed that because the new arena was still under construction, the city legally had the right to veto any deal—but reinforced that it was unlikely to happen. "A sale to Comcast with Ralph and Brian Roberts, two people we have abundant confidence in, we'd have no problem approving."

Snider was the clear short-term beneficiary of the deal. Just by signing on the dotted line, he would be relieved of nearly $200 million of long-term debt, along with all of the personal guarantees and collateral he had put up in order to get the financing to build the new arena in the first place. As part of the agreement, Snider also got the Phillies on board to sign a television deal with Comcast once the new network was established. Almost overnight, the cable giant had secured themselves the broadcast rights to three of the four biggest players in Philadelphia sports, all broadcast on their eventual network. They had guaranteed over 300 major league sporting events on a network that did not yet even exist. They had miles to go but were already in a position to have incredible success.

As time progressed, it was clear that Comcast had made the winning move. And when the NHL Board of Governors met at Devils owner John McMullen's house in New Jersey to discuss the Comcast acquisition (any ownership change of an organization requires league approval), everyone involved was ecstatic at the possibility of bringing a partner such as Comcast into the league. The vote was unanimous.

Shortly after the deal was signed, Brian Roberts and Snider began spending time together, getting to know each other as business partners should. Roberts was a diehard Flyers fan and had even attended the Soviet game in 1976, in addition to both Stanley Cup parades. He had rooted for the team his entire life and was thrilled to now essentially own the franchise. He also attended many games at the beginning of the partnership, using them as opportunities to better acquaint himself with his partner and begin a relationship that ultimately lasted until Snider's death. In that relationship, like all others, he quickly learned about the positives and negatives of Snider's passion for his team.

Roberts joined Snider for a Flyers-Rangers playoff game the first year after their partnership began. Sitting in the visiting team's owner's suite at Madison Square Garden, Roberts asked Snider if an old friend, an HBO executive, could sit with them. Unbeknownst to Roberts, his guest was a diehard Rangers fan and was not shy about making it known throughout the game. When the Rangers tied the game at 1–1, Snider listened to the intruder clap and holler and shot Roberts a glare. When the Rangers tied the game at 2–2 with only a few minutes left, there was celebratory screaming as the chairman seethed. Fortunately for everyone involved, the Flyers scored with just seven seconds left to seal the game. But when the game ended, as they walked toward the parking lot, Snider grabbed Roberts by the shirt and before storming off, said, "Don't you ever bring a Rangers fan to my box again." Business partners or not, Snider still did not mess around when it came to his team. You were either with him or you were against him. Roberts was certain never to make that mistake again.

The two quickly became close friends and confidants. While Snider was left with full management rights for the organization, he would still run every major decision by Roberts out of respect. And Roberts would, more often than not, make Snider his last call before making a major decision at Comcast. The two had incredibly different backgrounds regarding how they achieved their current levels of success, but they also contrasted each other perfectly in running both Comcast-Spectacor and the entirety of Comcast itself.

As the years progressed, they were each the other's most important business asset, which was crucial as the business was set to rapidly expand. Snider now had an even larger empire to oversee: the Flyers, the 76ers, the Center, the Spectrum, Comcast SportsNet, and all of the related subsidiary companies beneath. Each segment would have a dedicated executive to run it (Pat Croce would ultimately run the 76ers for the first five years), but Snider would be at the top of the corporate hierarchy, as he had been since 1967. It was a huge undertaking, one in which he would certainly see mixed success, depending on who was polled. But there is no doubt that this new empire had more potential than he had ever seen in his 30-plus years in the business.

14

Expanding the Empire

WITH CONSTRUCTION OF the new building underway, Snider was finally able to turn his attention back to business. He and Peter Luukko were beginning to spend more time together discussing business opportunities. Luukko had worked his way up the ladder through a long relationship with Snider, leading to his appointment as president and CEO of the Spectrum. They met in the '80s when Snider was living in California full-time, and the two had formed a brotherly bond in the years since he had started working for Snider's companies.

Snider's entrepreneurial spirit was not something he kept to himself. Rather, he looked for like-minded people so that his ambition and excitement for new ideas would rub off on those around him. He not only accepted minor setbacks, but he encouraged them, so long as they came honestly and with the right effort. When Luukko first came to Philadelphia to work directly under Snider, he was tasked with finding an event that could draw people to the Sports Complex in the dog days of summer, when both the Flyers and 76ers were in their respective offseasons. The consensus was a barbecue festival in the parking lot next to the Spectrum.

The organization contracted with some of the top rib restaurants from around the country, along with bands and carnival companies. When the day finally arrived, the temperature was close to 100 degrees, which felt even more scorching on top of the black asphalt of the parking lot. Few people attended, leaving the team with a $50,000 loss for the event. Nonetheless, Snider was exuberant. He barged into Luukko's office, expressing his excitement. "I love this," he said. "It's great, it's so creative, it's so fun." He reassured his executive that the idea was worthwhile and that they would not get hit with bad weather two years in a row.

The following year, the organization arranged the same event, but even bigger. They amped up their marketing campaign and contracted with even more vendors. The day of the event saw pouring rain and tornado warnings and the organization lost close to $100,000. Snider returned to Luukko's office with his same enthusiasm. "I love this rib festival," he repeated, before his executive interrupted him.

"Look," Luukko said, exasperated, "if you're trying to fire me, make it quick."

Snider laughed and assured him that he really was in favor of trying these new ideas. The two had a conversation during which they agreed that a food festival was not their forte. But the logistics and the business model stuck in the back of their minds for many years, lying dormant, before a new opportunity arose. In the late '90s, the idea came to hold a block party during the Flyers and 76ers playoff runs, inviting fans to come down to the Sports Complex and the new CoreStates Center to celebrate in the hours before the games. They took what they had learned from setting up the rib festival years earlier and created the first of what would be many block parties at which thousands of fans attended. The first year, the organization grossed over $600,000 from the block party and utilized its success to develop ideas for how to grow the company even more.

That regular event led to the eventual expansion of the Center (with what became known as the Pavilion), which allowed them to hold similar parties during the winter. It also sowed the seeds for what would be known years later as Xfinity Live!, a sports and entertainment venue for use during events. The bottom line was that Snider was perfectly willing to lose exorbitant sums of money in search of the next big idea that would work for them. He did not throw money away, but if he felt an executive did the proper research, put in the right amount of effort, and made an honest attempt at a new idea, he was happy to invest and was never upset if it failed. He knew that it was small failures that often led to the largest successes.

But in the early '90s, with Luukko working in a managerial role in the Spectrum, Snider got frustrated. He saw potential in Luukko, but was not convinced Luukko himself understood his own talent. Unprompted, the chairman walked into Luukko's office one day and laid it all out there. "I think you could be the greatest arena manager ever," Snider said. "I think you are. I think you can help me a lot with the Flyers. But I think you can do more." Luukko was a bit surprised—he was ambitious and knew he was doing good work, but here was his boss hinting that it was not enough. "You're my entrepreneur," Snider continued. "If you look at the roles, you're the entrepreneur here."

Snider had seen something in Luukko that he seldom saw in others in his decades leading the organization—he saw himself. With Snider's resources and Luukko's drive and intelligence, he foresaw the future of what is now Comcast-Spectacor. The two discussed the management structure of the company (as it was before the Comcast acquisition) and where Luukko could fit in the long term. "Listen," Snider said, "when I first started the Flyers, I had to make every decision. But then as I got older and got into more things, I began to let people make decisions. As long as the outcome is right, does it really matter how they got there?" He pointed at Luukko and made an accusation that set the company on a path to much larger success. "I think you're too involved in everything. You need to expand. You can create a lot of things here. But you can't have your finger on every button. Because I think you can do great things and we can build a bigger company than we have now."

The turn of events was unexpected for Luukko. With his ambition, he envisioned an even larger role one day, but to have the chairman of the company walk into his office unannounced and tell him that he had what it took to lead? That was something that Snider did not do too often—but if that was what the chairman wanted, that was how it was going to be. Very few people said no to Snider. It was textbook Snider management—Luukko was deeply involved in every aspect of the company, but eventually Snider felt his involvement was on the verge of micromanagement. Did he want to be involved in the legal side? Well, the company had a lawyer already. Did he want to be in the financial side? The company had a CFO already. Each segment of the company was already running smoothly—what Snider needed was for someone to oversee the entire management tree and look at everything from a broader perspective. Snider was only one man, and with the company looking to expand exponentially, there was no way he could do it himself.

With Luukko taking a larger role, he became attached to Snider, shadowing him and becoming a second head at the top of the organization. He developed a similar love and passion for the Flyers as the chairman. Although the two would be in meetings most of each day strategizing about the various companies right up until game time, when it came time for puck drop, there was only one thing that mattered. "For those three hours," Luukko explained, "we didn't give a shit about anything but the Philadelphia Flyers. That's all we cared about."

The two even saw eye to eye when it came to the Flyers—especially when it came to perceived mistreatment by the officials. On May 2, 1999, the Flyers were fighting for their season, down 3–2 in games to the Toronto Maple Leafs and facing elimination from the first playoff round. The two teams fought valiantly through nearly an entire game without a goal being scored. When referee Terry Gregson called a late elbowing penalty on John LeClair with under three minutes to go, Snider jumped up from his seat, infuriated. His anger mounted when the Leafs scored with 60 seconds left in the game to clinch the series and send the Flyers packing.

On the walk down to the locker room, Snider made a beeline to the officials' room and barged through the door, blowing past league security, who were not nearly quick enough to keep up with him. Luukko, always supporting his boss's passion, held the doors shut behind him, leaving the guards unsure how to handle the two men. Meanwhile, Snider stood in the middle of the officials' room and launched into an explosive tirade against Gregson as the shocked referee sat in silence waiting for the soliloquy to finally end. When the chairman had finally gotten it off his chest, he walked out to the reporters and continued ranting publicly against Gregson—actions that led to a $50,000 fine to Snider and thousands of dollars more to other members of the team who also spoke out in the press against the call.*

Luukko began joining Snider on business trips and in meetings that Snider normally attended alone. The management move forced Luukko to begin thinking outside the box and looking for expansion opportunities. With the Flyers and 76ers preparing to move into the new building in 1996, in addition to the scheduling of some major concerts and events, Luukko was charged with filling the Spectrum's schedule, so it would bring in sufficient revenue to warrant its continued existence. He found partners in the Major Indoor Soccer League, which had awarded Philadelphia an expansion franchise— the Kixx. He opened talks with the Arena Football League, although

---

* Years later, at an NHL General Managers meeting in Florida, Snider found himself next to Gregson on a bus transport to dinner. At first, Snider didn't recognize the now-retired referee, who was trying desperately not to be noticed. When the chairman realized who he was sitting next to, he leaned over and simply said, "Hey, sorry about that." Gregson later admitted that he was still deathly afraid of Snider after the verbal flogging he received all those years ago and was certain he was going to be chewed out yet again.

the Philadelphia team would not become a reality until 2004. He scheduled multiple collegiate basketball teams to play their games at the South Philadelphia stalwart. Still missing was that single, major tenant to fill up a good chunk of the building's schedule.

It was 1995 when Snider and Luukko were together on a train to New York, en route to an NHL Board of Governors meeting. Luukko was reading *USA Today* and scanning through the sports section when he came upon the scoresheets from the International Hockey League, a rival to the American League at the time. He noticed that the attendance numbers were fairly strong for cities he felt had much less passion for hockey than Philadelphia: Denver, Houston, Milwaukee, Cleveland—all of these cities (plus Detroit, an Original Six city) were selling an impressive number of seats for what was essentially a third-tier hockey league. With the Flyers' AHL affiliate residing in Hershey, Pennsylvania, at the time (and owned by the Hershey Corporation), Luukko had an idea.

"Hey, Ed," he said, "if we're planning on keeping the Spectrum, we might want to consider putting our farm team there."

"Well, okay," Snider responded. "But why would we do that? Wouldn't it be competition with the Flyers?"

Snider's memory jumped back to the early '70s, the last time the Flyers found themselves with any semblance of serious competition to their product. The WHA's Blazers were just a blip on the radar: the Flyers were selling out every game with no problem at the time, and the Blazers could not figure out how to properly run the team, from the marketing office to the on-ice product. But it was different now. Salaries had skyrocketed, along with ticket prices. Although Flyers attendance was still good, sellouts were no longer a guarantee. While an affordable Flyers ticket hovered around $40 at the time, an AHL ticket could be had for under $10 in some markets. Snider thought that would potentially take away from the major league squad, but Luukko disagreed.

The competition for a minor-league ticket, he believed, was not in NHL hockey, but in other inexpensive family activities: the movies, the shore, a theme park. Giving families a way to introduce their children to hockey at an affordable price could turn them into Flyers fans and garner new season ticket holders as they aged. Snider recalled the early days of his partner in the Flyers, Joe Scott, getting students and other young fans into the Spectrum to help build the foundation of what would be lifelong Flyers fans.

From a hockey perspective, the move made perfect sense. Why bus minor-league players back and forth to Hershey when they could own their own team and also have those players simply walk across the parking lot? Not only did it allow for more oversight of their farm team and the development of their young players, but it also allowed said players to get a taste of NHL life. From a business perspective, it made even more sense. They spent up to $1 million per year just to execute their affiliation agreement with the Hershey Bears—they would save that cost, while also adding the revenue the new team was sure to bring in.

After discussing with other executives in the company, it was agreed that they would reach out to the AHL to gauge their thoughts on the idea. League president Dave Andrews was pleasantly surprised at the phone call he received. The league, battling with the IHL for minor-league supremacy, was looking to expand into larger markets. At the time, the AHL was mostly in small-market towns: Providence, Rhode Island; Hershey, Pennsylvania; Syracuse and Rochester, New York. If he could get Philadelphia to join, it would be the largest AHL city in the league and would most likely convince other major league cities to consider a franchise for themselves. The Flyers organization paid an expansion fee believed to be in the range of $1.5 million and were granted an AHL franchise. They would drop the Hershey Bears and run their own farm team across the parking lot.

Martha Snider was put in charge of creating the color scheme, logo, and other designs for the new team. Using her artistic expertise, she helped lead the process that developed the Phantoms' purple and black color scheme, along with a logo that echoed the Flyers' longtime, recognizable features. With the backing of an NHL franchise and an organization now owned by Comcast, the Phantoms were destined for success. In that first year, they immediately achieved that success at the box office and on the ice, as they advanced to the division finals against their new rivals, the same Hershey Bears who represented the Flyers up until the 1996–97 season. In a rough, but entertaining play-off series, the Phantoms were eliminated in seven games.

The following season, 1997–98, the Phantoms dispensed with their rivals and advanced to the Calder Cup final against the St. John Flames. With the team looking to clinch the championship on the road in Game 5, Snider told his executives that he was bringing as many of them up to St. John as he could—they would purchase a suite for the night and watch one of their teams win a championship for the first time since the Mariners in 1979. Laughing and enjoying themselves the entire time, the group was disappointed when the Phantoms could not close out the series that night. But Snider was going to make sure they made a splash anyway. When the arena pulled the winning ticket for the night's 50-50 raffle, it had Flyers president Ron Ryan's name on it. Embarrassed, Ryan refused to go collect his winnings, before Snider grabbed his arm and dragged him to the booth in the middle of the arena, smiling for a photo op. When the Phantoms returned home a few nights later for Game 6, Snider's smile grew even wider, as they won the Calder Cup in just their second season—only the second time a Philadelphia hockey team had won a championship on Spectrum ice.

But as much as Snider loved his new minor league squad, the Fly-ers continued to be the bread and butter of his corporate umbrella. His passion for them had far from subsided—if anything, it was growing even stronger with age. That passion was mirrored by the fans. In a 1997 fan poll by the *Daily News*, the Flyers were a close second to the Eagles in the race for Philadelphia's favorite sports team—and in the important under-34 age group, the Flyers were the top team with nearly 46 percent of the vote. And the same poll found that just 7 percent had an unfavorable opinion of Snider himself.

Part of the reason that the fans were so enthusiastic about the Flyers and Snider is that he continued to spend to the limit in order to put his team in the best possible position to compete for a championship. After a 1997 season in which they reached the Stanley Cup Finals, the pieces were in place to continue contending for years. In the months after that playoff run, Snider spent nearly $90 million to secure the services of Eric Lindros, Chris Gratton, Luke Richardson, and John LeClair. Since the mid-'90s, Snider continued to ensure the Flyers outspent nearly all other teams in pursuit of the Stanley Cup. From 1995 to 2004, the Flyers' payroll was always in the top tier of the league, with the team paying over $65 million in 2003–2004, nearly triple the league's lowest payroll.

While the Phantoms were one source of ongoing revenue, it became crucial to expand the core businesses of Comcast-Spectacor to help finance the Flyers. In 1997, Snider was forced to sell his one-third stake in Spectacor Management Group (SMG) when his business partners refused to be bought out during a disagreement. At the time, SMG was the largest facility management company in the world, and Snider instantly regretted needing to remove himself from the company, as he often did when he sold a stake in one that he owned. Years earlier, he sold his stake in PRISM, then continued to look for ways to get back into the television business. The buying and selling of similar businesses was typical for Snider throughout his career and part of the entrepreneurial spirit that drove him each day.

But the sale of SMG included a two-year non-compete clause, giving him two full calendars to plot his reentry into the business. One of the ways he tried to get around the restrictive covenant was by going directly after sports franchises—if he owned the team outright, it would not be a violation of the deal. One of those teams he seriously pursued was the NFL's Minnesota Vikings. With the cost uncertainty of hockey becoming an issue with which he constantly struggled, in 1998 he saw an opportunity to enter a sport that not only had a hard salary cap but also a television contract worth billions of dollars. The football club was losing a little bit of money, but upon further review, Snider and his executives believed it was because the organization was being mismanaged—something they could fix with their years of experience. The NFL owners were thrilled at the potential to welcome Snider back into the league after a 30-year absence, with one anonymous owner telling the *Philadelphia Inquirer*, "He's the kind of guy the NFL needs right now."

Snider flew to Minnesota along with Luukko, Phil Weinberg, Sandy Lipstein, and other executives to meet with the Vikings owners and tour the Metrodome and its facility. The group was extremely interested in moving forward with the transaction, but the asking price was, frankly, too high (it would eventually sell for $250 million). Although Snider was willing to put up a fair amount of his own money, he could not afford the entire transaction alone. If there was one weakness of Snider's business acumen, it was his lack of desire to raise money from other investors. His executives suggested that he only buy in at 40 percent and obtain the balance of the financing from others, but he just couldn't see doing so. The other option would be to get a loan for the rest, but that would leave him so highly leveraged that he worried it could affect his ongoing business opportunities in Philadelphia.

It is interesting here to note the dichotomy of Snider's willingness to take great financial risk in some parts of his business life but not others. While he was perfectly willing to put nearly a quarter-billion dollars on the line to build the new arena in Philadelphia, the same amount was far too much for something outside the city limits, in this case the purchase of the Vikings. There are many theories one can suggest, perhaps none more plausible than his fear of losing his Philadelphia empire at the hands of an unrelated project, similar to what happened with Jerry

Wolman in the 1960s. Snider was willing to risk his Philadelphia companies in order to expand them, but was often unwilling to risk those same companies in a new venture that was mostly unrelated. With the new arena having just opened and too many irons in the fire, he simply wasn't comfortable putting up more money—one of the few times in his life one could accurately say that about him.

As the arena management restriction came close to ending in 1999, Snider and his executives confirmed it was a business they wanted to get back into. They began signing deals to operate arenas and, by 2001, were managing 12 arenas, six convention centers, three minor-league baseball stadiums, and three ice rinks. To aid in their management of these arenas, they established four companies: Global Spectrum, Global Stadium Services, Ovations Food Services, and Front Row Marketing Service. Within a decade, they would also invest in Paciolan Systems, a ticketing company. All of these expansions allowed Comcast-Spectacor to essentially run the entirety of the operations of any arena in the country. At the same time, it gave the Flyers additional revenue streams and the ability to run its operations at a lower cost, bolstering its already strong financial position. By the time of Snider's death, Comcast-Spectacor was managing hundreds of arenas throughout the country, making that segment of its business one of the largest.

But in the '90s, Snider was on a spending spree. Along with the Flyers and the other core businesses of Comcast-Spectacor, the new toy that the chairman had to play with was the 76ers. Never a huge fan of basketball, Snider nonetheless dove into the new entity headfirst, wanting to understand the ins and outs of the sport and, of course, desperately wanting to win at all costs. Similar to the rest of the organization, he was not shy about spending money on the basketball team. He dropped $25 million on a contract for coach Larry Brown in 1997. And although the team's payroll was just under $24 million when Comcast-Spectacor took control in 1996, it had ballooned to over $51 million by the 2000–2001 season in which the 76ers advanced to the NBA Finals.

Despite admittedly not being as passionate about the 76ers as he was about his Flyers, Snider was intrigued by the sport. He did not fully understand the culture of basketball, but he understood business and marketing and knew that the team had to win to draw fans. When he saw thousands of empty seats in the early days of his leadership of the team, he approached 76ers chief operating officer Lara Price with an old idea. He reminisced back to his early days of giving tickets to schools and youth programs to grow interest in the hockey club. Basketball should have been even easier, he thought. Philadelphia had a proven track record of loving the sport of basketball, yet the population didn't seem to be taking to the team.

"What are we doing to give tickets to kids in school?" he asked. Price explained to him a few small programs they were working on.

"How many tickets are you giving out?"

"Probably a couple thousand." It wasn't good enough for the chairman.

"Lara, I had to build hockey from the bottom up. We bussed in kids, we got them here. That is how I built the fan base for the hockey club, and I know we can do it for basketball." He sent Price on her way, with marching orders. Price increased the reach of the program a bit, but was trying to be fiscally prudent and not go overboard. A few weeks later, he called her back in.

"So, where are we on this?" Price explained that they were trying, but there were transportation issues, and other minor snags. Snider interrupted her mid-sentence.

"It's not moving fast enough," he said, getting annoyed. "I have the blueprint. Get the buses, get the kids in here. They deserve to see it. They deserve to be here."

Still new to working with Snider, Price was just learning what others had known for years: when Snider told you to do something, you did it, regardless of the cost. She worked with Luukko and drastically expanded the program, busing students from all around the city to 76ers games so they could experience a professional basketball game. Their attendance began to rise almost immediately.

He also was not averse to stealing some tactics from basketball to benefit the Flyers. Shortly after the Comcast acquisition, Snider took his teenage daughter Sarena to a 76ers game. Despite the team not having the same success as the Flyers, Sarena felt the game presentation was much more entertaining than that of a Flyers game. Snider was a purist and a conservative, and felt hockey should be presented in a very simple way, with the on-ice product being the star. But the 76ers were operating well before Snider had control and did it their own way: loud music, on-court stunts during commercial breaks, in-arena contests. It was a very different event than a typical sports game Snider was used to presenting. When Sarena informed her father of this opinion, he didn't miss a beat. He went to Price's office and asked for help making a Flyers game experience just as entertaining as his daughter found the 76ers.

But his clear placement of the 76ers as second fiddle to the Flyers angered many diehards, including those in the media. Those inside the basketball team never felt he had shortchanged them, but always understood that hockey would forever be his biggest passion. Nonetheless, when someone publicly criticized him for his treatment of the 76ers, he took it quite personally.

One day with no warning, Snider was blasted in a small market Philadelphia magazine for his handling of the basketball and hockey teams. The publication's circulation was quite small, but Snider didn't care. He wanted to hit back hard so the message would get across. He called Price up to his office and said, "I want to write a rebuttal to this, and we're going to send it to him."

"Mr. Snider," she replied, "this thing has zero publication. If you respond, it becomes a story."

"I don't care," he snapped back. "I want to do it."

While disagreeing vehemently, she returned to her office, constructed a letter, had it approved by the team's attorneys, and brought it to Snider's office, certain it was the wrong move but also frightened for her job if she disagreed with him while he was in such a passionate mood. She handed him the letter and waited a minute while he read it. Before he could finish, she interjected.

"I'm not doing my job if I don't tell you that if you do this, you give him all the power he wants," she said. "No one cares that he wrote that. As soon as you respond, everybody cares. I strongly recommend you do not respond."

Snider looked up at her with a glare that could send the toughest person into a sprint. "Fine!" he yelled, as he tossed the letter onto his desk and turned his attention to other matters. She left the office, certain she was going to be fired. Snider, within hours, had calmed down and was grateful for her honesty and for stopping him from doing something he might have later regretted.

Despite how hard he tried, Snider could never quite develop the passion he wanted for basketball (he sometimes referred to it derisively as "round ball" to those close to him). Although he put on a good face for those he worked with, he would consistently tell others in the NHL how much he hated the sport and the business model. He would be at every home game, sitting courtside in a dress shirt with the top button undone—a much more casual appearance than his Flyers games, where he donned a full suit. He provided every resource available to his staff and was not afraid to spend upwards of nine figures on star players, but he simply could not find it in his heart to become as devoted to the team as he was to hockey.

His exorbitant spending was not limited just to his businesses, either. As he cashed out a chunk of his Comcast shares and his wealth grew exponentially from the success of the businesses, he began indulging in some personal fantasies that he had never been able to afford. The first was a private airplane, which he had always wanted. He hated flying in the first place and certainly did not like doing so commercially. Instead, he joined forces with Philadelphia businessman Sidney Kimmel, with the duo together purchasing a brand-new Gulfstream IV (GIV-SP) in 1999 for shared use (more on their friendship in chapter 15). The tail was marked with the number 143KS (Kimmel-Snider) and allowed Snider to travel at his leisure across the country and to Europe with friends, family, and business associates.

The following year, at a cost of $12 million, the Flyers built a state-of-the-art practice facility in Voorhees, New Jersey, complete with two NHL-sized rinks and offices for the entirety of the Flyers hockey operations squad. Even amid all of this corporate expansion, questions from the media began suggesting Snider should be close to retirement. His eyes would narrow and sometimes his cheeks would turn red, as he controlled his anger and responded poignantly. "I want to win a Stanley Cup," he once replied to the *Courier Post*. "What else would you like me to do, grow flowers?"

Part of the expansion of the business required Snider to rethink the management structure at the top of the organization. For many years, he had had the same executives running various parts of the company, but he wanted to formalize the leadership group so that he could properly supervise what was going on in his company. That led to the creation of the Office of the Chair, which included four others: COO Peter Luukko; executive VIP and general counsel Phil Weinberg; vice chairman Fred Shabel; and CFO Sandy Lipstein. The four of them were some of Snider's closest colleagues and had garnered his trust and friendship over the many years they'd worked together. That closeness also led to some amusement that illustrated the pros and cons of Snider's management style.

One of Lipstein's regular duties was to open Snider's personal mail and handle all of his personal financial obligations. He would write and sign a pile of checks, put them in a folder, and send them to Snider's office with a cover sheet detailing each one for approval. Each October, Lipstein would write a check for Snider's life insurance policy, to which Snider would send the cover sheet back with a note, "What's this for?" Lipstein would walk to Snider's office and answer him. Each October, Snider would send the same note back for the same check, and Lipstein would save the note, remind him what it was for, and return to his office.

By the fifth year, Lipstein laughed. He had had enough. He brought the pile of notes to Snider's office and said, "Ed, you do realize you ask this question every year."

"No I don't," Snider replied.

Lipstein tossed all five sheets on Snider's desk and said, "Here's the sheets from the last four years." Snider laughed so loudly, heads rose from his outer office. He knew he had a tendency to forget the minutiae, and always appreciated Lipstein's no-bullshit attitude and willingness to walk right into his office and tell him he was wrong.

At one of the first meetings of the Office of the Chair, Shabel hosted the group in Atlantic City. Before Snider arrived, Shabel, a regular witness of his boss's reliance on ketchup for any meal, jokingly set up a pyramid of ketchup bottles on the table in the shape of a flower arrangement. When the rest of the group arrived, they burst out in laughter, including Snider, who said, while trying to hide a smile, "Don't you ever do that again." Even some of the women in Snider's life would carry a bottle of ketchup in their purses in case there was ever an "emergency" at a meal. And when several executives were at a restaurant in the Caribbean with Snider one night, they made the restaurant crew go on a goose chase to find ketchup before the meal was served.

In their meetings, the running joke among the four executives was that they each had one vote, while Snider had five. However, they knew their boss well enough that if they all fervently believed in something, they were usually able to sync up their thoughts beforehand and present them in a way that made it almost impossible for Snider to say no—even if he knew the game they were playing. "You guys are ganging up on me again," he would often say. And the other four steered into the skid. "Yeah, we're ganging up on you," they would say. "We think you should do this." And more often than not, he did. Snider always laughed, knowing deep down how difficult it was for people to disagree with him.

Often times, meetings of the Office of the Chair would get testy, but not without humor. When the organization was looking to partner with the Phillies on a shared parking lot deal, Snider was in California as the final details came into focus. While on the phone with his four principals, who were all in the office together, he revealed he was not happy with the results (though his executives believed it was because he was not a personal fan of the owner of the Phillies). The chairman began berating each of his executives in colorful terms, pointing a virtual finger at each of them for the pieces of the deal that he believed they messed up. In the midst of his rampage, he stopped midsentence and said to someone on the other end, "Excuse me, there's no sauce on that sea bass, is there?" Unbeknownst to the group, he was in a restaurant in California, having lunch with his wife as he laid into his staff.

As a general rule, though, the meetings were friendly, professional, and productive. It gave them all an opportunity to share ideas and explore options when there was a business decision to be made. One of Snider's great management techniques was allowing his employees to figure out answers for themselves. When someone brought a problem to him, he would ask all the right questions, allowing them to answer their own question. And when that point in the conversation arrived, Snider would smile and say, "I knew you could." Snider also was better at seeing situations from a different angle than most. It was this intuitive mind that forced those around him to constantly be at their best—a huge factor when you consider how many companies he started and that a vast majority of them were successful.

His closeness with the members of the Office of the Chair also extended to their families and gave others a unique view into Snider's treatment of his longtime, loyal employees, as well as his perception of his own role as the head of the company. One night, when Weinberg had his 10-year-old son, Zack, at the game, they were eating dinner in the director's lounge as usual. Zack approached Snider and asked, "Mr. Snider, are you my daddy's boss? Or is my daddy your boss?"

Snider sat back in his chair for a moment, thought deeply about how to respond to the question, and replied, "Well, Zack, this is my company and your dad's my lawyer, and he works for the company and for me, so I'm his boss." Zack nodded, but Snider continued. "But there are some things that I just won't do unless your dad says it's okay to do them. So I suppose in some ways, he's my boss, too."

But even his top executives were not immune to Snider's ire, especially when it came to the Flyers. With Snider and his usual crew in Toronto to take in a crucial playoff game (Game 6 of the semifinals in 2004), they settled down in an Air Canada Centre suite. Everyone was on edge about Snider's usual superstitions, especially with a trip to the conference finals on the line. Before the game went into overtime, Shabel ran to the arena's basement to grab a drink from their underground bar. He got stuck in line, and while down there, Jeremy Roenick scored his famous goal that sent the Flyers to the third round—perhaps the biggest Flyers accomplishment since their run to the Eastern Conference Finals in 2000.

Embarrassed at missing this moment and certain that his boss would not be happy, Shabel hung his head as he met the other executives at Snider's plane. As he started walking up the stairs to board, Snider appeared in the doorway with that look on his face. "Don't you ever get on my plane for an away game and miss an overtime goal," he said, before turning around and returning to his seat for takeoff. Shabel made sure to heed that advice for the future. As became even more evident as the years progressed, Snider forever lived and died with the successes and failures of his Flyers. Nonetheless, he still found that he needed a place outside of Philadelphia to escape the stressors of everyday life. That's how he ultimately ended up spending even more time in California.

15

Grappling with Success

SNIDER'S FRIENDS WERE of the utmost importance to him. From a young age, he'd always had a group of guys he hung out with, whether it was his Playboys posse, his camp friends, his players (in the early years of his ownership), or business colleagues. Whether he was in Washington, Philadelphia, or California, there was always a group of people waiting to welcome him with open arms. On top of that, he developed extremely close, fraternal bonds with a select few, one of them being Philadelphia businessman and philanthropist Sidney Kimmel. The two had met back in the 1960s at a meeting for Philadelphians born under the Capricorn astrological sign. Kimmel was still a lower-middle-class young man, desperately trying to make ends meet, while Snider was the debt-ridden owner of a new sports team, still struggling to turn a profit.

They hit it off despite their different views on society—Snider a staunch conservative, Kimmel a bleeding-heart liberal. As he did with most friends, Snider tried unsuccessfully to push his objectivist beliefs on Kimmel, while Kimmel made Snider laugh hysterically with his jokes and light personality. The two went on double dates (Myrna first and Martha later) and vacationed together as well. They had the sort of friendship where they could go years without chatting, and then pick up exactly where they'd left off.

Kimmel worked on building the business of his dreams, while Snider worked on expanding his business empire. The two often went extended periods of time without speaking, but they were always there for the other when needed. One day in the '80s, Kimmel called Snider, alarmed and struggling with his collection of businesses. Snider dropped everything and went to New York with some of his executives. They sat in Kimmel's office all day until they all agreed on a plan to help the budding entrepreneur fix the issues. As Kimmel became vastly successful in his clothing businesses, he began donating large amounts of his wealth, of which Snider took note. While he did not go to the same length as Kimmel in taking Warren Buffett's and Bill Gates's lead in pledging to give away most of their wealth by the end of their lives, Kimmel's immense generosity surely had an effect on Snider, who in the 1990s, exponentially increased his philanthropy.

As much as Snider had individual friendships with those he had known for decades, he was still much more comfortable in a group. Being just a few years older than many of his players in the 1970s, he became close with guys like Bob Clarke, Joe Watson, Bernie Parent, and Paul Holmgren. At the end of their playing careers, they would often vacation together. One photo shows Snider with a group of players, after a fishing trip, standing on the docks next to Holmgren as the longtime Flyer holds a 450-pound fish caught just minutes earlier. Snider knew how to have fun, how to celebrate, how to enjoy life. That rubbed off on those close to him.

And Snider's group of friends did not always evolve with his success. As is common, certain friends came and went, but he always held his Camp Cody friends near and dear to his heart. Even once he had moved to Philadelphia and reached the pinnacle of his career, those childhood buddies were always some of the first people he would call when he needed someone to talk with. He would invite them to his suite for a Flyers game and joke around about old times and would write letters to them on their birthdays to tell them how much he loved them. Each year, he would drive to Baltimore to meet up with them at Obrycki's, a famous crab restaurant. He would order buckets of crabs for everyone and pick up the check (but not before getting an additional pile of crabs on dry ice to take home for later).

Through these friendships is where you can most see Snider's generosity. He regularly wrote beautiful letters to old friends, expressing his love for them and gratitude for the life they shared. Whether it was picking up the tab, taking a group of friends to a fancy dinner at The Capital Grille, or paying for a vacation for them and their families, Snider would do anything for those close to him. Conversely, however, he would also then expect the same loyalty in return and never considered that anyone would do otherwise. This gave him a naïveté that often extended to those who ran parts of his business. There are many stories where it was discovered that someone was skimming funds off the top or taking kickbacks, often for many years, prior to being caught. Snider's loyalty to those for whom he deeply cared left him open to being exploited.

Many times throughout his life, an executive, a friend, or even a family member had to shatter the glass in order for Snider to see a situation more clearly, for he was easily blinded by his own feelings of friendship or love. It even led him to lend money to those claiming to be in need, much of which he would never see returned. Regretfully, he often became close to people who had ulterior motives. It was a weakness that he never seemed to overcome throughout his life. The more successful he became, the more often it seemed to happen—it was unfortunate for someone who gave his employees the autonomy to succeed on their own and who would give everything he owned for a friend in need. At his death, multiple people still owed him upwards of six figures from loans he made that were never repaid.

When it came down to it, though, Snider was generally a happy person. He had his moments and was certainly fierce and frightening at times, but at the end of the day he loved to sit back and enjoy himself. He loved dancing and singing, often spending rides home from work blasting Billy Joel on the radio and dancing his way up the driveway to his front door. He would spend time chatting with his grandchildren, some of whom he would invite to join the fantasy football league he and his California friends had already established. He would put up the money for their teams and allow them to keep the winnings from the pot if they won—all he wanted was for a Snider to be a winner.

But despite their love for Malibu, Snider and Martha were not certain that it was where they wanted to reside in the long term. At a Los Angeles party David Foster threw one night, the music star coincidentally introduced the Sniders to composer Barry Devorzon and his wife. Foster brought the foursome together and said, "Ed, meet your new best friend, Barry." The group hit it off immediately, garnering the Sniders an invite to the Devorzons' home in a beautiful region to the northwest called Montecito. Nestled just between the mountains and the ocean, some of the wealthiest and most successful people in the Greater Los Angeles area have called the Santa Barbara suburb their home over the years, including Oprah Winfrey, Ellen DeGeneres, and others.

Driving through the neighborhood each time they went to visit their new friends, the Sniders fell in love with the area and began shooting each other glances that said, "Are you thinking what I'm thinking?" After exploring the region and tossing around the idea of relocating yet again, in 1994 they nervously bought a home on 9.4-acres of land next door to Oprah for $7.2 million.

After a few years, Snider and Martha were growing antsy with the house. The couple lived in their Montecito home for a while, but when they purchased the property they knew that it would one day need to be reconstructed. Not satisfied with a simple renovation, they decided to demolish the home and start from scratch. Martha spearheaded the project, securing supplies from around the world. The hardwood floors came from Belgium. The roof tile came from Southern France. The paneling in the library was from Paris. Every detail of the house, down to the specific hardware used in each door frame, was painstakingly chosen. Reminiscent of the Italian villas of Lake Como, the home boasted a view of the mountains out one side and an ocean view on the other. The home itself was over 21,000 square feet, and also had a poolside cabana and a guest house. Also included were a library with leather ceiling, a downstairs theater so Snider could watch movies and Flyers games, a wine cellar, a bar/pub, and a private tennis court at the far end of the grounds. The fountains on the front lawn arched in a way that framed the mountains behind them. Meticulously manicured, the home quickly became what he called his favorite place in the world.

But even the beautiful new grounds on which they lived did not stop the family from adventuring across the world. Using his shared Gulfstream jet, they would fly to several small islands in the Caribbean, where they would partake in some of their favorite activities: reading on the beach, dining on gourmet food, and sailing. He would take not only Martha, but members of the entire extended family— children, grandchildren, friends, and business associates. His life now seemed perfect, and he wanted to be sure to share it with everyone he loved.

One of those individuals was well-known Philadelphia-area businessman and philanthropist Lewis Katz. Introduced during a potential parking deal between Katz and the Flyers in the early '90s, Snider was not originally a fan of his. Katz was a liberal and a close friend and confidant of Ed Rendell, then the district attorney of Philadelphia (and eventually its mayor), and a politician Snider regularly excoriated in private. Katz was also a practical jokester, something that did not necessarily endear him to a man who was extremely intense and focused when working.

But Snider and Katz eventually became best friends. The two realized that they had much more in common than they originally thought. Both had built their success from nothing and, despite their differences in political and societal views, they each had similar morals and a strong sense of family that the other could appreciate. Katz would regularly show up at Snider's workplace unannounced and, before barging into the owner's private space to schmooze with his best buddy, make everyone in the outer office laugh hysterically. When they talked on the phone, Snider and Katz would regularly end conversations with, "I love you, man." The two would see each other as often as possible, eventually vacationing together and going to charity benefits around Philadelphia alongside each other. Snider and Katz became like second fathers to each other's children.

Despite his love for old friends, Snider's life in California had introduced him to some of the movers and shakers around the business world, giving him a much different circle of friends than he was used to. Over time, he became involved with a makeshift billionaires' boys club in Montecito. Through Barry Devorzon and David Foster, he became friendly with some of the most successful people living in the region—real estate magnates Herb Simon and Jimmy Argyropoulos, actor Rob Lowe, Lucky Brand founder Gene Montesano, investor Bob Fell, and many more. The group began hanging out at Lucky's Steakhouse, a joint owned by Simon, Montesano, and Argyropoulos. On Sunday mornings they would open the place up for their group, and the boys would hang out for hours. The bulk of the discussion was about the week's NFL games, on which they would all bet wildly. As was typical for men of their ilk, it was not about the money, but rather about beating everyone else in the room. They would tell stories, poke fun at themselves, and of course, rag on each other when someone lost their shirt on one of the games.

At the end of each football season, they would give out awards, some good and some bad, as just another way to rib each other. Snider would also tease Foster and Devorzon over their successes in their respective fields. Telling stories from his record company days, he would joke, "I was in the music business, too. You're not the only fuckers around here who can make music." The competition did not stop, even when he was doing something nice for his buddies. Snider was one of two sports owners in the group, as Herb Simon owned the NBA's Indiana Pacers. Simon had invited the group to a game in Indiana, which they gladly accepted, landing at the airport, taking a cab to the arena, and sitting in the owner's box. Snider then invited the group to a Flyers game, but when they landed in Philadelphia, there was a police escort waiting to bring them to the Center. The group spent the night elbowing Simon and saying, "See? This is how you do it!"

Something interesting happened, though, when Snider would invite friends from outside Philadelphia to one of his games. Although they all knew what he did for a living and how successful he was, no one ever quite realized it until they saw him in action. In California, he was just "Ed." But in Philadelphia, he was "Mr. Snider." As one of his friends explained, "The seas parted when he walked down the street." None of them had ever seen him treated like a king, but in Philadelphia, that's essentially what he was. Although the ribbing would never stop, it added another layer of understanding for his friends to see what he meant to the city.

Yet, those two sides of him were also arguably the cause of his personal undoing. As his group of friends changed, so did his personality, his behavior, and how he treated those closest to him. This evolution ultimately led to the devastating conclusion of his marriage with Martha, an ending that saddened those around him. Their love for each other never truly burned out for the remainder of their lives, but the two sides of him were sometimes too much to bear to remain in the marriage.

At this point, it is important to stop and reflect on the fact that Snider had romantic involvement with countless women throughout his life, even while married. He would ultimately be married four times (Myrna, Martha, Christine Decroix in 2004, and Lin Spivak in 2013), but certainly there were many others who weaved their way into his world during the many decades since his high school days. And it would also be naïve to suggest that his wives were forever unaware of the amorous behavior he exhibited toward other women. His marriages dissolved not necessarily because there was no longer love in the relationship, but because his behavior was simply too much for his partners to accept.

A question that can easily be asked is, why? Did some of his wives simply understand that a life with Snider included everything that came with it: incredible pain that was often balanced by the immense love and affection he provided, along with the intelligence, charm, and life that he brought to the table? One can easily look at Snider's actions and jump to a conclusion that he never truly cared for any of his wives—two of whom were mothers to his children—that the emotion he showed for them was simply a cover. But that would be an oversimplification. Snider had deep love for each of them, especially Myrna and Martha. Even years after the marriages had ended, he would often tell those close to him—sometimes the ex-wife herself—about how he messed up what he believed were perfect marriages. As he got older, perhaps he understood it better. But as he came of age and went through the first few decades of his financial success, it is certainly possible that he felt he needed two types of love: the domestic type and one that was much more dangerous and exotic. As he began to associate more with those of his ilk in California, the behavior unquestionably did not improve.

That dichotomy between his Philadelphia and California personas is one that truly defined Snider in his later years. His personality could be vastly different depending on who he was with and where he was. Yet, deep down, he was always a Philadelphian, no matter where he spent the bulk of his time. In Philadelphia, he would consistently ask those who worked with him to call him by his first name, yet everyone, save for some of his top executives, refused. Even Bob Clarke, one of his closest business associates, called him Mr. Snider, and continues to do so years after his death. Those who speak about him do so with such reverence, even acknowledging that they were told to call him Ed, yet most could never muster the courage to do so.

While most had nearly endless respect for him, they certainly knew how to joke with him as well. He was very tolerant and accepting of those times and knew how to be self-deprecating toward his own flaws. When he married for a third time in 2004 and a fourth time in 2013, he would humorously tell his friends, "I'm getting married *again*," emphasizing the last word and laughing. When Clarke was invited to one of his weddings, he politely declined. "But I promise you," Clarke said with a smirk, "I'll come to the next one." Even his children poked fun at him on this subject. During one of his temper explosions, he told one of his kids that they would not be invited to his wedding. The snappy reply came quickly: "It's okay, I'll just wait for the next one."

That family side of Snider's life is perhaps the one with the most contradictions. From a young age, the importance of family was instilled in him by his parents. Even though time did not always permit him to be at home, he did truly feel passionate about being with his family. That is part of the reason he and Myrna originally decided to create a home base in Maine for themselves, their kids, and eventually other members of the extended family. Snider spent so many hours tending to his businesses that he often felt the need to physically remove himself in order to reconnect with those he loved.

With such a large family, there would never be enough time for Snider to regularly keep in touch with everyone. Yet he loved when those moments did occur. For years, the second Passover Seder was a makeshift Snider family reunion, often with upwards of 80 people in attendance. Any time the Sniders would visit Washington, they would stay with Phyllis and her family. When Phyllis or Earl Foreman visited Philadelphia, Snider would insist they stay with him. There was always a deep love among the extended family, and Snider cherished the times they could spend together.

He even loved using his vast array of experiences to help younger members of the family. He once took aside a youngster to discuss the difficulties of peer pressure and how to overcome it. "You know what's going to happen," he said. "You're going to be with a group of kids. They're going to be smoking a joint. They're going to pass it to you. You need to say no. And then they're going to call you a pussy. And that's called peer pressure. The way you handle peer pressure is, you punch them in the nose, you stand over them, you say, 'Who's a pussy now?' And then you walk away." The tough guy from his childhood, embedded deep within the entrepreneur, never truly left him.

Having come of age alongside the Flyers, the first four Snider children had become used to their father's tough quirks at an early age. However, as young adults, they may have better understood the reasons behind their father's parenting style, but that didn't mean his remarks were any easier to accept. Recalling his experiences as a high testosterone man for some years, Snider was overly protective and extraordinarily judgmental when it came to his daughters, who admittedly were looked at with a harsher eye than his sons. If they came downstairs for school in an outfit that he thought showed too much, he would immediately send them back upstairs to change. And when they reached dating age, he sat them down and explained to them how teenage boys think. "Why buy the cow," he would often warn them, "when you can get the milk for free?"

Whether fair or not, he fervently believed that, regardless of how society evolved, men were men and would always look for an opportunity to satisfy an evolutionary desire. He would teach them to hold out for the best and never accept any man who treated them like anything less than a princess. And when one daughter brought home a high school boyfriend who had long hair and an earring, Snider was not happy one bit and did not hide his disapproval. He was the metaphorical dad with a shotgun when it came to his daughters.

But he had a softer side as well that occasionally revealed itself. As time permitted, he would drop everything to do a good deed. When his daughter, Tina, was having a difficult time determining the best college for her education and suggested that the University of Colorado seemed like a good fit, Snider booked a flight for the next day and flew her to Denver, toured the campus with her, signed her up for classes, and made sure she was fully prepared.

Even if he could not visit or call, he always seemed to know what was going on with various family members. His grandchildren often went months without speaking to him, but Snider was always aware of their activities, what they were doing, and the next steps of their lives. Simultaneously, Snider compensated for his lack of time by financially supporting numerous members of the family. He did so not because anyone asked, but because he felt it was his duty to share his success with those close to him. This generosity was certainly learned from watching his father do so in his youth and even by watching Jerry Wolman during the years of their partnership. Whether it was buying someone a car, paying for their home, covering a medical expense, or even simply sending someone money if they could not get to the next paycheck, Snider took great pride in being able to help his family. Never, however, would he publicly reveal that he was doing so.

At the same time, Snider certainly had a dark side as well when it came to his family, a side that could be classified anywhere from poor prioritizing to simply cruel. As previously mentioned, he would often miss important family events because he was preoccupied with a Flyers home game. That often gave the impression that he cared more about his work than he did about his family. And if anyone called him out, his stubborn side took over. At one point, he and his sister did not speak for years, over a squabble so minor the family does not even recall what it was about. Only when their mother, in one of her final breaths on her deathbed, made a comment about how disappointed she was in the two of them, did they finally bury the hatchet and remain closer than ever for the rest of their lives.

But Snider would also cut off any one of his children for any reason with no warning. He could go years without speaking to them if he perceived a serious problem—whether it was there or not. He would often lie to them about life choices that he knew they would disapprove of, and even when it was indisputably evident that he was not being truthful, he abhorred being challenged on it. Those who did, paid the price. One of his children described it like this: he could be holding a red shirt, look you straight in the eye and swear that he was not holding a red shirt. That trait, more often than not, created serious problems among the Sniders, which only got worse when you called him out on his behavior.

Even in business, Snider was far from a star father. His experience with Jay aside, nearly all of his children, at some point, worked for the organization in some capacity—a few even spent many years at high-level positions. He would constantly refer to it as a family business, but at the same time would make unilateral decisions that would adversely affect the next generation. He could bring them in, mentor them, and then suddenly drive them away. As a young, first-time father, he gave his (at the time) four children ownership stakes in Spectrum Limited, an early venture that owned the Spectrum lease and charged rent to the Flyers, so that he could begin building a solid financial position for each of them. And before the Comcast acquisition, each of his six children held about 5 percent of the company, allowing them to cash out at the same time he did.

But Snider's generosity often hid a bitter ruthlessness. "He would give you the world," one of his kids described, "but then he wanted it back." His children all loved working for the company—but more often than not, they simply did not like working for him. His tendency to create exorbitantly stressful situations for those close to him while he was making major decisions was debilitating. Despite their partial ownership, the children were totally unaware that he was even negotiating to sell the organization to Comcast in the 1990s. He created unnecessary personal conflict between some members of the family, then when relationships hit bottom, he dropped the bomb of the sale. In essence, he used the conflict as a makeshift excuse, despite the fact that he had already made the decision beforehand to sell out.

It is quite difficult to make heads or tails of Snider's behavior when it came to his personal life. He could treat those close to him poorly, then at the same time say he cared for them deeply and wished that everything could be better. It is a black cloud, a complexity, that hangs over his legacy. As he got older, he progressively mellowed, began feeling closer to his children and, as the number of grandchildren increased, he, like many other grandparents, found a new lease on life with his family.

While he often had difficulties balancing his family life, he almost always made time for those friends who had stuck by him during the ups and downs of his recent life. He yearned to share with them the passion he still held for all aspects of his business. He would often take those friends to 76ers games, sitting courtside to take in some basketball, and even there could not avoid some humorous antics. Late in his ownership of the 76ers, Snider and Jack Williams sat courtside to enjoy a game. In the midst of a controversial officiating decision, an unruly fan threw two cans of beer from the upper level. They whizzed by Snider's and Williams's heads, landed on the court, and exploded loudly. While listening to the radio wrap-up of the game on the drive home, the broadcasters described the beer incident, saying, "They just barely missed hitting two elderly gentlemen sitting courtside." The two burst out laughing, while Snider simultaneously yelled at the radio. He hated the characterization yet couldn't help but smile at the humor.

One time, he sat at the Center with Lewis Katz, then the owner of the New Jersey Nets, to watch their teams play each other. Katz egged his buddy on all night as the Nets dominated the 76ers. With Snider getting redder and angrier with each passing minute, Katz finally turned to him and said, "Hey, if you want, I'll go in at halftime and talk to your team for you." Snider exploded, walked off the court, and spent the rest of the game watching from the tunnel, Katz laughing in the background.

Win or lose, at this point Snider was exorbitantly successful in his business life. He had wealth beyond his wildest dreams and ran companies that had influence over almost every aspect of the North American sporting world. Part of that success came from his grit and determination to ensure the game of pro hockey was healthy. He constantly complained about how often ticket prices had to be raised, so he was ecstatic when the 2004–2005 NHL lockout introduced cost certainty to the sport, allowing him some flexibility in determining how he could properly present his team. In fact, he lowered Flyers ticket prices up to 20 percent the month after the lockout ended, in the hopes of drawing back the fans who were irate about the work stoppage.

One of the benefits Snider enjoyed from this financial success was the use of his private plane. By the end of the 2000s, however, he felt limited by his Gulfstream IV's range, which allowed him to make transatlantic journeys, but which needed to be refueled more often. He also now had the ability to buy his own plane, instead of sharing it with a friend. So, in 2011, he relinquished his ownership portion of the plane and purchased his own Gulfstream V. Built in 2001, the aircraft was initially designed by Ralph Lauren, who had sold it elsewhere before it ended up in Snider's hands. Number 629 in Gulfstream's records, it cost $22.5 million and had a range of over 6,000 miles, allowing him to go back and forth between Philadelphia and Santa Barbara without refueling.

The elliptical windows were trademark Gulfstream, but naturally, any plane owned by Snider would not be complete unless it was
customized to his specifications. The interior of the aircraft was left
mostly the same, but the outside is where the chairman was particu-
lar. He kept it simple—an orange and black line painted horizontally
across the entire fuselage. The most important piece, however, was
the prominent Flyers logo on the tail, with every alteration painstakingly supervised by his pilot to ensure the specs were correct and that
the shade of orange was precise. The tail number was 188ES—his
lucky numbers and his initials. The second it rolled out of the hangar,
he fell in love with it.

His pilot, Chris Mattie, would fly him all over the world to vacation in exotic locations: Tahiti, Bora Bora, Hawaii, Sardinia, Israel,
Rome, and more. They would travel throughout the Caribbean, often
to Anguilla, one of Snider's favorite islands on which to vacation. And
the use of the plane was not just limited to himself and his family. He
would often invite friends and business associates on lavish trips so he
could share his success with those around him. Sometimes, he would
not even invite them—a trip was sprung on them after they were
already airborne. One time, Snider had Fred Shabel and some of the
other team executives on his plane to head to a Phillies spring training game in Clearwater, Florida. The plan was that they would catch
the game, grab dinner, and head home the same night. When Shabel
arrived to the plane, not only were all of the wives on board—including his own—but the entire plane began singing "Happy Birthday"
to him for his 70th. Surprised and humbled, Shabel laughed along with
the others as they partied lightly on the flight south. A few hours into
the flight, he looked out the window and noticed nothing but water
beneath them. He asked where they were actually going, a question
Snider pretended not to hear. When the plane landed and the passen-
gers disembarked, Shabel was greeted with a WELCOME TO ANGUILLA
sign. When he mentioned that he didn't pack for a Caribbean vacation,

Snider pointed to his suitcase being unloaded from the plane. The crew spent a week on Snider's favorite Caribbean island, paid for by the chairman, in honor of their colleague's birthday.

Historically not a fan of flying, Snider grew to love his plane and his time on board. It was one of the few times in his life that he did not have to be in charge. When he was on the airplane, the pilot was admittedly the boss. A stickler for safety, he made sure every pilot knew that safety protocols came first and that he would never ask them to fast-track their procedure to get airborne quicker. In fact, for a successful man running so many companies, Snider was surprisingly laid-back and introspective on cross-country trips. One of his favorite sayings, which he uttered often to his pilots, was, "We never have to be anywhere." It was just one more way that he always enjoyed the present and appreciated what he had.

Planes were not the only luxury in which he indulged—he also had a love of fancy cars. He did not own a lot of them, but the ones he did purchase, he loved dearly. He owned a Mercedes McLaren, on which he spent close to $500,000. He also bought a beige Cadillac Escalade that his driver used to take him around Philadelphia. He had one of the first Porsche Panameras in the United States. He purchased a Ferrari, which a girlfriend of his crashed, causing $45,000 of damage—enough to trigger the famous Snider temper. A Mercedes S Series stayed at his home in Pennsylvania. He was once asked why he only purchased new cars, rather than classic cars. "For what?" he would reply. "I'm classic. I don't need anything old." He loved his cars new, fast, and beautiful.

Despite his easygoing attitude when it came to leisure activities, he was often the opposite in the office, even as he neared the age of 70. His reputation had preceded him, especially when it came to his jumpiness and temper. Many employees were deathly afraid of him, and some got dressed down quite efficiently by a man who often demanded perfection. The tangents were never personal—he never called anyone names or insulted them. It was always about the work and the business. Nonetheless, he still intimidated almost anyone who walked by.

Even scheduling meetings became a problem at times. Those unfamiliar with him were so nervous, they would actually end up wasting his time by either not cutting to the chase or stammering at a time when the chairman needed the information. His assistants began prepping them using pointers and suggestions in order to make them more relaxed and the meetings more efficient—those who worked with Snider knew his time was so valuable that they did not want to waste a single minute.

But through the many parts of his sprawling business empire, everything started and ended with the Flyers, even after all those years. No matter what other issues might arise, when it was game time, nothing else in the world mattered. That mindset trickled down through the entire organization. Everyone's work lived and died with the success of the Flyers, whether their work was directly related to them or not.

And it went even deeper than just hockey. Like a typical Philadelphian, he defended his team and his city to the death, and to a fault. He was too passionate and too committed to think any other way. "He genuinely loved the Flyers and Philadelphia," said Wayne Gretzky. "He thought that they were No. 1 and the rest of the world was No. 2." That passion for his city, his team, and their success was regularly on display, whether he was willing his team to victory or preparing to say good-bye to an old friend.

16

A Building Falls, but the Memories Remain

THE FLYERS ALWAYS held the highest place in Snider's heart. His passion never ebbed—if anything, it grew with age. He always referred to the team as his "baby," acknowledging proudly that he cared more about them than any other part of his empire. Everyone knew that the Flyers were what made him successful in the first place and understood the staunch connection he had with his franchise.

More than anything, Snider had a deep love of and appreciation for Flyers fans. Likewise, Flyers fans generally had a deep care for Snider. No matter how angry fans may have been when the team played poorly, they always knew there was someone who was even angrier than they were. Snider was a fan at heart, and because of that, he knew how important it was to show the fans his appreciation. Seeing Flyers fans attending away games gave him great satisfaction. Even if someone moved across the country, they often remained a Flyers fan and attended the games when the Flyers played in their city. By the turn of the century, Snider was certainly more publicly involved with the team than in the previous decade, yet he still stayed one step away from the spotlight, not wanting to take the focus away from his players. However, in the event it appeared the Flyers could be a serious Stanley Cup contender, he could easily be drawn right in front of the camera. Before the 2001–2002 season, *The Hockey News* picked the Flyers to win the Stanley Cup. Despite his superstitious nature, Snider could not keep a poker face. "I don't like it," he said, grinning ear to ear. "I don't like it at all."

At the end of the season, however, having scored just two goals in five games, the team was knocked out in the first round of the playoffs. With the players publicly calling for the removal of head coach Bill Barber, Snider angrily acquiesced and announced that he would become even more involved in the hockey operations department going forward. Barber's firing created an aura around the organization that did not portray the team in a positive light. With five new coaches in five years, the Flyers were perpetuating a culture of impatience and desperation, willing to do anything to have even the slightest chance to win the Cup. Snider bristled at the thought, but it hung over the organization like a black cloud for many years.

There was always an assumption that Snider ran the show, that the chairman made all of the hockey decisions. If a coach was fired, if a player got traded or signed, it was assumed to be Snider's doing. And, while there are anecdotes and snippets of Flyers history that would support that theory, dozens of former executives, coaches, and managers passionately refute that characterization. Bob Clarke (who had returned to the organization in the 1990s and served as GM a second time from 1994 to 2006) said it best in a 2001 interview with the *Courier Post*, when asked about Snider's perceived meddling. "He doesn't really interfere," Clarke said. "But he asks a lot of questions, and I don't find that offensive. I think it's good, actually. He's obviously a bright man. He knows players, and when we're doing something, he's always informed. But he's never stopped us when we've wanted to do something.… He'll support us, even if he doesn't agree. Sometimes we've disagreed, but he'll say, 'If you think we need it, go ahead.' And that's important."

This notion seems to be the most accurate portrayal of Snider's management style when it came to hockey. If his mantra in his business was, "Hire the right people and let them do their jobs," an appropriate mantra for his view of the hockey team would be, "Hire the right people and let them do their jobs, but make damn sure they are doing everything in their power to win each night." When a manager informed him that they wanted to make a coaching change, Snider would, as expected, ask dozens of pointed questions, ensuring they were 100 percent certain of the decision they wanted to make. The chairman wanted no wavering, no uncertainty. If an executive came to him, having thought deeply through the repercussions of his actions and could show that it would benefit the team, Snider would always accept it, even if he disagreed. But if there was any inkling of uncertainty, he would send the executive back to the drawing board. Those with less self-assurance might crack under this pressure, but the truly great ones, with a passion rivaling that of their chairman, would walk through the fire and come out stronger for it. To them, Snider wasn't just another Broad Street Bully, but an intelligent owner who cultivated an atmosphere demanding no less than their best efforts.

His passion often showed itself when the Flyers were struggling. A horror to work with the day after a Flyers loss, Snider was particularly difficult during seasons in which the Flyers piled up more losses than wins. The 2006–2007 Flyers season was dismal—they finished in last place, and Snider's emotions boiled over. It was rare that the Flyers were one of the worst teams in the league, and for the chairman, living through that season was akin to being stabbed on each of 82 nights. After one particularly frustrating game, he called COO Peter Luukko, who heard the angry voice of the chairman on the other end. "John Stevens can't coach our fucking power play!" Snider yelled. Luukko, as angry as his boss, shot back, "Fucking God couldn't coach our power play!" The two went back and forth before pausing, laughing, and realizing that the answer to a difficult season was not constantly bashing their team, but rather making a plan to move forward. They met with GM Paul Holmgren, figured out a long-term plan to

get back to the respectable level they knew was attainable, and progressed from there. The following season, the team advanced to the
Eastern Conference Finals.

As the years progressed, Snider continued to show that he would
do whatever it took to help the Flyers reach the lofty goals he set,
even if it was irrational. His superstitions were well-documented,
but none of them were more apparent than during Flyers games.
Even if he was watching by himself, he still had to wear his lucky tie,
lucky cuff links, and have his lucky coin in his pocket. His executives
understood his passion, and the players generally loved working
for him. Players consistently spoke publicly in glowing terms about
Snider's care for them. They loved his passion and loved the fact that
he would spend hundreds of millions of dollars if it gave the team a
chance to win at all. It was not about the money, it was about finding
a way to be the best.

That notion was not hyperbole. If he believed it would help them
win the Cup, Snider would spend huge sums without even blinking an
eye. In 2011, with Tampa Bay Lightning superstar Steven Stamkos a
restricted free agent, the Flyers considered offering him a deal worth
close to $115 million to lure him to Philadelphia. Snider was happy to
provide that level of financing, but after discussions with the hockey
operations staff, they were concerned that, with the salary cap and
draft-pick compensation required to be sent to the Lightning, the deal
would hamper their ability to properly fill the rest of the Flyers roster.
They declined, and Stamkos remained in Tampa.

However, the next summer, Snider decided to put his money
where his mouth was. He authorized Holmgren to offer restricted
free agent Shea Weber, a superstar defenseman playing for the Nashville Predators, a 14-year, $110 million deal. The contract was heavily
front-loaded with eight-figure bonuses in the hopes the small-market
Predators would not be able to match the offer and keep their asset.
It was a rare occasion that Snider guessed incorrectly, but in this case,

Nashville matched the offer and Weber remained with them. "To me, every year we want to win the Cup," Snider said to the *Philadelphia Inquirer*, summarizing the philosophy that guided him for so many decades. "So, if we don't win the Cup, it's an unsuccessful year."

During the 2011 playoffs, the Flyers went through an untenable goaltending carousel, a constant for the Flyers ever since Ron Hextall retired from tending their net in the '90s. With his usual conviction, Snider made a bold statement. "We are *never* going to go through the goalie issues we've gone through in the last couple of years again," he said, according to the *Philadelphia Inquirer*. That off-season, the Flyers brass stunned the hockey world by trading their captain, Mike Richards, and their top scorer, Jeff Carter, and by signing goaltender Ilya Bryzgalov, all on the same day.* Snider did not specifically instruct his hockey operations executives what to do here. Rather, he set the goal (no more goaltending problems) and asked them to come up with their own solution.† It is surely a fine line between the two, but his long-term employees became used to his public statements and were rarely intimidated. Instead, they realized this was a passionate owner who wanted to be sure the organization was on the right track for the future. But there is also no doubt that Snider's presence always loomed large over any major hockey decision, even if his executives did not consciously notice it.

---

* Bryzgalov's signing turned into an unmitigated disaster that resulted in the team buying out his contract just two years later, resulting in them paying him seven figures each year through 2027.

† The principals involved at the time remember Snider calling a meeting in which they discussed every possible option that would result in the ultimate goal of improving the team's goaltending. Incredibly, this is the only instance since the 1960s that any of those close to him can remember Snider being so involved in a hockey decision—yet at no point did he tell his staff which option to choose. He solely wanted to ensure that they were, indeed, considering all potential routes to achieve the end goal.

Not only was Snider willing to pay anything to win, but he often developed deep love and loyalty to those who wore the orange and black. When it came to player transactions, Snider was not only passionate and empathetic toward the harsh realities of the business, but at times even more emotional than the players. When a player was traded from the Flyers, more often than not Snider was the next person to call after the general manager, expressing his regret for the transaction. Depending on the situation, he might even do so in person. When fan favorite Bernie Parent was traded to the Toronto Maple Leafs in January 1971, Snider, with tears in his eyes, walked into the locker room to tell the star goaltender. The two cried with each other as Parent said good-bye to his teammates. The chairman felt loyalty toward the players who gave so much to him, and trading players was one of the few parts of the business he hated, though he understood the necessity.

Consequently, one of Snider's biggest flaws in hockey was that he always expected the same loyalty from his players that he showed to them. As the business evolved and the expansion of unrestricted free agency allowed players to leave their teams and sign freely with another organization, Snider often felt betrayed when a player opted to do so. When top defenseman Mark Howe, now a member of both the Flyers Hall of Fame and Hockey Hall of Fame, saw his on-ice role about to be diminished as he approached his late thirties, he became unhappy, believing he had more left in the tank. A call from the Detroit Red Wings piqued his interest, and he approached Snider about his desire to accept a larger role with another club before his career ended.

Howe loved Philadelphia and was not keen on leaving, but he understood that a professional athlete's career lasted only so long and he needed to capitalize on his time remaining. When the two met, Snider was shocked. Instead of his typical anger, Snider simply expressed hurt and betrayal. He looked at his star defenseman and said, "Look at all we've done for you." Howe, saddened at disappointing his boss, but understanding that it was a two-way street, replied, "With all due respect, Mr. Snider, look what I've done for you." Even though the two remained on friendly terms for the rest of Snider's life, he continued to harbor the pain of a player leaving of his own volition. About five years later, Howe saw Snider for the first time since that conversation took place, and although Snider gave him a huge bear hug and invited him to join his dinner already in progress, he looked Howe in the eye and said with a grin, "You know, I'm still really pissed at you." Perhaps Snider was naïve, perhaps it was the one part of the NHL's business model in which he was old school, instead of progressive. But it was something that bothered him throughout his life.

That personality trait was not limited to players, either. In the 1990s, when Snider contemplated bringing Mike Keenan back as the team's coach, he brazenly went as far as placing a contract in front of the fiery coach at the chairman's Radnor home in the hopes he would sign on the spot. Keenan asked to think about it and ultimately signed with the rival New York Rangers instead. Snider was irate that someone not only spurned his offer but had the chutzpah to sign with a divisional foe. Years later, at the 2010 alumni game between the two teams, Keenan walked over to Snider and stuck out his hand. Snider took one look and sneered, "I'm not fucking shaking your hand."*

Nonetheless, business still called quite often. As the first decade of the new millennium came to a close, Comcast-Spectacor found themselves in a bit of a structural pickle. Although the Phantoms and the Spectrum's other tenants were seeing great success, the Spectrum was falling apart from the inside. At over 40 years old and built quickly and simply, it was essentially at the end of its useful life. The

---

* Though it is interesting to note that, while Snider's anger toward those in business was rarely personal, he often took others' actions personally, especially when it came to his Flyers.

public-facing portions of the building were okay—the exterior was the same as always, and the concourse was usable. But the back of the house was in desperate need of upgrading. HVAC systems had to be replaced, electrical and plumbing lines needed to be updated to modern standards—popcorn machines would regularly catch fire because the circuits were outdated and unsafe. The building was also not compliant with the Americans with Disabilities Act, which would need to be fixed if they undertook construction. The cost of repairs would have been upwards of $30 million, and the building did not bring in nearly the kind of revenue to support such a complete renovation.

But the bigger issue was that no individual wanted to be the one to suggest to Snider that they demolish the Spectrum. It held a near and dear place in his heart—he had said so multiple times throughout the years. In fact, Comcast-Spectacor executives later acknowledged that the only reason the building stayed standing for so many years was for that exact reason: no one wanted to be the one thrown out of the Center after giving that opinion to the chairman.

Fortunately, the organization had development rights to the land on which the Spectrum sat as well as the adjacent parking lot, which stretched all the way back to the construction of the Center. By framing it as a business expansion opportunity, this allowed Luukko to make the suggestion to Snider. The Spectrum would not simply be razed; they would be replacing it with an attraction that could bring even more revenue with less maintenance costs. As expected, Snider was very emotional about the suggestion. People associated him with the Flyers, but he associated himself just as equally with the Spectrum. His idea to bring a hockey team to Philadelphia started the whole endeavor, and it was his pitch to the city that made it a reality. And it was the Spectrum's design plans that convinced the NHL to choose Philadelphia at the last second over Baltimore for the sixth and final expansion squad. By demolishing the building, he momentarily felt that it would demolish a part of his legacy.

As conversations progressed and evolved, Snider came around, as he always did when one of his executives brought him a well-thought-out and intriguing business proposition. To have an old building lose money each year solely because Snider had an emotional connection to it was not how an entrepreneur should be thinking. An entrepreneur always looks for new opportunities and ways to grow their business empire. His next question to Luukko and the other members of the Office of the Chair was: what should they do with the development rights?

His executives presented various options: a movie theater, a Bass Pro Shops, a Hard Rock Café, and numerous other suggestions. But the group kept coming back to the same issue: it was in the heart of the Philadelphia Sports Complex, so it had to be loosely related to what was happening in that area. Who was going to come to a movie theater well outside the city, pay for parking, and sit in traffic with the tens of thousands of people who were at that night's sporting event? Who was going to do the same to walk into a retail store? And why would anyone drive to South Philadelphia for either of those options when the entirety of Center City was overflowing with similar, perhaps even better options? And what would happen to the Phantoms if the Spectrum was no longer in existence? There was no room in the schedule to make them a tenant of the Center, and there was no suitable arena in the region to properly house and support an American League franchise.

At that point, Snider received two nearly concurrent calls. The first call came from the Cordish Group, a development company based in Baltimore. They suggested a dining and entertainment complex at the corner of 11th and Pattison Avenue to complement the three stadiums that surrounded the property. The proposal, called Philly Live!, would have an outdoor plaza, multiple restaurants, and plenty of big-screen TVs so thousands of fans, who did not have tickets to the night's sporting event, could congregate and together cheer on their squads.

The second call came from the Brooks Group, a financial company that owned parts of the Pittsburgh Penguins, Pittsburgh Pirates, and the AHL's Wilkes-Barre/Scranton Penguins, along with some minor-league baseball teams. They pitched an idea that would have them purchasing the Phantoms, constructing a state-of-the-art minor league arena in the middle of Allentown, Pennsylvania, and relocating the minor-league club to a city that they believed was starving for a professional hockey team. Allentown was filled with Flyers fans, but few were making the 70-mile drive down the Pennsylvania Turnpike to South Philadelphia.

When Snider convened meetings to discuss their options, there was a clear consensus: selling the Phantoms and demolishing the Spectrum were the best financial options for the organization. Not only would the Phantoms be sold at a financial gain, but Philly Live! was expected to bring significant revenue to the club. In addition, they would also be able to utilize many of the companies under the Comcast-Spectacor umbrella to help manage the Phantoms ongoing. When the deal was closed, the Brooks Group had paid close to $4 million for the AHL club, while also signing contracts with Global Spectrum, Ovations, and Paciolan to manage all of the operational aspects of the new building to be completed in downtown Allentown in 2014.

When the organization finally made the painful, but necessary decision to close and demolish the Spectrum for good, ideas were discussed about how they could best utilize the event for their public relations benefit. The Spectrum was so iconic and meant such a tremendous amount to Philadelphians and the entire sports world that Snider wanted it to be done right. Everyone agreed that nostalgia was the best way to go. They brought Snider into the Spectrum for a "last walk-through," and he was interviewed on camera about his memories. Video clips were taken, chopped up, and distributed to all of the media outlets in the region at the time of the announcement. Despite the city's sorrow at losing their beloved arena, reporters and television networks fawned over the footage and clamored for more, praising the opportunity to do historical pieces on the Flyers, the Spectrum, and their illustrious history. "This has been one of the hardest decisions I've ever had to make," Snider told the *Courier Post* when they announced the decision. "The Spectrum is my baby. It's one of the greatest things that has ever happened to me."

As time progressed and final events were scheduled in the building, news outlets were banging down the Flyers door looking for access to the building's custodian. Amid many final concerts, Snider began taking interviews with *Philadelphia Magazine*, all of the daily newspapers in the region, and the major Philadelphia television networks. At one point, while walking the Spectrum with Comcast SportsNet, he stopped outside one of the dressing rooms and said with great pride, "It was right here, when I told Clarence Campbell, 'Tell them [the Soviets] they're not going to get paid.'"

On top of the numerous interviews, the organization agreed on three major pieces of marketing: a website to honor the Spectrum, a documentary on the Spectrum, and a book on the Spectrum. With those three accomplished, they would be able to document and secure the memories of the building before finally knocking it down. The work culminated in the RememberTheSpectrum.com website, the book *God Bless the Spectrum*, and a documentary produced by Comcast SportsNet honoring the building's legacy and memories.

Even amid what became a joyous time, with everyone in the city recalling their personal memories of the Spectrum with a smile, Jerry Wolman came out of the woodwork to take some shots at his former business partner. He called the decision a "disgrace" and even hinted that he would ask the Philadelphia Historical Society to protect the historic building from demolition. Decades later, Wolman still had a bitter taste in his mouth from his debacle in Chicago and his perception of the role that Snider had played in it. "I took him out of the gutter," Wolman said to the *Philadelphia Daily News*, "and then he fucked me."

Not that the bitterness wasn't reciprocated from the other side as well. Since Wolman was instrumental in constructing the building over 40 years earlier, reporters were curious. When asked if Wolman would be invited to the Spectrum demolition, Snider smirked and replied, "Yeah, if he's inside the building!"

With the Spectrum set to close for good, numerous famous acts returned to the venue for one last hurrah, including Bruce Springsteen and Pearl Jam. At the Pearl Jam concert, the last official event the building held, Snider wiped a tear from his eye as he watched the show come to a close. As one of his friends put their hand on his shoulder to comfort him, he couldn't believe that this was the end. His friend suggested that it did not have to be the end—what if they threw a final party for him, his friends, and family at the building that gave him everything? With bright eyes, he pounced on the idea and got to work.

Snider wanted to ensure that everyone (on his good side) who had anything to do with the Spectrum over the years had the opportunity to experience the arena one last time. He invited hundreds of people for a major gala that he wanted everyone to remember for the rest of their lives. Using his connections, he quietly secured the services of Earth, Wind, and Fire to play the gala as a surprise to the attendees.

The night of the gala arrived, and the inside of the building was beautifully decked out. Everyone was dressed to the nines. With high-top tables, hors d'oeuvres, and an open bar, those closest to Snider over the course of his life gathered in black tie attire to party in the building. The organization put together a video message from Bruce Springsteen, who had a long relationship with the Spectrum after performing there numerous times over the previous 40 years. They mixed with it highlights of the greatest moments in Spectrum history for everyone's enjoyment.

When the video finished running, Snider got on the stage and thanked everyone for coming to his party. Then he pointed to the curtain and said, "I want you guys to get up and dance and have a good time—say hello to Earth, Wind and Fire!" The curtain rose, and the building erupted. Everyone ran onto the dance floor and partied for hours, laughing, smiling, and dancing. During one set, Snider's grandson, Jacob, an aspiring musician, was asked to join them on stage, eliciting an enormous grin as Snider witnessed the legendary rock band jamming with a member of his family. The demolition of the Spectrum was going to be one of the toughest times of Snider's life, but for one night he was able to let loose, remember the good times, and share them with everyone near and dear to him.

As the time for the wrecking ball loomed closer and closer, Snider found himself doing more interviews than ever before. Despite being such a known public figure in Philadelphia, he wasn't one for the spotlight. The Flyers organization as a whole was always the premier attraction to him. Yet, with the news of the Spectrum's impending demise, everyone wanted to hear directly from the chairman, and he grudgingly obliged.

But after dozens of interviews and press events, with everyone repeatedly asking similar questions, he became fed up. He returned to the office one day from an interview and called Ike Richman, his spokesperson, up to his office.

"I'm done," Snider said. "No more. Done."

"Today?" Richman asked, confused.

"Forever."

"What do you mean?"

"Interviews. No more, I'm done."

Richman tried to interject, but Snider didn't allow it. "Ever," he repeated.

Nodding, Richman returned to his office to cancel the remainder of the interviews that were on Snider's docket. Minutes later, his phone rang. It was George Roy from HBO. The closing of the Spectrum was major news and the famous movie studio was interested in doing a 60-minute documentary on the Flyers, called *Broad Street Bullies*. Roy asked to come to Philadelphia and interview Snider. Richman put his head on the desk, allowing himself one indulgent moment of self-pity, then headed back upstairs to his boss's office. Snider lifted his head, took one look at Richman, and glared at him before either said a word.

"You don't listen, do you?" Snider said. "I said 'ever.'"

"I have an opportunity," Richman said.

"I'm not doing it."

The two went back and forth, before Snider relented. "Ten minutes," he said. Richman nodded and ran back to his office to set up the interview.

In January 2010, Roy and his filming crew set up shop outside the Flyers dressing room as they prepared to best utilize 10 minutes of Snider's time, hoping to be granted a small extension. As Snider rounded the corner, he was blindsided by the look of the hallway: lights brighter than he'd ever seen, hundreds of wires strewn everywhere, cameras all over the place. It looked like a miniature movie studio.

"What is going on here?" he asked. After being walked through the process, he changed his tune. "This is unbelievable," he said as he sat down.

Within seconds, Roy began asking him casual questions about Snider mortgaging his entire life to start the Flyers back in the '60s. Snider quickly warmed up and the two began a deep, pleasant back-and-forth discussion about the early days of the Flyers. After a few minutes, Snider said, "Are they ever gonna start the interview?"

Roy smiled and said, "Ed, we've been rolling the whole time." Snider nodded and motioned to continue. Nearly 90 minutes later, the conversation was still going strong. Roy finally looked down at his notes and said, "That's everything, Ed."

Before leaving, Snider looked Roy straight in the eye and said, "George, I have one ask. I want to see it before anyone else sees it."

"Absolutely," Roy replied.

Snider then turned to Richman and said, "That was a fast 10 minutes."

Richman looked at his boss and, with a smile, said, "Ed, it was an hour and a half."

"Wow, that was great," Snider replied, walking back up to his office.

Months later, when the piece was finally completed, Roy phoned the Flyers on a Tuesday evening. He was scheduled to be in Gary Bettman's office on Friday to get the league's approval, but remembered the promise he made in Philadelphia back in January. He wanted to return south the next day to give Snider the first viewing. Snider, however, was in California at his Montecito home. Unfazed, Roy caught the first flight out to Santa Barbara and was at Snider's doorstep Wednesday evening.

A bit nervous, Roy phoned Richman from the driveway and asked him for his thoughts. "One of two things is going to happen," Richman said. "He's either going to hug and kiss you or he's going to kick you out of his house." Roy laughed at the two possibilities, then went inside to show the chairman the finished product. With Snider sitting in the Montecito home's theater, the chairman was glued to the screen as he watched decades of memories rush in front of his eyes. He responded to each part with the fire that anyone who knew him would expect: he laughed at all the funny parts, fist-pumped every time the Flyers accomplished something extraordinary, and yelled with pleasure every time someone appeared on the screen to ridicule the Broad Street Bullies' rough style of play. When the documentary ended, he sat silently for a few minutes, reflecting on the incredible film he had just seen.

When Roy left, he phoned Richman. "He hugged and kissed me." Richman was thrilled, but had little time to celebrate as a phone call from Snider interrupted them.

"That was fantastic," Snider gushed to Richman. "I really loved it. I want you to set up a private screening. Get a movie theater, rent it out. I want our team to see it before everybody else."

Sure enough, the Flyers rented out the Ritz Theater near their practice facility in Voorhees, New Jersey, and the entire team, coaching staff, and management crew watched the first public screening of *Broad Street Bullies*. He then arranged for a public screening of the film at the Center for a few thousand fans. Snider's pride and joy was forever on display for everyone to see.

This time period was one of the more curious ones of Snider's later career. While he was always extraordinarily proud of his accomplishments, he wasn't one for living in the past, nor was he one for career nostalgia. His eyes were always looking ahead and he was always interested in the next big thing, but in this instance he finally allowed himself time for reflection. Perhaps he saw on the horizon the reality that, at some point, he would no longer be the one running the team. Maybe he even simply reached a point in his life where he could sit back and appreciate all he had accomplished. Nonetheless, his outlook seemed to change.

Amid his brief indulgence in the past, he still had a job to do. The Flyers season had not gone too well up to that point. Their fall left Snider fairly dejected as he watched his team plummet to the bottom of the league standings by December. In his Montecito home, he received a call from GM Paul Holmgren, who wanted to discuss firing coach John Stevens in favor of Peter Laviolette, who he knew was willing to take the job. As usual, Snider asked many pointed questions of Holmgren before acknowledging that, if he felt a coaching change was in the best interest of the team, then that was his decision to make. The move was executed at the start of the month, and although it took the team a few games to get used to Laviolette's new system, the club began winning games, slowly climbing up the standings.

By April, they were sitting on the playoff bubble and challenging for the final spot. The regular season came down to a final game against the rival Rangers—the winner would advance to the playoffs, while the loser would end the season on the outside looking in. In one of the most dramatic games in Flyers history, goaltender Brian Boucher shut the door in a shootout against future Hall of Famer Henrik Lundqvist, clinching the playoff berth for the Flyers and igniting a boisterous celebration in the Flyers dressing room after the game. Snider, as always, was one of the first people to burst through the door, and with a huge grin on his face, gave hugs and handshakes to every player. "This one ranks No. 2," he said to the *Courier Post*, referencing the game in which the Flyers clinched the 1974 Stanley Cup. "My heart can't take any more of these."

The run continued when, in the second round of the playoffs, the Flyers fell behind three games to none to the Boston Bruins. Over the following week, they accomplished what only two other teams had ever done in NHL history—win four in a row to take the series in Game 7. To add drama to that last game, they fell behind 3–0 before coming back, winning the game, and clinching the series. A jubilant Snider could barely contain his excitement. "These guys are unbelievable," he kvelled to the *Philadelphia Daily News*. "It's incredible. They never quit. I never, ever, in my wildest imagination thought that we could spot the other team three goals in their building and come back and beat them.... I've never seen a team like this. I've seen a lot of teams.... They have just done such an incredible job, it's unbelievable."

His pride in his team was infectious and continued as they beat the Canadiens in the third round to secure their spot in the Stanley Cup Finals against the Blackhawks. "These guys have shown so much courage and so much heart and so much not quitting," he said to the *Delaware News Journal* after the team was crowned the 2010 Eastern Conference champions. "I just admire them tremendously, no matter where we go from here."

Through that entire playoff run, Snider was exuberant, perhaps more so than he had ever been. With Father Time slowly making himself known, gone were the days of him stressed and angry with each goal scored against his team or each loss. Instead, it was replaced by permanent pride in the remarkable achievements of that season's squad. One team staffer described him as "a 20-year-old kid" with "so much energy." On top of his usual postgame handshakes, he developed a love for the Black Eyed Peas song "I Gotta Feeling," which often played in the dressing room after wins. He would burst into the dressing room, screaming, "I want to hear my song!" The team would crank up the volume as their 77-year-old chairman danced through the room and high-fived his players, showing his love perhaps like never before.

When the team flew to Chicago for the first two games of the Stanley Cup Finals, Snider brought his entire family, wanting to share the wild ride with everyone close to him. Eating dinner at the famous Carmine's, he spilled spaghetti sauce on his white dress shirt, whereupon his daughter ran next door to a sports shop and found a XXL T-shirt that said "Broad Street" on it. She bought it, and he slipped it on with an enormous grin, saying, "This thing is great!" He joined his players at a bar across the street to have a beer and dream about what might happen over the following two weeks. Even though he yearned for just one more Stanley Cup, it was more about his players, more about being with them and showing them how proud he was of their accomplishments and knowing that he cared so deeply about each member of the team.

The magical run ended in the sixth game of the final as the Flyers lost in overtime, giving the Stanley Cup to Chicago at the Center—a bitter pill to swallow for the chairman. With the doors closed to the locker room just after the game, Snider came in with a smile on his face, pushing through the hurt. He told his players that he was prouder of this squad than any other iteration in Flyers history. Despite his disappointment, he never expressed anything but joy and pleasure at the men who had worked so hard to even get within two games of a championship, which was the closest the Flyers had gotten in over 20 years.

It was a special team, one that will forever hold a dear spot in the hearts of Flyers fans everywhere. But it also proved that Snider still had the same passion for his work. Even after 40-plus years, he still looked at his organization with immense pride and never once considered leaving—which speaks volumes for his love of the team, considering how many other businesses he had bought and sold over the years. "I've been forced to be a little more patient," he acknowledged to *Philadelphia Daily News* writer Bill Fleischman. "But if I lost the passion and the drive, I would definitely retire. A lot of friends think I'm nuts. If the people around me think I'm slipping, and I'm not good at it any longer, then I'll have to face up to it. I believe that no matter how old you are, you have to keep your mind working."

This feeling was something that sat deep within Snider's psyche. His fear of retirement was known. Forever dreading his own mortality, Snider refused to stop working, believing it would be the eventual cause of his death. If he could keep his mind sharp, he thought, his body would follow. And he was having the time of his life, so why change anything?

As was often the case, though, Snider's high came crashing down when his old foe once again came out of the woodwork. Jerry Wolman had commissioned a biography, titled *The World's Richest Man*, and as part of the book's release he was making the rounds, as expected, to everyone in the media. The public, understandably, still had an old love affair with the former owner of the Eagles. His generosity had made waves for decades, even long after his fortune had diminished and he was forced to sell all of his major assets, including the football club.

But in his book, he made many claims regarding the founding of the Flyers that were demonstrably false according to documents that Snider still possessed (and that the family still has to this day). This included Wolman's claim that he provided the $2 million down payment for the team. When Wolman began repeating such claims in interviews across the region, Snider exploded. Within the confines of his office in the Center, he went on tirades to his closest advisors, demanding retribution. He asked numerous people to go through the book and highlight every single questionable claim Wolman made about him. He then went to his attorney, Phil Weinberg, and demanded that they sue Wolman for defamation. Through a series of conversations, Weinberg conveyed that it was not a fight Snider could ultimately win in any meaningful way and suggested he back down. The chairman grudgingly obliged.

Snider then suggested he talk to the media and refute every claim that the book made about him. He was talked off the ledge by Lou Scheinfeld, who was with him from the team's first days. "Ed, it's his story, you have yours," Scheinfeld said, trying to calm his friend down. "You don't want to answer this, you don't want to get into a battle in the press 40 years later." After finally taking a deep breath, Snider grudgingly agreed, instead providing a generic statement to the press and refusing to comment further.

The statement did nothing to heal his internal scarring, of course. Snider was always bitter about the end of the partnership, even occasionally reminding those close to him, "That son of a bitch fired me."

Even when members of his family, including his children, would ask about the events of October 1967, he would simply direct them to previously written articles or books, refusing to go deeper into the pain of that era. As always, he managed to move forward, looking toward the next item on his agenda.

As the calendar progressed, Snider continued to have a bit of anxiety about tearing down the Spectrum. The event at which the wrecking ball would make first contact with the structure was scheduled for Tuesday, November 23, 2010. The organization arranged for such legendary Philadelphia athletes as Bob Clarke, Bernie Parent, Julius Erving, and others to attend the historic event. They erected a stage between the Spectrum and Center and prepared for a short ceremony at which Snider and others would reminisce about the building and what it meant to the city.

The morning of the event, Richman was in the parking lot preparing for the 11:00 AM start time. At 10:45, his phone rang: it was Snider.

"Where are you?" Snider asked.

"Outside."

"Come on up, I want to see you for a minute."

"Really?"

"Come on up."

Richman ran upstairs, hoping to make it back down by the start of the program. He ran into Snider's office. "Hey, you wanted to see me?"

"What's going on today?" the boss asked.

"Well, we're having the press conference, we're going to have the wrecking ball."

"Is the media here?"

"Yeah, they're all here."

"Are there fans here?"

"Yeah, probably a thousand fans here."

"Dr. J here?"

"He's here."

"Bob Clarke and Bernie Parent?"

"They're both here."

"Sounds like you got it all set."

"Yeah."

Snider thought for a moment and said, "Do it without me."

Richman was taken aback at the thought. "What?"

"Do it without me," Snider repeated.

"Ed, in five minutes they're all waiting for you!" Richman exclaimed. "This is your baby, how can you not be out there?"

"I'm not gonna do it."

"Ed, you've got to be kidding me," Richman said, desperately trying to save the event. "Everyone is here because of you. We're all here because of you!"

"Well, you can do it without me."

"Ed, you've got to do it, they're counting on you."

Snider thought about it for a moment. "Well, I'm not gonna watch that wrecking ball hit the Spectrum. I just can't do it. There's no way. I can't do it."

Richman could work with that. He said, "Okay," then arranged for Snider to be driven over to the event and whisked away before the demolition started.

Sure enough, when Snider arrived, he went up to the podium to speak to the throngs of fans, media, staff, and alumni that had gathered to say one final good-bye. With his car waiting just a few feet behind the stage, Snider regaled the crowd with his love for the building that helped launch the success he now enjoyed. "I come with mixed emotions," he said. "On the one hand, I'm really sad to see the Spectrum go. But on the other hand, I know we'll all always have the memories." He also took a humorous shot at the Center, whose name had changed three times in 13 years as banks continued to acquire each other, referring to it as the "Wells Fargo, or whatever it's called, Center" and drawing enormous laughs and a cheer from the crowd.

When he was done, he mentioned he was not staying for the wrecking ball, saying with a smirk, "Let me know what happens." He left the stage, got right back into the car, and drove away before the ball had a chance to make contact with the Spectrum. A chapter of his life was ending, but he knew it was for the greater good. As difficult as it was for Snider to overcome emotional attachments, he knew he had put the proper people and structures in place for his dream to continue operating without him. This welcome development gave him the time to step back, as he initially intended to do in the 1980s, and focus his attention on more pressing issues within the Philadelphia community.

17

Bringing Hockey to the Inner City

AS FAR BACK AS 1976, Snider was determined to find a way to get hockey into the inner-city communities of Philadelphia. The Flyers started programs such as Hockey Central, where they would go to schools throughout the city and introduce students to hockey. They continued this and other such programs by creating a Learn to Skate program, putting minority students on skates for free and guiding them toward attending college. By the 1980s, the program's budget had ballooned from $20,000 to six figures. Snider fervently believed, as proven by his and Joe Scott's work in 1967, that introducing hockey to students who wouldn't otherwise have the opportunity would provide major benefits to the local communities. To him, the most important benefit was the ability to get those kids off inner-city streets, which he felt very strongly about. He wanted to help his city and was always searching for ways to do so.

Snider's programs continued to evolve through each Flyers season. The organization conducted school assemblies, which Flyers alumni would attend to teach young students life lessons through the lens of hockey. Still, deep down, Snider knew he could do more, but he wasn't precisely sure how to go about doing that. With his focus fully on running his now massive business empire, he often didn't have the time to ponder what more he could do for the community.

It was in the early 2000s, as Snider began to take a step back from day-to-day business operations, when Fred Shabel brought him to the Arthur Ashe Tennis Center, a Philadelphia nonprofit to which Shabel was devoted. The center focused on tennis instruction to inner-city kids, with a main goal to improve their lives: help them with their schoolwork and put them on the path to success. Snider was mesmerized from the moment he walked into the building for the first time. For decades, he dreamed of helping his community, and now the reality was in front of him in the form of tennis.

Snider had been a huge fan of tennis, having played it endlessly since he was first introduced to the game in the late 1980s. After Shabel introduced him to the Arthur Ashe Center, Snider donated a large chunk of money, for which the organization named one of the courts in his honor. He regularly met with Scott Tharp, the executive director, and eventually got a grand idea of his own.

What if, he asked Shabel, they could utilize the same business model with hockey? The resulting conversation eventually led to the creation of the Ed Snider Youth Hockey Foundation. Throughout his successful career, Snider always refused to put his name on any part of his business. It was always more about the company and those who worked for it, rather than himself. However, he realized that this foundation would be his opportunity to create a legacy much larger than any he could with the Flyers.

At the beginning of October 2005, Snider held a press conference where he announced the official start of Snider Hockey. Surrounded by local reporters from the *Philadelphia Daily News*, the *Philadelphia Inquirer*, and local television networks, Snider stood at the University of Pennsylvania's Class of 1923 Arena, where the foundation would spend much of their time operating on the ice, and introduced his dream. "Hockey is the greatest game ever invented," he said, "and my hope is to provide a chance for a whole new generation of children to learn and play the game.... This is something I've always wanted to do. I just had to bring it together in the right way."

One of the difficulties Snider knew he would face in creating on-ice programs for students was the availability of ice time. On top of the hefty price of ice time, as well as equipment, perhaps the most inconvenient part of playing hockey is that most youth teams have to practice either very early in the morning or very late at night, in order to avoid school conflicts. Snider knew that he was not going to be able to create a foundation that required inner-city students to be up at 4:00 o'clock in the morning, so he went directly to the school districts themselves and worked out a deal. They were thrilled to have one of the city's biggest movers and shakers support their students, especially when it came to helping them with their physical education programs. Snider Hockey, in exchange, would operate during the school day, in place of certain physical education programs at school districts throughout the city. The foundation would finance the ice time, equipment, and the travel from the schools to the rinks and back. This would give students the opportunity for physical exercise, along with an opportunity to be involved in a sport that they otherwise would not have the chance to play.

The programs would be held in a series of four-week clinics running through the winter. Designed for school children aged 7–12 and operated out of the Class of 1923 Arena, the Flyers Skate Zone in Northeast Philadelphia, as well as other rinks located throughout the city, the foundation also would provide scholarships for students to join local youth hockey clubs.

Immediately, Snider enlisted those who worked for his organization, including some of the most popular players at the time. Flyers captain Keith Primeau and fan favorite Donald Brashear were two of the early participants to attend clinics, working with the inner-city students through Snider Hockey, helping to spread the excitement of the game. From the start, Snider made very clear his ultimate goal in starting the foundation. "Wouldn't it be a thrill if someday a kid came out of this program and went to college on a hockey scholarship?" he asked rhetorically to the *Philadelphia Daily News*. "But really, with all of the problems in the cities in the schools, if you can give kids the opportunity to have fun, progress, and accomplish things, it's just a big satisfaction to me."

Moving forward, Snider Hockey events would consistently draw some of the most famous names in the region and in hockey: Claude Giroux, Wayne Simmonds, Gary Bettman. Even Wayne Gretzky attended an event to work with some of the Snider Hockey kids. "Anything for Mr. Snider," was the constant refrain. If there was anything in his career he cared more about than the Flyers, it was Snider Hockey.

One of the requirements for students to remain involved in the foundation was to keep their grades up and most importantly, to stay in school. Snider wanted to introduce hockey to the inner city, but he wanted to do it in a way that helped the children lead upstanding lives. What Snider really wanted was to create a better life for those he felt needed more of a purpose. Getting them to finish high school and go to college, he thought, would be the best way to accomplish this lofty goal.

It quickly became evident that, although the foundation was doing great work, it didn't seem to have enough staying power. Students were partaking in the programs and having a great time, but there was no continuity and no road map for the foundation to accomplish Snider's desired goal. He reached out to the only person he thought could fix the issue, the person who turned the Arthur Ashe Center into the success that influenced Snider Hockey: Scott Tharp.

Snider invited Tharp for a meeting and asked his thoughts on the foundation. The reply was not what Snider expected. Tharp made it clear that, although the intention was great, it was possible that the foundation was doing more harm than good for the students. The programs that Snider Hockey was conducting were indeed fantastic, but there was no endgame. The foundation would come in, introduce the students to hockey, show them a great time, and then the program would end—more often than not they would never see the students again. It could be that they were giving the students false hope by ending the program without any continuity. That surely wasn't Snider's intention, but he wasn't sure how to fix the issue. By the end of the meeting, he had offered Tharp the position of running Snider Hockey to impart his own experience and expertise on his legacy.

Tharp was overwhelmed by Snider's commitment to the ideas. The chairman offered all of his help, as much financing as the foundation needed, and any other resource to make Snider Hockey successful. With that in mind, Tharp accepted the position, and Snider Hockey entered its second chapter, one that was destined to be much more successful than the first.

Almost overnight, Tharp adjusted Snider Hockey programming to include much more than just hockey and physical education. In fact, one issue that was brought to their attention was why they were pulling students out of school for the programming. If the goal was to keep them safe and off the streets, they should be doing it after school ended. Since they had adult supervision, the hours that students spent in school were often the safest of their day. Snider and Tharp devised a system to bring students into the program after school and retain them for many years, helping guide them on the path toward graduation and even college. By doing so through the lens of hockey, they would have a much higher success rate in improving the futures of the students and giving them a chance to experience their own success. If students remained on top of their schoolwork, they would be rewarded with the continued opportunity to play hockey for free, with the foundation footing the bill.

From the beginning, Snider had a greater involvement in the foundation than he had in his business. While he always managed every part of his life with the mantra of "hire good people and let them do their jobs," he was much more hands-on with the foundation and wanted to be apprised of any developments, issues, and ideas. If there was a problem, he did not want to find out about it days later—he wanted to know right away, so he could help. In fact, he would smile immensely any time the foundation asked him for his direct help. Unlike his businesses, in which he wanted his executives to solve the issues, he relished being intimately involved with the foundation.

It was during the foundation's second year that Snider increased his visibility by doing what he loved most of all: going to the inner-city rinks and watching the students partake in the programming. It not only warmed his heart to see underprivileged kids partaking in the sport he loved, but also made him confident that his foundation would accomplish the goals he initially set. One time, in West Philadelphia, Snider and Tharp entered a rink and saw a group of Black students skating alongside Hispanic and White students, while all of the parents in the crowd cheered wildly. He couldn't understand exactly what they were yelling, so he turned to Tharp and asked what the chant was. Tharp informed him they were chanting in Spanish. Snider was exuberant and couldn't contain his happiness. "I've been in hockey for over 40 years," he said, his eyes bright and his mouth agape. "It's the first time I've ever been to a hockey game and heard cheers in Spanish." He looked through the crowd and saw the parents standing shoulder to shoulder, cheering on their kids. None of them knew much about hockey, but they were there to learn, share, and support the children, who were doing something of which they could be proud, most of them for the first time in their lives. It was at that moment that Snider had the realization: they were uniting neighborhoods. It was something he never envisioned being able to achieve, especially that early in the foundation's life. Immediately, Snider changed the foundation's mission statement to include "building lives, uniting communities."

It was just a couple of years later that Snider began planning ways in which to expand the foundation's footprint. He and Tharp began discussing plans to create a center, similar to Arthur Ashe, at what is now the NovaCare Complex in South Philadelphia. The plan was to erect a hub that would house all of Snider Hockey's operations, allowing them to run their programming from one building.

But around that time, the city of Philadelphia announced a plan to demolish some of the city's recreation centers that they felt were not pulling their weight. Some of those centers included ice rinks that Snider Hockey was utilizing for their programming. With ice time already at a premium, Snider was concerned that their foundation would struggle to operate with fewer locations available for their programs. In a meeting with Shabel and Tharp, Snider expressed his perplexity. "Why are we putting money into one facility?" he asked. "Why don't we try to move this around the city? Let's buy them, let's take them over." While it was technically feasible, the cost would be astronomical, and the foundation still wasn't quite successful enough to finance that decision.

Instead, the three of them traveled to Harrisburg to meet with former Philadelphia mayor and then governor Ed Rendell. Pennsylvania had a program called the Redevelopment Assistant Capital Program (RACP). The state earmarked a certain amount of money each year for grants to cities throughout the state, to be used to repurpose parts of their communities for the public good. The group requested an RACP grant to purchase and redevelop the rinks so the foundation could continue operating them for the kids. While most of the rinks were enclosed from above, they had chain-link fences surrounding them, making them susceptible to the elements. Because of the Philadelphia climate, this made the ice rinks usable for only a few months each year. Part of the grant money, in addition to purchasing the locations, was to fully enclose the ice rinks so that they could be used up to 12 months a year in order to further expand and enhance Snider Hockey's programming.

Despite their political differences, Snider and Rendell were on the same page right from the beginning, having gone through the Spectrum II ordeal years earlier when Rendell was the mayor. Rendell, having grown up in Philadelphia, had a hometown bias. He had served the city for many years before ascending to the governor's mansion. Together, they enjoyed a similar vision for improving Philadelphia's inner cities and giving students the opportunity to succeed in life. Subsequently, the group went directly into the inner city to address the parents of these students, to present to them their plan for the next chapter of Snider Hockey. They wanted not only to bring hockey to the students, but they wanted to provide life coaching. That included homework help, tutoring, mentoring, life lessons, and coaching—including how to properly introduce themselves at a job interview, how to make positive first impressions, and other advice to help the students become productive members of society. Rendell agreed to provide the grant, so long as Snider matched it with his own contribution. He happily accepted and from his own pocket added $6.5 million to the foundation's coffers without blinking an eye. Rendell provided $6.5 million of RACP grants, and the foundation was suddenly in a position of great strength.

Around that time, Johns Hopkins released a research report that focused on the poor state of education in Pennsylvania. It specifically singled out Philadelphia, where less than 49 percent of the kids who entered ninth grade graduated from high school. Each time Snider and his executives went into the inner cities to chat with parents, the No. 1 concern was always the dropout rate. Parents wanted their kids to graduate from high school so they would have a better chance in life, but they all seemed helpless in figuring out how they would actually achieve that goal. Snider determined that the new goal of his foundation would be to have every enrolled student graduate high school.

As the programs were being redeveloped, Snider was always involved in the day-to-day strategy. In fact, he would insist that he get a call from Tharp once a day with updates on what was happening—he would be upset if he missed even one of those calls. As was typical of his management style, he allowed Tharp to make all of the decisions but still asked all of the correct, pointed questions to make sure that his executive was on the right track. "Why is our retention rate only at this level?" he would ask, or, "Why are some of these students dropping out of the program after a few months? That's a waste of our investment, we need to figure out why." A charity was still a business, and had to be operated as such, regardless of the good intentions. If the program was not being financed or operated properly, the amount of good they could do would be limited. Snider wanted the foundation to be limitless.

With the foundation entering this new stage of its life, students who entered the program would be retained and develop close relationships with those who worked and volunteered in the foundation. One of those, of course, was Snider himself. Particularly in his later years, nothing would make him happier than a Snider Hockey event where he had the chance to interact with the kids and watch them skate around on the ice. He began cultivating personal relationships with some of those who went through the program, learning about their families and understanding the difficulties they faced in their daily lives. Often times, when someone would come into his office for a meeting, he would excitedly grab a letter he had just received from a Snider Hockey student. The person opposite his desk would then listen to Snider read the note thanking him for Snider Hockey and how their life had changed because of his foundation. He wanted to show off to everyone the great work his foundation was doing. Those who knew him recognized that he was always proud of everything he had created in his life, but it was quite evident that nothing in his professional life made him prouder than Snider Hockey. He was able to see the tangible effect that he was having on people's lives and knew he had made the right decision where to direct his philanthropic efforts.

Those funds were earmarked in a way that few but Snider could have planned. He was fully committed financially to supporting this foundation not only through the end of his life, but for decades beyond. Therefore, he needed to ensure that the foundation was financially self-sufficient and not completely reliant on him to operate properly. He wouldn't be around forever, but he wanted to ensure the foundation was. He created a fundraising plan in which, for the rest of his life, he would match any donation to Snider hockey at a 2-to-1 ratio. He was committing financially to the foundation, but only as a reward for the organization being run properly. If they could raise the funds to finance the operations, Snider would be there to triple it and provide even more opportunities for Snider Hockey.

As the years progressed, the foundation grew, along with its influence and effect on the city of Philadelphia. Even during the 2012 NHL lockout, Snider utilized his newfound free time to become more involved with his foundation. He visited more rinks, met with more students, and created even loftier goals. He announced that he wanted 10,000 kids to be involved in the program and to ensure that some of those students attend college, graduate, and become successful in the real world. In 2013, the foundation saw Ricky Lucas receive a college scholarship—the first time a Snider Hockey student had accomplished this. Snider was over the moon about this new achievement. "We are very proud of what Ricky has been able to accomplish," Snider said. "When I created the foundation, this was exactly what I had envisioned—helping to produce scholar/athletes who understand the importance of staying in school and accessing post-secondary opportunities."

The foundation continued to garner additional media attention, not just in the region but also nationally. The NHL and the NHL

Players' Association began donating hundreds of thousands of dollars to Snider Hockey to support the vision Snider had created. The foundation also received awards over the years for work they did in the Philadelphia community. Furthermore, the Flyers began leveraging media access to Snider through the foundation. Those who wanted a quote or story on one of the Comcast-Spectacor businesses were advised to ask Snider about Snider Hockey before the interview even started. Not only would it give the foundation more exposure, but Snider was always in a much better mood after talking about the foundation's success. Even in press conferences, his trademark glare that he often showed while waiting for the first question turned into a bright-eyed smile when somebody asked how everything was going at Snider Hockey. The chairman would then ramble for a few minutes about all of the successes and accomplishments of the students, often times name-dropping the most recent example of someone who graduated high school and went to college. It regularly gave Snider the opportunity to speak freely about what he considered his greatest achievement.

One of the ways in which he was able to help spread the word was through one of the highest honors he received in his life, his 2011 induction into the U.S. Hockey Hall of Fame. Over 23 years after his induction into the Hockey Hall of Fame in Toronto, he now had six grown children and many grandchildren with whom he could share the honor. Nearly the entire family joined him in Minnesota for the festivities, one of the highlights of his later life. For someone who spent much of his early of fatherhood screaming phrases like, "I have so much respect everywhere, except in my own house!," Snider used the opportunity to finally see the pride his family had for him. That pride reflected on his face, which exuded immense happiness and comfort by having his family supporting him after many years of various familial struggles. He attributed that honor to all of them, and it was something he cherished dearly in the final years of his life.

At his press conference for the induction ceremony in 2011, Snider, in front of the national media for the first time in a while, spoke lovingly of Snider Hockey. Some of the reporters in the room were unfamiliar with the foundation and how successful it had been in its mission. The next morning, there were multiple stories in national media outlets about Snider Hockey and its effect on the city of Philadelphia. The chairman was ecstatic.

Snider would always drop anything for the Ed Snider Youth Hockey Foundation. If he wasn't certain about attending a meeting or an event, the argument that it might help Snider Hockey would immediately convince him. When there was a group of kids from the organization preparing to be sent to Oshawa, Ontario, for a hockey camp, Snider not only insisted they give each kid a Flyers hockey equipment bag, but he personally delivered them to the bus and saw them off as they were getting ready to leave.

In 2015, the *Philadelphia Business Journal* called the Flyers offices and told them they wanted to award Snider their Philanthropist of the Year award. They invited him to appear at their annual breakfast to accept the award, but when Ike Richman approached Snider with the offer, he rejected it. "I don't do breakfasts," he said. As Richman was returning to his office to let the organization know Snider wouldn't be attending, he stopped for a moment, before turning around. As he walked back into Snider's office, the chairman looked up and said pointedly, "I just told you no."

Richman immediately explained the opportunity they had. There would be more than 500 people in the room, many of whom probably had never heard of the Ed Snider Youth Hockey Foundation. Just by talking about it for a few minutes, Snider would have the chance to spread the word about his philanthropic legacy. In addition, the *Philadelphia Business Journal* had agreed to donate a portion of the event's proceeds to the foundation. Wasn't that worth more than any hassle of attending the event?

Snider thought about it for a moment and said, "I'll do it." Of course, Snider had a fantastic time at the event, as was always the case. And hundreds of people were introduced to Snider Hockey and the wonderful work they continued to do each day.

Even after Snider's death, it was stipulated that Snider Hockey would receive a nine-figure endowment, but they only had access to it at the same 2-to-1 ratio that he had established while he was alive. While the foundation now had the financial means to be sustainable for many years, it needed to continue operating efficiently on its own, raising its own funds, in order to access the money that Snider had earmarked for them. Those in the foundation continued to joke for years that Snider still found a way to control them even from the grave. It was his vision and business acumen that has allowed the Ed Snider Youth Hockey Foundation to continue running to this day as one of the most successful inner-city initiatives that Philadelphia has ever seen.

Philanthropy and
Spreading Capitalism

SNIDER HAD ALWAYS utilized a charitable arm within the businesses, be it the Flyers Wives Carnival, Flyers Charities, Comcast-Spectacor Charities, or any other event the organization held for the benefit of a nonprofit group. But one way to determine if a businessman is truly charitable is whether they are running all of their charitable work through their business for public relations purposes, or if they also do so using their personal finances.

Not only did Snider contribute personally from his wealth, but more often than not his charitable giving was never even publicized. The first time Snider was publicly lauded for a donation was in the 1980s, but that was more than a decade after he first began supporting causes in the Philadelphia region at a financial level he never imagined when he was younger. In the 1970s, he and Myrna started the Snider Foundation, to be used as an arm of the family's giving for the remainder of his life. He funded the foundation from his pocket, utilizing it to make donations to several causes the couple cared deeply about.

Snider was a staunch conservative, so many of his donations were political in nature—though he was admittedly not a political creature himself. He only voted a few times in his life, which suggests his donations to conservative political causes were more about protecting his businesses than anything else. But more importantly, he ensured his charitable work—even years before the youth hockey foundation was in existence—made a positive impact in the Philadelphia community.

From a company perspective, Snider used Spectacor to support his community for the duration of his ownership of the organization. In the 1980s he invited 12,000 underprivileged children from around the Delaware Valley to take in a Disney on Ice performance at the Spectrum. He heavily supported the Flyers' Hockey Central program, one of the precursors to his eventual youth hockey foundation. And of course, the Flyers Wives Carnival has raised millions of dollars for cancer research and continues to do so each year.

One of Snider's personal passions was the Philadelphia Museum of Art, a renowned institution that he and Myrna started supporting in the 1970s, and which he and Martha continued to support through the '80s and '90s. The Snider Foundation appeared as one of the museum's corporate sponsors nearly every year dating back to the late '70s. Snider supported the Philadelphia Music Foundation, along with the National Conference of Christians and Jews. His foundation was one of the many donors that helped construct the Kimmel Center, a modern Center City music and arts venue—an organization that continued to receive Snider's support even after his death.

Snider regularly supported anything relating to Holocaust education, including the United States Holocaust Memorial Museum in Washington, D.C. His devotion to cultural Jewish causes was legendary, especially when it came to the National Museum of American Jewish History. He supported the organization for years, even hosting a gala with Martha in 1986 for its benefit. When the museum began a fundraising campaign for a new location in Center City on Independence Mall, Snider donated $5 million to help construct the building. He was recognized across the region for his philanthropy. His charitable work was multifaceted: through the Flyers and Comcast-Spectacor, he donated millions of dollars each year; his youth hockey foundation remained a steadfast part of inner-city Philadelphia; and between his family foundation and personal contributions, Snider's philanthropic footprint was all over the city.

Snider also was involved in a deeply personal cause—Celiac disease. Since his twenties, he was often hampered by stomach distress and in addition would constantly become red in his face—issues he often attributed to other causes. Doctors had prescribed medications and other remedies, to no avail. In 2003, though, during an endoscopic exam, his doctor discovered he had the immune disorder in which gluten damages the small intestine. Having finally become mainstream by the turn of the 21st century, Celiac was a disease that, at the time, was still not getting the widespread support it needed. As was typical of Snider, he dove in head-first to attempt to help himself and others who suffered from the same malady.

Through his niece, he was introduced to Alice Bast, a woman trying to start a nonprofit to help those like Snider, who knew little about the disease and how to manage it. He quickly became the first donor to the new National Foundation for Celiac Awareness (now known as Beyond Celiac). As a founding board member, he spent endless hours and dollars to create awareness of the disease that hampered him his entire life (and which he passed down to some family members, as well). As always, he went all out in creating awareness, even creating the first gluten-free food stand at the Center, for patrons suffering from the same disease.

But perhaps the most important contribution he felt he could make to society as a whole was to pass along his beliefs in capitalism and individualism, bolstered by his love of Ayn Rand and objectivism. In the 1980s, he wanted to honor his recently passed father in a way that his mother could appreciate while she was still alive. With a soft spot in his heart for the University of Pennsylvania, he arranged for a donation that would create a building within their Wharton School of Business named in Sol's honor—the Sol C. Snider Entrepreneurial Research Center. The entire family, including Lil, attended the opening event and, by teaching students about entrepreneurship and capitalism, celebrated Snider's father in a way that would make him proud.

Unfortunately, Penn began naming multiple buildings after donors and refused to keep Snider involved with the curriculum and objectives of the center he funded. The Sol Snider Center was getting buried under the additional buildings Penn named. The move upset Snider very much, and he considered it an insult to his family and his father's name. No matter how much pushback Penn received from Snider, the university was going to continue doing it their own way.

Unused to being told no at this stage in his career, an angry Snider backed away from academia and for many years focused his philanthropy elsewhere. Yet he was perpetually bothered by his inability to properly spread Rand's philosophies and his own views of capitalism. Since 1967, it was not often that he failed at anything. But his discovery of the stubbornness of university politics was frustrating. He still held out hope that one day he would be able to achieve his goal. In fact, in the early 2010s, he mentioned to his oldest son, Craig, that after he was gone, he wanted him to do something big at his alma mater, the University of Maryland. He was not exactly sure how it would happen, but he knew he wanted to find a way to support his vision of business academia to help mold it in the way he felt would create future entrepreneurs.

In June 2014, Craig, in the midst of a fundraiser for the Koch Foundation, met someone who mentioned that the University of Maryland was looking for a donor to support a new center that would teach capitalistic principles and entrepreneurial studies. Intrigued, Craig began discussing with his father the potential to create this center within Maryland's Smith School of Business. Although Snider was skeptical based on his previous experience, he listened openly and discussed it with his son, ultimately agreeing in principle to go along with the idea. Craig suggested that they donate half of what the university needed to build the program, but Snider refused to do anything halfway. "We should do more than half," Snider replied. The Koch Foundation was going to monitor the program to ensure that it met the goals they all desired, so Snider wanted to be all-in. The agreement was that he would donate $5 million and continue funding it through his family's foundation, along with a $1 million donation from the Koch Foundation. There were two conditions that Snider put on the deal: first, the new school would be named the Ed Snider Center for Capitalism Studies; second, he would get to meet the person who would run the center to ensure an alignment of vision before agreeing to the donation.

Immediately, the dean of the Smith School of Business at Maryland knew who had the best chance to connect with Snider. His first call was to Rajshree Agarwal, who was the Rudolph P. Lamone Chair and professor of strategy and entrepreneurship at the university. Agarwal was born in India but, like Snider, was inspired after reading *Atlas Shrugged*. With just two suitcases, she left her family in 1988 and traveled to Buffalo, New York, where she continued her education, eventually obtaining a Ph.D. in economics and embarking on a career in academia. Her firm objectivist views and belief that capitalism was the greatest system in the world convinced her to pursue her dreams in the United States—something the dean knew would resonate deeply with Snider.

In early discussions between Agarwal and the university, she raised objections to the proposed name—she wanted it to be called the Ed Snider Center for Enterprise and Markets. She was concerned about the public perception of capitalism and did not want to spend her days confronting the negatives, fighting bad press. Rather, she wanted the focus to be on academics and curriculum. Nonetheless, she was told that it was non-negotiable—that it was Snider himself who insisted on capitalism being part of the name. Agarwal traveled to Philadelphia, where she ironically gave a lecture at the Wharton School prior to going to the Center to meet with Snider in his executive office. The meeting would allow Snider to determine if he had enough confidence in the director of the new program to allow him to finally sign off and move forward on the project. On a sunny morning in June 2014, she arrived early for her 11:00 meeting that would include herself, members of the Koch Foundation, members of the university, Snider, and Craig. She had never met Snider before, nor did she know much about him other than his career success and that he had been a friend of Ayn Rand. She was also told by people who knew him that first, Ed Snider did not suffer fools; and second, despite the meeting being blocked out for a half hour, she would have just 10 minutes to establish a rapport. Historically, Snider had been known to make up his mind within the first 10 minutes of a meeting, and if he was not impressed, he would stand up and declare the meeting over.

At 10:45 AM, as Agarwal sat in the waiting room outside his office on the top floor of the Center, Snider walked in early, made eye contact with her, then disappeared behind his office door. Just a couple minutes later, his assistant informed her that Mr. Snider would see her now—before anyone else had arrived. She entered his office, and the two hit it off instantaneously. They bonded over their views of capitalism and their love of Ayn Rand's work. Snider was enthralled by the story of her coming to America in search of a better life. She loved his entrepreneurial spirit. By the time the other participants arrived, Snider and Agarwal were already chatting as if they had known each other for years.

Their main point of discussion was Rand's famous article, "For the New Intellectual." In that piece, Rand discussed how professional businessmen and professional intellectuals are siblings born out of capitalism. Yet it is the responsibility of the intellectual to work with the businessman, or else the two will perish together. With Agarwal as the intellectual and Snider as the businessman sharing the same world view, the two found themselves to be kindred spirits who could achieve their joint goals.

But then the meeting got down to business. All was in place, and Snider, after approving of Agarwal as the director, was ready to give the entire project the green light. In typical fashion, he immediately ran through a list of questions, without even waiting for the answers: "What do we need to do to get this moving? Isn't this great? Have we decided on a name?" Craig responded, "Yes, it's the Ed Snider Center for Capitalism Studies." Snider looked at Agarwal and said, "What do you think?"

Knowing the background of Snider's insistence on the name, Agarwal asked candidly, "Do you really want to know?" He nodded, always looking for honesty from those who worked with him, even if he didn't like what they were going to say.

"I don't like it," she said. He questioned her, wanting to know what she would call it. "I want it to be the Ed Snider Center for Enterprise and Markets," she replied, reiterating her previously rejected request from months earlier.

"Why don't you want to call it the Center for Capitalism Studies?" he asked, getting a bit fiery.

"It's not because I disagree with the principles," she said. "Of course, I agree with them. But the reality is that today, *capitalism* is a dirty word on university campuses. And what I want is to do the good work, I want to channel the positive, rather than confront the negative." She explained that in her view, capitalism was comprised of two twin engines: enterprise and markets. Enterprise is about individuals acting to their highest ability to pursue their aspirations and coming together within businesses. Markets, defined very loosely, enabled them to engage in voluntary and mutually beneficial trade— whether it is the trade of money, or resources, effort, or of ideas. Agarwal was also cognizant about the impending backlash on campus about the Koch Foundation's involvement. Most college students were well aware of the Koch family's regular donations to conservative causes and would already be inclined to reject their presence on a liberal college campus. Agarwal wanted to circumvent these negative issues.

Snider immediately disagreed. "But Ayn Rand would tell you that this is exactly why you need to call it the Center for Capitalism Studies," he said, pounding his fist on the desk, "because you need to reclaim the word *capitalism*."

Agarwal agreed with the sentiment. But she also reminded him that, like it or not, Ayn Rand's name was also considered a dirty word in many social circles and particularly in academia. The two continued to exchange back and forth, both sparring with equal passion and conviction, while everyone else in the room watched, speechless, as a giant of industry and a giant of academia went at it right in front of their eyes. After nearly 15 minutes of heavy argument, Snider signaled an end to the conversation.

"You know what," he said, leaning back in his chair, "it does not matter what I think. You're the director. You're running the center. What matters is what you think. So let's have it be named the Ed Snider Center for Enterprise and Markets."

All in the room were stunned by his sudden turnaround. For Agarwal, Snider had just established himself as her hero, and as a person who lived his ideals and principles. "He had me with that one sentence," she recalled years later. "Think about what he said to me, and think about the history up until then. He was reluctant to give any money for a center that would carry his name until he was convinced the right person was at the helm. And once he was convinced, he was going to trust their judgment." The action was consistent with one of his most important management philosophies: hire good people and let them do their job.

The two continued to chat casually until Snider looked at his watch, which was reading 1:00 PM. The half-hour meeting had lasted over two hours. He stood up and said, "I am so sorry, but I have to take this 1:00 meeting. I can't cancel this one." Unbeknownst to Agarwal,

Snider had signaled to his assistant to cancel each meeting as the start times passed, so he could continue to focus on their vision and alignment for the center.

A few months later, in November 2014, with the university's president there to introduce both Snider and Agarwal to the cheering crowd, the new center was inaugurated. When Snider introduced Agarwal as the center's director, he described her to the audience by saying, "When I talk to her, it's like I'm talking to Ayn Rand." Agarwal teared up, recognizing this to be the highest compliment he could pay her, and which she had ever received.

A beautiful relationship blossomed between the two, as they each called the other on a regular basis, discussing their life philosophies and sharing their viewpoints on the world. And their in-person meetings were based on mutual invitations—not only did Agarwal invite him to various events at the school, but Snider invited her to watch a Flyers game in his owner's box with him and his wife. Having never witnessed a hockey game in her life, Agarwal came to the Center in February 2015 to watch a matchup against the New York Islanders. After dining in the director's lounge as Snider's invited guest and watching as Snider meandered around the room, greeting everybody in his lounge that night, they retreated to his suite. She was offered the "hot seat"—the one next to Snider in the front row—for the duration of the game. "If the Flyers are winning, that's fine," she was warned by Snider's wife, Lin. "But if they're not, then know he's going to be very upset and you're going to have to deal with that."

Agarwal agreed, and Snider, like a loving father, carefully explained all the rules of the game to her, walking her through the sport as the game got underway. Midway through the game, when she recognized and called out an icing play, Snider turned to her with wide eyes and a doting smile in a reversal where the professor was now the student, making her tutor proud. The game went into overtime, causing Agarwal to miss her train and eventually arrive at her home past 2:00 AM.

And although the Flyers had lost in the shootout, Snider called her twice that night, just to make sure she was safe. To allay his concern, Agarwal told Snider that she had missed her scheduled train in full knowledge, and that she had not stayed out of respect for Snider, but because she simply had to see the exciting game to the end. Snider responded that she had passed the test of being a true fan.

A few months later, in October 2015, Agarwal invited Snider for a marquee event of the Snider Center to give a talk on capitalism, ethics, and leadership to hundreds of students and faculty. Snider declined, stating that he did not like public speaking, but she insisted. She responded by offering to create a "fireside chat," where she would utilize his own prior quotes to steer the conversation, so he would not have to worry about preparing a specific speech or agenda. "We have to do it for the students," she said. "It is important that they hear from you how you have lived your principles so they are inspired to do the same." Snider finally agreed. His admiration dictated that he could not say no to her.

One month before the event, she received a call from Snider's assistant. The NHL Board of Governors had planned a meeting for the day of the event, and Snider needed to attend. With Snider having recently become chronically ill (more on this in chapter 19) and regressing faster than the public knew, he was aware that it may be his last opportunity to attend a league meeting. Agarwal was asked if the university event could be rescheduled. But the venue was already booked, the university president and other key administrators were already committed, and the program had been heavily advertised all over campus. Five minutes later, Snider's assistant called back and informed her, "Mr. Snider said, don't worry. He'll come."

And so Snider, looking much thinner and older than the last time he was in the public eye, spoke with Agarwal for the entire 90 minutes, as hundreds of Maryland students and faculty hung on his words. The conversation ranged from his entrepreneurial beginnings, the creation of the Flyers, his love of capitalism, and his appreciation for the important work being done at the center in his alma mater. Many Snider family members attended, all wearing big smiles on their faces as they watched their industry giant share his wisdom with those in attendance.

"Business is what makes this country great," he said, responding to a query as to why business was viewed so negatively in the media. "The fact that we have growth in our businesses, all the innovations, all the companies that are doing remarkable things around the world, they should be held in high esteem. It's really a shame and it's something I'm hoping a program like ours will show young people and other interested parties exactly how great this country is and how wonderful business is. Most all businesses are run with honesty and integrity, I believe. Some lose their way and become crony capitalists, where they hire lobbyists and seek government favors. That's not capitalism. A lot of people think that's capitalism, but it's not. Capitalism is when companies have nothing to do with the government."

He went on to discuss another of his philosophies in life, that money is the reward, not the reason. Once you can safely feed and provide for your family, he explained, money should never be the reason to do anything. "You're doing it because you enjoy it and you love it," he said. "Growth is something you get great satisfaction out of. The reason is because you enjoy creating things, you enjoy building things, you enjoy making them better. Therefore, the reward is the money."

He talked about the dangers of government regulation, reminiscing back to when he built the Spectrum in the '60s, with the paperwork for the loan and with the city being two small packets. He contrasted that with the building of the Center in the '90s, when paperwork was piled so high he couldn't see the people on the other side of the conference table, despite the fact that he didn't utilize any public funds to build it, either, unlike nearly every other major league stadium in Pennsylvania at that point.

At the end of the chat, he reiterated his lifelong belief that capitalism is beautiful and that everyone should understand what true capitalism is and why it was important. University of Chicago president Hanna Holborn Gray once said, "Education should not be intended to make people comfortable. It is meant to make them think." It was and remains one of the pillars of philosophy behind the Ed Snider Center.

"Man left to his own device is pretty innovative and pretty talented," Snider concluded. "What we've accomplished is amazing."

Two months before Snider died, Agarwal wrote him a letter to express to him how much he meant to her and the effect he had on her life. Included in the letter was a story about her father, from whom she was estranged after she left her family years earlier. A Hindu expression loosely translates to, "When a peacock dances in the forest, who sees, so who cares?" This had been her father's response to her success in America. In her final letter to Snider, she wrote, "When I look in your eyes, I see the pride of a father watching a peacock dance. Thank you for that."

When the talk in October 2015 ended, Snider received a standing ovation and a beaming smile from Agarwal. She knew it was probably the last time she would see him. When she walked him to the waiting limousine, she talked about what they could do the next time he came down for an event. A very tired Snider looked at her and, for the first time in their relationship, said no. "This is it," he said sadly. "I'm going home now. I can't say yes to you anymore." The next morning, he flew back to his home in California. It was the last public appearance he ever made.

Fighting through the Final Days

IN HIS FINAL YEARS, Snider's life often threw very trying situations at him. He was becoming increasingly entrenched in the Flyers hockey operations, more so than he had in previous decades. He was prominently at the team's draft table in 2013, a seat he had not occupied since the early days with Bud Poile and Keith Allen. The press had been hammering him for meddling with the team's decision-making and for creating a culture of impatience, one in which it was accepted to sacrifice the future for a chance to win now. As he aged, the criticism became even more rampant.

It came to a head in October 2013 when, just three games into the season, the team fired coach Peter Laviolette, who had taken the Flyers to the Stanley Cup Finals just three years prior. The Stanley Cup–winning coach was well respected by the fans and media as one of the brightest minds in the game, and when it was announced that the Flyers were going to fire yet another coach, there was an immediate uproar. Sitting at the press conference alongside Peter Luukko, Paul Holmgren, and interim coach Craig Berube, Snider seethed as the media pegged the group with accusations about the team's culture. "We've been in the Stanley Cup Finals a lot of times," Snider said sternly. "And we've been to the playoffs a lot of times, and the culture is to win. Thirty teams are trying to win the Cup, and we're doing our damnedest to do it. That's our culture." When a reporter attempted to ask a follow-up, Snider's eyes narrowed and stared daggers at him, as he repeated himself, this time with some bite: "That's our culture!"

His frustration was palpable. He was thrown for yet another loop when, just a month later, Luukko left the organization. A longtime executive and one of Snider's closest business confidants over the previous 20 years, his departure left Snider's company with a gaping hole at the top of the management chain. One would not blame the chairman if, during this span, he felt like everything was falling apart.

That stretched into his personal life as well. For decades, Snider had no time for illness or injury. Even when his children were young and cut themselves playing outside, he was always the one to hand them off to their mother to ask her to make it better. With his aging, the typical health issues arose, and he did not have the patience for them. Even when he was diagnosed with thyroid cancer in the early 1990s, his attitude was essentially, "Let's fix it and keep going." He had no time to dwell on the negative; he wanted to find a solution for the issue so that his life could progress with his usual optimism. He always had too much on his plate and too many things he still wanted to do to let any illness sideline him from his work or his family.

So, when he started experiencing some hip pain in early 2014, it was typical of him to be annoyed with the inconvenience. The news was not good when he received the results of his scan: he had bladder cancer. The illness disproportionately affects the older population, and when the doctors told him of his malady, Snider was 81—well above the average age of 73 for a bladder cancer patient. The disease often afflicts those who spent years smoking—and Snider's 40-some years with the habit surely contributed.

With his diagnosis, for the first time in his life, he was faced with a life-threatening problem at an age when cancer is much more difficult to treat. And though there were surgeries available for bladder cancer patients, they were highly invasive and the complication rate was often over 50 percent. Instead, Snider did the only thing he knew how to do:

dive fully into the topic with a focus so strong that those around him had no choice but to join his efforts. He leaned on everyone he knew who could possibly help, no one more than Larry Kaiser, a prominent physician who was married to his daughter, Lindy. Autonomy was one thing that Snider cherished throughout his life. Cancer would not rob him of that now. He would find every possible option available and only he would make the final decision regarding his treatment. For years he trusted that, when he made a decision, it would prove to be correct. This time, he thought, it would be no different.

Snider found an alternative treatment in Switzerland that was meant to prepare him for any future procedures, and when he returned stateside, he scoured medical research journals looking for additional guidance. For the last 50 years, his main job was to gather information from all those who worked for him and make a decision. He attacked his cancer with the same mindset. Throughout his life, Snider would send newspaper and magazine snippets to his family whenever he found something of interest. Now it was his family's chance to return the favor, as they flooded him with clippings from newspapers, medical journals, and anything else they thought would be of help to him as he pondered through his medical options. One research article he found was a 2013 joint UMass-Harvard study on a treatment called Trimodality Bladder Preservation Therapy, a form of chemoradiation specifically tailored for muscle-invasive bladder cancer. After reaching out to those who had a deep knowledge of it, he contacted Fox Chase Cancer Center in Philadelphia to start the treatments that he hoped would be his saving grace.

All the while, Snider continued to be involved in overseeing the Flyers organization. With his age advancing and his recent illness fresh in the public's mind, the Philadelphia media pressed him about their theory that he was desperate for the Flyers to win and would sacrifice their future in order to achieve that goal now. "I want to celebrate another one," Snider admitted to the *Philadelphia Daily News* in

2014. But at the same time, in the midst of a 2013–14 season in which the Flyers were competing for a playoff spot, Snider refused to take the bait. "We want to protect our draft picks, our kids," he insisted to the *Philadelphia Inquirer*. "I would never sacrifice the welfare of the Flyers because of my age."

But despite his public claims, the aura around the organization was that Snider insisted the Flyers make an attempt to win the Cup every year. So, in May 2014, it was of interest when GM Paul Holmgren got a call from Trevor Linden, the Vancouver Canucks' president of hockey operations. The organization wanted to interview Flyers assistant GM Ron Hextall, an up-and-coming superstar in the world of NHL management, for their open manager position. Holmgren immediately called Snider. The two agreed that they did not want to lose their rising executive. Holmgren stepped aside and was named the team president, while Hextall replaced him and was given the reins of the club. Snider invited his new manager to a one-on-one meeting to see if they were on the same page. But Hextall had an issue: he wanted to take the Flyers through a full, multiyear rebuild, something they had not done in over 20 years, and he knew the chairman was not going to be keen on that.

When the meeting got underway in Snider's Philadelphia office, he simply asked Hextall if he needed anything from him. The new manager replied cautiously, "Mr. Snider, I need one thing from you, and it's patience."

Snider was taken aback, responding, "You think I'm not a patient man?" Hextall, knowing the previous pattern of Snider and the Flyers, sat silently, unsure of what to say. The silence felt endless, as Hextall squirmed, expecting considerable blowback from his boss.

But on the other side, Snider became introspective. He stared straight ahead as thoughts rushed through his mind: the near-half century that he ran the team, the most successful first decade in the history of an NHL expansion club, followed by over 40 futile years chasing the goal of bringing a championship back to Philadelphia. And now, with his cancer diagnosis suggesting that he may not be in that seat five years later, he had a decision to make. Was he going to risk the future to continue taking annual shots at a distant Stanley Cup, or would he continue to follow his mantra of letting the people he hired do their jobs? He took a deep breath.

"You know," he said quietly, "we won two Stanley Cups because I was patient. And I don't know what the hell happened to me since then." With one sentence, he expressed perhaps the most complex, yet dedicated conclusion of his entire life. On one hand, he expected he would not be around to see the results of Hextall's rebuild. But the Flyers were not his—they belonged to the city of Philadelphia and the fans who continued to support them. It would not only be irresponsible to reject his manager's decision, but also selfish. By placing his trust in a long-term rebuild that would ultimately be to the organization's benefit, he was essentially stating that the most important thing to him was the long-term success of the Flyers, regardless of whether he would be around to experience it.

Snider was not the only member of the family dealing with a potentially fatal illness. Just a year before his ailment was identified, Myrna was diagnosed with lung cancer. Snider immediately contacted Kaiser, who had performed a life-saving lung procedure on Eric Lindros in the '90s. Ironically, Snider and Myrna ended up doing their treatments at Fox Chase at the same time and on the same floor. On friendly terms at this point in their lives, Snider kept on top of her treatment and condition—the dichotomy of their long, past relationship coming full circle as each was fighting for their lives is a visual that almost seems too coincidental. It was bad enough that he was in pain, but he was extremely upset that she was going through similar hardship as well. After a few months, Snider completed his treatment and his scan was clean—it appeared the cancer was in complete remission.

But 2014 was evidently going to be the year that knocked Snider to the ground in a way he had never before experienced. He never let anything stop him in life, but death was a topic with which he was uncomfortable, and that year was a constant reminder of its quiet presence. He struggled as he watched Myrna slowly go downhill, before finally succumbing to her lung cancer in May 2014. On his own difficult days, he would sometimes ask family members if she was experiencing the same pain he was at that moment. He was already struggling with his own battle, but her death was a crushing blow to his fragile mental state.

Come June, disaster struck again, when he woke up to the news that seven people perished in a plane crash in Boston. While attempting to take off, the plane rolled off the end of the runway at a high speed, crashing into a ditch and bursting into flames. The crushing blow came when Snider discovered one of those on board: Lewis Katz. Stunned and devastated, he immediately phoned his pilot, Chris Mattie, who had also just heard the news.

"What happened?" was all Mattie heard on the other end of the line. As always, Snider wanted information and he needed it immediately. There would be plenty of time for emotional reactions later.

Mattie tried to explain that it was much too early to know, but that he would gather all of the information as quickly as possible and pass it along. In the meantime, the press was filling up Snider's call sheet, looking for a quote from Katz's best friend. "He was like my brother," Snider said to the *Philadelphia Inquirer*, calling Katz "the epitome of the word *mensch*." The public was not privy to much information ahead of the investigation's full results being unveiled, but Mattie, as a pilot under the guidance of the FAA, continued to glean bits of data that helped him piece together the picture of exactly what caused the tragedy.

Airplanes have a control called a gust lock—essentially a parking brake—that keeps the rudders from moving in the wind when an aircraft is parked outdoors. During a pre-flight checklist, the pilots must ensure that the gust lock is disengaged. One of the pieces that became clearer as the FAA investigation progressed was that the flight crew on Katz's plane was not always properly performing their pre-flight tests. In fact, of the plane's previous 147 flights that the FAA examined, Katz's flight crew had performed a proper flight control tech (the required pre-flight check) just three times. After they failed to disengage the gust lock, the aircraft did not respond when they pulled back on the rudder to get the plane airborne. The aircraft simply kept accelerating down the runway while the pilots, instead of bringing it to a stop and figuring out the issue, continued to try to get the plane up in the air with only seconds to spare. On a wet runway, with a dark night overhead, and a mechanical issue unbeknownst to the pilots until the final seconds, the plane sped off the end of the asphalt and struck a small antenna, igniting the fuel tanks and causing the plane to settle in a ditch just past the airport.

When Snider discovered this, he again called Mattie. Already a stickler for aircraft safety in his Gulfstream, Snider was extremely shaken and asked what more they could do to ensure his own plane was safe for himself and his family. Snider always had a policy: on the plane, the pilot was in charge. He would never be caught demanding a rush job on safety protocols. He knew the limitations of his own knowledge, and air travel was surely not a strength. He trusted those he hired. But this time, he insisted Mattie take any precaution available, asking him to fly the plane to the Gulfstream factory to have whatever maintenance needed to be performed to ensure his plane's safety. He even had Mattie schedule the engines to be examined with a borescope, an expensive procedure that probably was not needed—though it illustrates just how large of an effect the death of his best friend had on him.

Katz's death was one of the few times in Snider's adult life that he cried. He had been through divorces, he had seen the death of his parents, he had lost cherished members of his Flyers team. But this one stung him deeper than anything else. There would be rides home from work where he would confide in his longtime driver the emotional toil that he was going through and would break down in tears. It is possible that, in his life, he had never experienced a loss as painful as that of his best friend.

At Katz's memorial service, Snider was one of many to speak of their friendship. With his voice quivering, emotion nearly getting the best of him, the chairman told a story about Katz once mentioning to him that, when people leave a funeral, other than the family, people generally never think about that person again. With tears welling in his eyes, Snider looked up and said with conviction, "Lew, I'll remember you every single day of my life." He became extremely involved with Katz's children, Drew and Melissa. He and Drew had been friendly for years due to Drew's love of the Flyers. But after his father's death, Snider took him under his wing and treated him like one of his sons, always there for guidance and comfort.

Just before the start of the following season, the Flyers announced that Snider was cancer-free and happy with the team's gradual but consistent growth under Hextall's long-term plan. But when his hip pain returned in fall 2014, his always-optimistic mind was suddenly thrown for a loop. He returned for another scan, and the news was as grim as could be: the bladder cancer had not only returned after less than a year, but it had metastasized into his bones, something for which there was no known treatment or cure. As he notified each of his six children with the news, the timbre of his voice changed for perhaps the first time. Snider always had a deep-rooted fear of death, as many do. But he had been quite healthy for most of his life and always had the resources to fight whatever came his way. This time, however, there was no amount of money he could spend to fix the problem. There was not a management team in the world that could find a solution. There was no amount of determination or stubborn willfulness that could aid him. His children could hear the slight quiver in his voice as he showed vulnerability and weakness, admitting he was unsure of exactly what to do. There was no way to fix it, but he had to find a way to keep going.

Once reality set in, Snider quickly repositioned his mental state to the optimism that always defined his life. Those around him were telling him it was the end, but Snider was certain he would still find an answer. And if he couldn't, then he surely was going to make the most of whatever time he had left. "I just have to keep living my life," he would say. As the 2014–15 season ended in disappointment, with the Flyers missing the playoffs, he began experiencing more and more pain in his hip, making it difficult for him to walk. When he appeared at the Flyers Skate Zone during training camp in fall 2015, he was his usual, optimistic self, putting on a brave face to hide the pain lurking underneath. He called the team's defense "better than it's been in years," according to the *Philadelphia Inquirer*, and predicted that "we're going to be a playoff team this year."

But for the first time in nearly 50 years, Snider was absent for the team's home opener in October, and the fans and media alike were apprehensive. If Snider was unable to make it, something must be seriously wrong. The team officially announced that he was in California "resting and recharging after recent medical therapy," but the reality was that the trip to and from Philadelphia from his Montecito home was now too much to handle. He was beginning to get physically exhausted just by walking, let alone getting on a plane and flying across the country. Yet, as was often the case in his business career, Snider cast the only vote that held weight by demanding he return to Philadelphia for a game in November. After dining in the director's lounge, he struggled mightily to get to his suite, instead staying in the dining area. As he sat there, catching his breath, with the color slowly draining from his face, his assistant called down to the locker room for a sports drink to help replenish his fluids. When he finally got home to

Montecito, a conversation ensued about his physical capacity to travel. Amid heated family debates and advice from various doctors, it was agreed that he would remain in California and not risk his health further by attempting to return to Philadelphia. Montecito would be his home for the final months of his life.

Snider refused to talk publicly or even confirm the return of his cancer. He did not want to be defined by the disease, nor did he want pity. He wanted the focus to remain on his team. In a fall 2015 conversation with one of the Flyers beat writers, he began to casually discuss his cancer at length. But when the interview ended, he thought better of it and requested that it not be published—the beat writer obliged, keeping the information under wraps. The Flyers players and staff were somewhat aware—they understood what was going on and knew it was possible he would not even make it to Christmas. His health was going downhill quickly, and no one knew how much longer he could hang on.

At that point, an old friend of Snider's called Flyers team coordinator Bryan Hardenbergh. If Snider was unable to see the team, then they needed to bring the team to him. The Flyers would be on their annual West Coast road trip at the end of December, and Hardenbergh wanted to arrange for the team to visit their chairman at his home. Discussions among the family ensued to determine if he was physically well enough to handle 30-plus guests, but Snider again broke the tie by casting the only vote that mattered. Once the idea was planted in his mind, there was no chance anything would stop it from happening. He was going to see his team, no matter the cost. He would call Hardenbergh almost every day, asking, "Are you guys booked? Is this happening?" It was finally put on the schedule, and Snider spent the next few weeks with bright eyes and his trademark grin, talking endlessly about how excited he was to see his team.

At the end of December 2015, the Flyers rerouted their Los Angeles flight plan to land in Santa Barbara first. They arranged to practice at the local Ice in Paradise rink, which Snider helped build just a few months prior. Snider tried to attend the practice to see his team skate, but as he struggled, he relented and figured it was better to save his energy for his hosting duties later that day.

After the brief practice, the Flyers team bus drove the winding roads in Santa Barbara and pulled up to Snider's Montecito estate. Snider spent the entire morning getting himself physically prepared, pulling himself out of the bed to which he had been mostly confined over the previous weeks, donning a suit and standing at the front door to welcome his team with a big smile and open arms. The players had exceedingly mixed emotions. Naturally, they were thrilled to set eyes upon their chairman—it had been nearly a year since he was last in the dressing room, offering his regular postgame handshakes. He was the face of the organization, even when not on site, and seeing him once again brought a smile to everyone's face. But he also was much changed from the last time they had seen him. In just a few months, he had lost a lot of weight and his age was beginning to show much more than previously. He was the same person mentally, but his cancer was markedly taking a toll on his body. His state was much worse than anyone knew.

But there was still cause for celebration. Most of the players and staff had never been to Montecito, and certainly not to his property. With the mountains on one side and the ocean on the other, the scene was gorgeous and something most of them had only ever seen on a vacation or in photographs. Tables were set up on the back patio, and a catered lunch for the team had been prepared. The circumstances created a joyous atmosphere for the players to commingle with Snider and some of his family, possibly for the last time. He excitedly took them on a tour of his home, proudly showing them his wine cellar, the theater where he would often watch hockey games, and every other part of the property. He brought them to the pool and his private tennis court, where some of the players grabbed rackets and began competing heavily in just the fashion Snider always expected from his teams.

He engaged in conversation with as many members of the team as he could. He spoke with Russian-born defenseman Evgeny Medvedev about his own father's upbringing in Ukraine and with captain Claude Giroux about taking a step back and enjoying life. He chatted with coach Dave Hakstol about the team's plans for the coming months and the potential for the club to make the playoffs and compete for a Stanley Cup. Snider wanted to make sure that the long-term plan was still being executed properly and that there were no short-term sacrifices being made. Some of the younger players on the team and even Hakstol himself were not fully familiar with Snider, having only known him for a short time. But it was evident to even those newcomers how special he was, how much he meant to the team, and more importantly, how much the team meant to him.

It was clear to the players and to Snider's family that he spent the day in a considerable amount of pain. But when asked, he refused to acknowledge it. The big, trademark Snider grin never left his face as he reveled in the most exciting day he had experienced in months. Any pain he had simply melted away in the company of his team. He not only got to see everyone but was also able to share his home with them, which he often called his favorite place in the world. After a few hours, Snider was visibly tired, walking less and sitting more to rest his weary body. Even though he was still just as mentally engaged and equally as excited as when the team first arrived, it was understood that they should let him get his rest. He pleaded with them to stay just a little while longer, but everyone realized that the longer they stayed, the more of a physical toll it would take on him.

As the team finally boarded the bus to pull away from Snider's home at the end of the day, there was a lot of emotion from the players and Snider's family. Everyone was trying their best to keep on a happy face—except Snider himself. He didn't need to pretend, his face was beaming. He had no time to dwell on the negative or wonder whether this was the last time he would see his team. They had just given him one of the best days of his life and he was going to embrace that memory with a smile.

The visit left him bedridden for the next few days as he recouped from the immense physical exertion it required. His body was struggling to keep up, but he had no regrets about pushing himself to the limit to be a gracious host for his team. The day gave some members of his family a further idea: if they could bring people to him to visit, it would keep him occupied and continue giving him days that he could look forward to. More debates took place as the family argued on either side whether he was fit enough to see guests, or whether they wanted people to see him in this frail state. Snider had always been a proud man, careful of the public perception he created for himself. Some wanted visitors monitored and controlled. But, as always, Snider broke the tie with his single vote. "Don't monitor any of that," he said. "I want my friends. I want my family."

About the same time the team visited, Snider invited Hextall to Montecito to watch a game and chat about the team. As the two settled into the downstairs theater to watch the Flyers take on the St. Louis Blues, Snider walked very slowly, evidently in much pain, down the stairs to his normal seat, propped up by a few pillows to support his aching body. As the team was quickly down by three goals, he looked dejected, angry, and clearly not happy about the night's activity. The two sat in silence as they watched what both expected to be another loss. But, as the Flyers turned it around and scored not one, not two, but three consecutive goals to tie the game, Snider jumped out of his seat and pumped both fists in the air. When the Flyers scored the game-winner minutes later, the chairman walked over to Hextall and high-fived him, moving at a speed none of his family had seen in months. The next morning, he came down to breakfast still talking about how excited he was about the previous night's win. In his final months, there was nothing that perked him up quite like watching his Flyers.

Snider's pain continued to be a serious problem, as it was preventing him from eating and causing him immense anxiety. At the advice of his nurses, the family explored medicinal cannabis, legal in California at the time. They ordered pre-rolled joints delivered to the house, and his daughters Lindy and Tina sat on his bed as they lit one and attempted to get him to puff a few times. As the room filled with smoke, Lindy's son entered the room, not knowing what was going on. When he smelled the marijuana and saw the room dense with smoke, and his grandfather with a joint in his mouth, he froze like a deer in headlights, while the rest of the room broke out in laughter. Nonetheless, the supplement worked as advertised. His pain was significantly reduced, allowing his appetite to return and his anxiety to subside.

The following months involved a parade of friends, longtime employees, and business associates being flown out in Snider's Gulfstream to spend time with him at his California estate as he and his family tried their best to manage his pain. (By this point, Snider's fourth wife, Lin, was no longer around, the couple having been separated just weeks before his death.) Snider flew in his bartender and waitresses from the director's lounge, to whom he had grown close over the decades they worked for him at both the Spectrum and the Center. He flew in Phil Weinberg, Sandy Lipstein, and Fred Shabel. Gary Bettman traveled across the country to say good-bye to his longtime partner on the Board of Governors—and Snider spent the day enormously upset that it was cloudy, thereby robbing the commissioner of the beautiful views. Sidney Kimmel had lunch with him on his patio, as the two reminisced about their long, fruitful friendship. Each of his visitors would become emotional, knowing it was likely the last time they would see their friend. But they were never able to properly say good-bye, since Snider would act as if nothing was abnormal. "See you soon," he would say, as they left from his home one last time.

Amid his struggles, he still regularly reached out to those he worked with, if nothing else just to stay updated on the day-to-day status of his business and his personal finances. His body may have been failing him, but his mind was as clear as ever. He would call his financial advisor, Scott Sommermann, on a Saturday night at 10:30, and Sommermann did not need to even look at his phone: he would simply answer and say, "Hey, Ed, how you doing?"

"How the hell did you know it was me?" Snider replied.

"Who else is calling me at 10:30 on a Saturday night?" Sommermann said.

Even when Sommermann had a day off, Snider would forget and call him anyway, not knowing where he was. It didn't matter what he was doing, Snider would still expect the call to be answered. "Where are you?" he asked.

"I told you I was taking the day off," Sommermann replied. "I'm waist-deep in the ocean."

"What the hell are you doing holding a cell phone?" Snider asked incredulously.

"Because I was waiting for you to call," Sommermann said.

Through his absence, Snider also remained devotedly involved with the team's performance. He would regularly call Hakstol to congratulate him after a win or talk through a difficult loss. He received daily phone calls from Brian Roberts to discuss the team, the company, and to keep his business partner apprised of all events going on at Comcast. Roberts felt it was crucial to inform the chairman of the day-to-day happenings and to make sure he continued to feel relevant. After what the two had been through over the previous 20 years, Roberts believed it was the least he could do. Snider spent each day looking forward to these calls—it kept his mood up and kept him going for one more day. The thought of people visiting him or checking in on him brightened his mood and gave him something to live for.

At the 2016 NHL trade deadline in February, Snider saw that the team was not in the best of shape and knew that Hextall was going to continue the slow rebuild that he assured the chairman would ultimately result in greener pastures for years. But nonetheless, Snider could not help himself. With just minutes left before the deadline and the Flyers having yet to make a single transaction, he phoned his general manager from across the country. There were no pleasantries or introductions—just the chairman on the other end desperately needing to know what he had to look forward to in his final days.

"Are we getting better?" Snider asked.

"No," Hextall said, sadly.

"Okay," Snider said, before hanging up. The conversation did not last longer than a few seconds. It was his way of trying to find one more piece of hope as his illness continued to take control of his life.

Just weeks before he passed, he welcomed Bob Clarke, Bernie Parent, and Joe Watson, three of the men who helped build the foundation of Snider's empire. Life rarely slowed down enough to allow him to gaze down at his life's work, yet finally he was now able to look back and appreciate his accomplishments. He walked his hockey friends through his wine cellar and toured them around his home. "Hey, Ed," said Parent, in his lovable French-Canadian accent, "I didn't know I was friends with Richie Rich!" The group roared with laughter as Snider slowly walked them to his theater to take in a Flyers-Blackhawks game, with Watson providing sarcastic color commentary. "Jesus Christ," Snider chuckled as the game went on, "this is like old times. You're still noisy."

As the Flyers won and secured another two points in the standings, they inched ever closer to the playoff spot that Snider was desperate to witness. This was the team that could finally do it, he firmly believed—as he believed nearly every year since 1967. He just wanted to hang on to see his team clinch. The group said their good-byes the following day, as they prepared to board a plane back to Philadelphia. With Snider in a robe, holding a cane, and struggling to stand, Parent simply embraced him, no words needing to be said. Each member of the group had tears in their eyes, hoping it would not be the last time, but understanding that reality suggested it was. Soon after, Snider was even visited by his old friend, David Foster, who spent the day serenading Snider on the piano as the entrepreneur sat in the living room with a smile. "It's a really shitty thing," he said to Foster, "just sitting around [waiting] to die."

Just weeks before he passed, Snider was visited by Drew Katz. Drew had developed an incredibly close relationship with Snider. The two were nearly as close as Lewis and Snider had been years earlier. A Flyers fan from the time he was a young child, Drew was concerned at the direction the organization might head once Snider finally passed.

In deep conversation about the state of the company, Drew pitched a last-minute idea to Snider. He had a deep respect for Comcast and the Roberts family and how they had taken care of the organization, but for the last 20 years, it was still Ed Snider at the helm. "Would there be a possibility of me to buy your interest," Drew said, "and just sort of be in your stead? Let it be Ed Snider's Flyers forever." Snider, with tears in his eyes, loved the idea and expressed how happy that would have made him. But arrangements had already been made, agreements had already been signed between Comcast and Snider to pass the organization along at the time of his death. It was a last-ditch effort to carry on Snider's legacy through the Flyers for decades to come and something that many Flyers fans would have likely enjoyed after the passing of their entrepreneurial giant.

With his condition worsening by the day and the pain progressively increasing to the point of confining him to his bed, Snider continued to defy medical odds. A week before he passed, his nurse informed the children that it was almost time, most likely within 24 hours. Yet 50 years of his always fighting to win prevented him from even considering it as an option—despite his physical state and the family's concern for his well-being. While some of his closest family and friends suggested it was time for him to finally end the constant agony, he quietly refused. "I don't know how to give up," he said, tears welling in his eyes. "I've never given up in my life."

As an April 9 matchup between the Flyers and Penguins arrived, the team needed one win to punch their ticket to the playoffs. Being the final home game of the season, the team brought out Kate Smith, their perennial good luck charm, as Lauren Hart prepared to sing a duet of "God Bless America" with Smith's famous recording to inspire the team to the win that would make Snider proud. As the game neared, Hart knew Snider was on his last legs and wanted to bring his Flyers to him one last time. Instinctively, she dialed Snider's eldest daughter, Lindy, who was by his side as he lay in bed, then filmed herself and the entire arena as she belted out the famous anthem. Although unable to speak and often unable to even open his eyes, a small smile formed in the corner of his mouth, barely able to express his eternal gratitude for the final outreach from an old friend—one of thousands in his last months.

Just after the Flyers defeated their cross-state rivals, clinching themselves a spot in the playoffs, Snider slipped into a deep sleep. With his nurse by his side, she had his children come to the house in preparation for the end. On the night of April 10, with his Flyers securely in the playoffs and his family surrounding him, it was finally time for him to accept his fate. His children were right there, holding his hands and his head. His breathing grew shallower as the family stood next to him in silence. With time to reflect and be grateful for all their father had given them, their eyes glistening as some tried to hold back emotion, they awaited the final moments. Just after midnight on April 11, Ed Snider took his final breath, sealing his legacy and giving birth to a legend.

Epilogue

Tributes and an Outpouring of Love

IN THE SHADE of a maple tree, around a sharp bend at the West Laurel Hill Cemetery in Bala Cynwyd, Pennsylvania, sits a sprawling plot. Up seven steps and past a stunning stone wall lays a small area of green grass, surrounded by its own collection of gray stones, with lush foliage around the entire area. In the middle rests Ed Snider, his headstone as simple as could be: his name, his dates of birth and death, and below it, his Hebrew name. Beneath it all, a small Jewish star. On top of the stone lay a dozen small rocks, a tradition in the Jewish faith, a reminder that, no matter how many years it has been since his passing, Snider is still regularly visited by those who loved him, be it family, friends, or fans. To the sides rest two beautifully crafted, simple yet elegant marble benches, inviting people to sit down and reflect—ironic for a man who rarely sat still in his decades chasing success to reach the pinnacle of his career.

Just a few feet behind his final resting place is a stone with the Flyers logo etched into it—the only other spot in the plot that has any sort of inscription or information about who this man was. The logo is beginning to be obstructed by the greenery beside it, having been left to mature for multiple years. It is a somber sign that, regardless of how much Snider loved his Flyers, they no longer belong to him. The thought is fitting, when you think about him. For various periods throughout his career, he regularly insisted that the Flyers were not his. Rather, they belonged to the city of Philadelphia. He was simply a temporary steward of their name. His headstone and cemetery plot do not say a word about his businesses, not a word about his success. Why would they? At the end of the day, Snider felt he was simply a young entrepreneur from Washington, D.C., pursuing his passion every day. In his mind, that was so much of what life was about: loving what you do.

Snider's death was handled immaculately by his family and his organization. With ample warning to prepare statements, photos, and a schedule of events, everyone was ready to move as soon as the news came that he had taken his final breath. The next morning, the Flyers sent out a press release as a giant shadow was cast over the Philadelphia region. Photos were sent to the media outlets and a memorial was scheduled a few days later at the Wells Fargo Center. It was only fitting that, 20 years after he mortgaged his entire life to erect the hockey arena, the city and its fans acknowledged his passion by filling the entirety of that arena, including the ice level, which was covered in seats. The only spot left exposed? The Flyers logo at center ice, visible for all to see.

The memorial saw a who's who of the hockey and business worlds come together to pay respects to a man they all loved. From Gary Bettman to Brian Roberts, along with dozens of Flyers players, past and present, the speakers went on about his vision, his entrepreneurial spirit, his humor, his passion. The Flyers added an "EMS" patch to their jersey during the playoffs as well as through the following season. In the Kensington section of Philadelphia, a mural of Snider and his youth hockey foundation was painted on the side of a home. The outpouring of love and passion for Snider stunned many, who, despite his accomplishments, perhaps still did not quite realize the enormity of his contributions to the city.

At his funeral, his family gathered to say good-bye one last time. A few words were said, perhaps none more poignant than those of his brother-in-law and former business partner, Earl Foreman. Less than a year away from his own death, the family patriarch struggled across the grass with his youngest son on his arm and said, "I was around, and I watched what these guys did. This man did everything and he did it on his own. What he accomplished is remarkable."

Shortly after the ceremonies were complete, the family went through the necessary, yet difficult process of handling Snider's enormous estate. His Montecito dream home was put on the market and eventually sold for over $30 million. His art collection, valued at nearly $10 million, was put up for sale, with the proceeds being donated to Snider Hockey. And in September 2016, as had been planned years earlier, Comcast purchased the remainder of Snider's stake in Comcast-Spectacor. Just over 50 years after Snider started Philadelphia Hockey Club, Inc., for the first time, the team's ownership ledger would not include his name.

A year later, Comcast announced they would erect a statue of Snider outside the Center. In October 2017, at the northwest corner, just below his former office, a nine-foot-tall bronze statue was unveiled of a middle-aged Snider, standing with his hands together, the Stanley Cup ring on his left ring finger exposed for all to see. He looks up at the empire he created, almost watching over it with the same dedication and passion he radiated when he was alive. Those who pass by rub the ring for good luck and smile at the memories. Those too young to remember can gaze upon the man who started it all, an opportunity to always see the team's past while working toward its future.

As time progresses, the memory of Snider remains, yet the flame certainly gets dimmer each year. In the concourse of the Center, in the press box up above, and in the streets below, you can always find at least a few people reminiscing during games about when the team used to be Snider's and how things have changed. "Ed Snider would never have let this happen," is a constant trope when the Flyers are struggling or when a controversial decision is made, be it a poor officiating call, a disappointing losing streak, or an unpopular business decision. That sentiment is often echoed from the most casual fan to executives at the top of the organizational chart.

Snider's life is difficult to sum up succinctly. It is well-established that he had fantastic upside but also troubling downsides when it came to running parts of his company. His upside is clear based on the honors he earned over the course of his career. They are endless but include being a member of the Hockey Hall of Fame in Toronto, a member of the U.S. Hockey Hall of Fame in Minnesota, a member of the Philadelphia Sports Hall of Fame, and the inaugural recipient of the Ed Snider Lifetime Distinguished Humanitarian Award. He also was awarded the Lester Patrick Trophy for contributions to hockey in the United States, the Irvin Feld Humanitarian Award, *Philadelphia Business Journal*'s Philanthropist of the Year Award, a Lifetime Achievement Award from the Global Sports Summit, the Philadelphia Chamber of Commerce's William Penn Award, the Ellis Island Medal of Honor, and many more.

But certainly Snider had his drawbacks as well. No matter how often it is refuted by those who worked with him, Snider had an aura of meddling. It is nearly impossible to find a specific example of him making a decision that was below his paygrade—he always left it to those he employed. Yet the perception did not come out of thin air. You can find an endless number of Flyers or 76ers fans or members of the media who are unhappy with the way he ran those teams. That is to be expected in a market such as Philadelphia, where millions of fans have passionate opinions and are not shy about sharing them.

Snider himself acknowledged that he became less patient as the years progressed. While he was willing to build for seven years to create the Flyers' championship-winning teams in the 1970s, that seemed to create a fervent belief within him that the team could challenge for the title every year. Even in years when it was clear that the team did not have the ability to contend, he pushed on. There is a certain level of respect one can have for someone who is willing to chase a dream so fervently, but at the same time, one can easily question the negative long-term effects that attitude had on his teams.

Nonetheless, whether one wants to argue either way, what is irrefutable is that Snider created an enormous organization in the style of a mom-and-pop company, a small, family-owned business that treated its employees like members of that family. That aura remained even as the company grew to thousands of employees. It was one of the perks of working for Snider for the many years he ran the company. If you could withstand his "heat," he would allow you to remain a member of his "kitchen" as long as you wanted.

In the midst of the research for this book, one of the themes that continued to arise was feelings toward the Flyers and its related companies now being completely owned and operated by Comcast, one of the largest public corporations in the world, as opposed to Snider, one man with more passion for the team than perhaps all of the fans combined. Those who previously worked for the organization and even some who still work there all had sentiments very similar to the millions of fans who have interacted with the Flyers in the years since his passing: it's not quite the same.

When Comcast became the sole owner of the organization, the Comcast staff, including Brian Roberts, said nothing but positive things about Snider and the effect he had on their management style. "I don't view this as a typical corporate structure," Roberts said to the *Philadelphia Daily News*. "This is an entrepreneurial company that has thrived.... We want the Flyers to be the Flyers. A family."

Yet, years later, it is evident that, despite their desires, the organization indeed has become much more corporate, as would be expected of a parent company that employs nearly 200,000 people as of this writing. There is a clear difference in the makeup of the organization and the culture of the place. That is not a comment on Comcast, but rather, a statement on just how specific Snider was in how he wanted his organization managed. One cannot simply replicate the brilliance of someone like Snider, no matter how many resources are available. It is impossible to replace the passion of the person who started a company, but specifically that of professional sports. It is because of this that his legacy lives on.

In the years since Snider's death, the Snider Foundation, run by his family, continues to do work that he would have approved of during his life. The foundation donates upwards of $10 million annually to hundreds of causes he believed in, from Holocaust education and Jewish organizations to conservative politics, along with continuing to fund the Snider Hockey program. It is a reminder that, in light of his immense financial success, it mattered deeply to Snider that it was not just about hockey, sports, or business. He took care of those around him and insisted on trying to make society, specifically his beloved city of Philadelphia, a better place, one step at a time.

At the end of the day, as with any person, there were ups and downs to Snider's life. But the best way to judge someone's time is by engaging with those close to him. When it comes to Snider, it is a gargantuan task to continuously listen to the dozens of close friends, family, and business associates who still look to Snider's legacy to this day for inspiration and guidance. Those closest to him understood his faults and accepted that no one is infallible. Everyone has some level of faults and parts of their lives they would like to do over. Yet, if one can look at the whole of a life and recognize the positive effect it had on those around them, then it is difficult to judge that life any other way. In reflecting on his final days, perhaps one of his closest friends, Bob Clarke, summed it up perfectly:

> He didn't feel sorry for himself, no remorse, no regrets. He's still talking hockey, still talking about women. I think his life was full right to the end. You regret losing him, but when you leave, you celebrate him, you don't feel sorry. Not

many times you run into people like that. I think everybody feels the same when you talk to them about Mr. Snider. They don't feel sorry. They're thankful that they got to spend part of their time with him.

Almost eerily, exactly four years to the day after Snider's death, his sister, Phyllis, passed as well. After a decades-long, up-and-down relationship between the two, it is ironic that fate would choose to bring them back together on the same day. It provided a beautiful reminder that, even amid some of the most difficult times of his life, he always tried to make time for his family, especially as the years progressed.

Ultimately, Snider's life revolved around three crucial things: Flyers, family, and Philadelphia. Perhaps the saddest story of the end of his life was how badly he just wanted to go back to Philadelphia. He knew his life was quickly coming to an end and, while he was over the moon to be visited by old friends, all he wanted was to just go "home," even though it was a medical and physical impossibility. He was born and raised in Washington, D.C., and for most of the final decades of his life he lived in California. Yet Philadelphia was always home. It was his adopted city, but he fell for it as hard and as passionately as it fell for him. Perhaps the king of all ironies is, if it were not for those like Snider, Philadelphia would not feel like home to as many people as it does and always will. Whether the Flyers win or lose their next game, whether they win their next Stanley Cup next year or never, it is Snider's contributions to the city of Philadelphia that will forever leave the greatest mark.

Which is important, because the Flyers and Comcast-Spectacor will be fine. After all, Ed's in the northwest corner watching over them.

Acknowledgments

TO DELVE DEEPLY into the life of Ed Snider is not a one-man project. Over the course of nearly three years, this book went from wild idea to completion due to the help of numerous people, both present and past. Through a 50-year public career, Ed was covered by a plethora of newspaper beat writers and columnists, along with various magazines and other media outlets. These articles, features, and videos exist in the public domain as an enormous library of information. I am extremely grateful to everyone who spent so many years covering Ed so effectively as to create this archive of knowledge that served as the basis for this book. I also thank all of the living writers who sat down with me to discuss their own memories of Ed, both in his role as the head of the Flyers, and in more personal moments.

There are only two entities on which Ed put his name while he was alive: Snider Hockey and the Snider Center. Both of these organizations continue to thrive and house many people who worked closely with Ed near the end of his life. Many people within each organization helped to color his philanthropic side and the final years of his life in a way that few others could. Specific thanks go out to Rajshree Agarwal, Scott Tharp, and Ike Richman for their help and guidance on this project.

In a life that spanned more than 80 years, Ed accrued a large number of friends and business colleagues, each of whom had a unique perspective. Whether it was childhood friends like Chuck Klein and Harvey Kasoff, Philadelphia friends such as Sidney Kimmel and Drew Katz, members of his California crew such as Barry Devorzon,

David Foster, or Wayne Gretzky, or members of his personal staff who became like family, such as Chris Mattie, Michael Barrino, and others, scores of these people enthusiastically got onto Zoom calls, phone calls, or met up in person to share all they could about Ed. These personal stories and memories helped add color to a manuscript that would otherwise have been solely about his life in business.

His business and hockey colleagues were imperative to understanding Ed's incredible business acumen. Special thanks go out to former and current employees, including but not limited to Michel Sauers, Ann-Marie Nasuti, Jack Williams, Lara Price, Leo Carlin, Ron Ryan, and Scott Sommermann, who spent endless hours with me to make sure this book was as in-depth and accurate as possible.

Ed's love was, of course, his Flyers and the NHL. In that respect, a great deal of the information in this book comes from those who were part of those two families, including Gary Bettman, Jeremy Jacobs, Bob Clarke, Paul Holmgren, Joe Watson, Mike "Doc" Emrick, Mark Howe, Mike Keenan, Ron Hextall, Zack Hill, Brian Smith, and many more.

Outside of his Flyers, Ed created a family, even within the large company that is now known as Comcast-Spectacor. Those executives who worked with him had the best view of his day-to-day work, along with some of the most entertaining stories and enlightening anecdotes that helped illustrate the man. Thank you to Brian Roberts, Peter Luukko, Phil Weinberg, Sandy Lipstein, Fred Shabel, Dave Scott, and the many other current and former Comcast executives that cooperated with this project from the get-go. Special thanks as well to those who provided access to the Comcast-Spectacor archives, including many of the photos you see in this book.

Perhaps most importantly, Ed's family was enthusiastically on board from day one. In my first conversations with his children, they were each initially cautious in a protective way, before quickly jumping on board with full support. My thanks go out to all six of